MW00512528

Bluenose Ghosts

Helen Creighton

This is a wonderful collection of those stories that many Nova Scotians like to tell when the lamps are lighted and long shadows haunt home and countryside. The stories are often hair-raising, and many are said to be based upon personal experiences. Certainly, as Dr. Helen Creighton tells them, they all seem real enough, and convincing.

The author, an anthropologist and folklorist of renown, approaches her theme with the casual reader in mind as well as the specialist. Most of one's friends these days seem to be in search of a chilling thrill! Her stories, both the mysterious and the macabre, are part of the cultural inheritance of the Maritimer, a field in which Dr. Creighton has specialized for over twenty-eight years.

These "ghost stories" deal with premonition, buried treasure, phantom ships, haunted houses, headless spectres, and with "things that go bump in the night." Underlying all this is the author's own personal attitude toward an unrestricted universe of the spirit, and the immortal spirit of man.

BLUENOSE GHOSTS

BLUENOSE GHOSTS

Helen Creighton

McGRAW-HILL RYERSON LIMITED

Toronto   Montreal   New York   London   Sydney
Johannesburg   Mexico   Panama   Düsseldorf
Singapore   Rio De Janeiro   Kuala Lumpur
New Delhi

Published October, 1957

ISBN-0-7700-0022-3

9 10 11 12 13 D-57 6 5 4 3 2
PRINTED AND BOUND IN CANADA

Prologue

THE telling of ghost stories was not a part of my early experience in life. These tales came as a new and unsought adventure when I began my search for folk songs in Nova Scotia in 1928. Once I entered the home of my first singer, Mr. Enos Hartlan, there was no escaping them. The high point of land on which he lived, overlooking the eastern approach to Halifax Harbour, proved a fitting place for an introduction to this subject, for there were spruce trees around most of the property and several small houses built near a larger abandoned and unpainted dwelling.

"You see that house?" old Enos said proudly. "That's our Ghost House. No one don't live there no more." Then he explained that the house had been built of wood washed ashore from wrecks, and that where there has been sudden death there is likely to be a return of the spirit. Standing as we were in an exposed spot, with the surf pounding on the rocks below and the fog drifting in from the sea and wrapping itself around the trees and dwellings, it would seem that anyone with imagination could see anything. But what of sounds like heavy knockings where no human stood to knock, and bedclothes ripped off the sleeper night after night as though the ghost objected to his occupying a bed?

Many were the stories centred around this Ghost House, some of which will be told later in greater detail.

We would sit of an evening beside the old deal table in the kitchen until Mr. Hartlan's voice would fail him and he would say, "I can't sing no more tonight." But even though his singing voice grew husky he could still talk, and he told story after story of "apparations" seen by himself or told about by his uncle. Then when I visited his brother Richard I was told more stories, and gradually I realized that I was not immune to supernatural manifestations myself. Through the tutelage of the Hartlan men I understood for the first time the meaning of a strange event in my own life that had occurred not too long before.

This had happened just prior to the death of my eldest brother's wife. It had been a long illness, one that was very hard on both the patient and her family. We turned to anything that would distract the children, and one evening three of us sat in the drawing-room playing cards. Suddenly we were interrupted by a loud knocking. We all heard it and stopped playing. I made the obvious remark, "There's someone at the door."

"There can't be," Kathleen said. "There isn't any door on this side of the house." That was quite true, for the house was built on a hill, and that side, although on the first floor, was high above ground. Neverthless to satisfy me Barbara went to the nearest door.

"There's no one there," she said in a tone which inferred this was no more than she had expected. We were mystified but I forgot about it until the Hartlans took on my education. Then I realized that what we had heard were the three death knocks. These are heard in certain houses or by certain people and they come as a warning of approaching death. Whether my sister-in-law died on the day following the knocks or a few days later, none of us could recall. Kathleen remembers the incident, but Barbara was too young. Certainly at the time, we all heard it—three slow deliberate knocks that insisted upon our attention.

I have heard the knocks only once since then, and in a different house. I was sitting at my desk one morning shortly before twelve o'clock when I was startled by three distinct knocks. In my house there are many noises caused partly by the steam-heating system, and partly by people in other apartments. But there was something about these knocks that disturbed me greatly. I rose at once and called to Susan in the next apartment. There was no reply. I then opened another door, one leading to the hall. She was passing through, so I asked if she had knocked. She looked surprised and said "no." So I said, "I just heard three knocks," but I did not say three death knocks nor even admit that to myself.

Earlier that morning I had been with a friend who was ill but her condition was not considered serious. Now I was alarmed. Surely nothing had happened to her. I jumped in my car and hastened to her house and, on the way, wondered why I was driving and not walking this short distance. After writing for an hour or more I needed exercise, but I was possessed by a feeling of urgency, and time seemed important. She was all right of course, so I returned home but found it impossible to settle down. I seemed to be waiting for something to happen. It came when the telephone rang. The husband of a very dear friend had died suddenly in his car. Checking up, the time coincided with the warning and, when his wife was asked whom she would like to have with her, she had asked for me. Knowing she would want me, and all three of us being very close, I suppose he had been trying to get through to me.

Some years ago we had in Dartmouth where I live an Anglican clergyman, Venerable Archdeacon Wilcox. He was a boyish, lovable man, greatly esteemed by people of all faiths and ages. To our grief he developed cancer, and the time came when death was imminent. One morning I awoke very early and then went to sleep again. I dreamed that I was walking along a street and that I saw the archdeacon walking towards me, but on the opposite side. Normally he would have seen me, for he loved people and was always aware of them around him. He would have waved his hand and then raised his hat in a friendly greeting but, on this occasion, he seemed to be unaware of anything around him. Instead he was walking steadily ahead with his eyes on a goal at about the height of the house tops. I said to myself in my dream. "Archdeacon Wilcox is much too ill to be out walking," and then still in my dream explained it to myself by saying, "That's not the archdeacon; that's his spirit," and I was satisfied. He had died during that second period of sleep, probably at the time when I had seen him.

In the summer of 1954 I was at Indiana University. I have a sister for whom I am responsible since she is not well and cannot look after herself. I had only just arrived when word came that she was ill. Should I return at once, or was that necessary? She was constantly upon my mind until one day while walking across the campus I was for a fleeting moment in the house where she was living, and I had a picture of life proceeding normally. Someone walked quietly through a room and no one was disturbed in any way. I knew then that the trouble had righted itself, and subsequent letters showed this to be true. It seemed almost as though I had been transported to that house in far off Nova Scotia long enough to witness its interior and to calm my fears.

It was during my twenties that I became aware of a guiding spirit, a hunch if you like, and surely everyone experiences hunches. One day in Halifax I knew I should cross to the other side of the street. There was no apparent reason and the side I was on was less congested and more pleasant. Nevertheless the urge was strong and, for curiosity's sake more than anything else, I obeyed. The reason was given immediately when a friend got off the tram and upon seeing me looked greatly relieved and said, "I've been trying all day to get you on the telephone." The message was important.

Ever since then I have listened when this advice has come. It is not a voice that I hear nor a vision that I see, but a knowing that a certain thing is advisable. If I heed it, the reason is soon apparent. If I decide to go my own stubborn way I soon see my mistake. This gift I believe may be encouraged and developed. Or it may be confused with wishful thinking, and that can be dangerous. But when it comes in the manner I so often experience, and usually when least expected, it is something to be treasured and respected.

If experiences of this kind are rare, I fancy it is because most people think a hunch is no more than a fortuitous thought that just happened to come along at the right time. Obedience does not mean that you think no longer for yourself, but rather than when advice comes from a higher source you apply your own intelligence to the help that is provided and work with this guiding spirit as a team. What, for instance, but guidance could have told me to duck under the bedclothes at the moment of the 1917 Halifax explosion when part of the window casing with the nails facing down imbedded itself in my pillow where my head had been seconds before? My own common sense? No, I was too inexperienced. And why do I so often know how a thing is going to turn out and whether or not I should attempt this or that? Something outside is helping me all the time. Haven't you felt it too?

Another strange thing happened when I went to Toronto in March, 1956, to do the narration in a special broadcast of folk songs. A number of the songs on that programme had come to me from the singing of a fisherman, Mr. Ben Henneberry, who had died five years before and, in introducing the songs, I had talked of him and his island home. I have always toiled against a handicap of exceptional fatigue, and I always get worked up over any performance in public. Consequently when we were about half way through I began to feel a little shaky. Then to my great astonishment Ben Henneberry was with me. I neither saw nor heard him, but I received a message and knew it was from him. It said, "You're doing very well. Just keep it up." How did I know it was Mr. Henneberry? That I cannot tell you for I do not know myself. I certainly was not expecting him to come to me in the middle of a broadcast, but come he did. He had never appeared before. I was all right immediately and the broadcast proceeded with no one else realizing what had taken place. It was an encouraging experience, and proves that if your mind is receptive those whom we have perhaps befriended in life or loved, can and do help us in moments of need.

This recital of my own phenomena may seem lengthy and personal, but I trust it has impressed you with the sincerity of my belief in them. The same sincerity lies behind every tale in this book. They have come from many sources and from all walks of life, for ghost stories are found among people of the highest as well as of the lowest intelligence and education. They all have one thing in common. The people who told the stories were convinced they had happened, just as I believe in my own personal experiences that I have outlined. They have not been added to for the purpose of lengthening them, for a true ghost story is nearly always short. Many are given exactly as they were told, and all are by word of mouth and not from printed texts.

I have heard it argued that a ghost story is of little value unless it can be substantiated, but how can you prove something that has taken place only once and may never occur again? For myself I consider well the integrity of the informant, if he is temperate in his habits, and how much his outlook upon life has been coloured by a superstitious environment.

Whether you read this book for entertainment or for

serious research, I hope you will be rewarded for the time you spend. The material covers the whole Province and has been taken down over a period of twenty-eight years. The diversity and extent of our people's belief will, I think, surprise you. Here you will find ghosts in the form of big dogs and little dogs, lights, balls of fire, phantom ships, a man on horseback with his head under his arm, a boatload of pirates wearing old-fashioned clothes, soldiers and sailors in uniforms of a past era, women in white and women in black, an old sailor sitting on a cannon wearing a split-tail coat, a man covered with eel grass from the bottom of the ocean, a woman with a pair of stockings in her hand who stopped and put them on, a dead mother who came back to advise a sympathetic stepmother in a child's illness, a horse, a kitten, a pig, a barrel of brandy, and so on.

I do not suggest that all the stories are actually true. Some are the result of imagination, superstition, and fear, but there are many others whose authenticity cannot be questioned. I have purposely refrained from making comparisons with similar cases from other parts of the world because this book is devoted to the thinking of our own people. Any conclusions I reach have been based on what they have taught me, and not from outside reading.

I wish to thank Dr. F. J. Alcock for his unfailing interest and co-operation during the ten years that I worked for the National Museum of Canada when he was its chief curator; Miss Phyllis Blakeley, Miss Marion Moore, and Mr. G. D. H. Hatfield of the Canadian Authors' Association, Nova Scotia branch, for reading this manuscript and giving helpful advice; also the people of this Province who have generously shared their supernatural experiences with me, even though it meant that I often left their homes with a tingling in my scalp and a too rapid heartbeat.

—H. C.

Contents

CHAPTER ONE

Forerunners

FORERUNNERS are supernatural warnings of approaching events and are usually connected with impending death. They come in many forms, and are startling, as though the important thing is to get the hearer's attention. The most common forerunners are a picture falling off the wall or a calendar dropping to the floor at the moment when a distant loved one has died. Or you may hear your name called as I did when the mother of a friend died, although she had not called me at all. The three death knocks mentioned in the Prologue are forerunners and, to my knowledge, nobody has ever been able to explain them. Many people who disclaim any belief in ghosts admit to having had a forerunner which, after all, is just as much a part of the supernatural as the seeing of a spirit.

Although forerunner is the usual name in Nova Scotia, these warnings are known occasionally as tokens or visions. Whatever the name, the stories run the same way. I remember how my breath stopped momentarily one day when Mr. Eddy Deal of Seabright finished the folk song he was recording for me and said, knowing my

1

interest in such things. "Did you ever hear of a man walking with himself?" I said no, I hadn't.

"Well, there was a man here," he continued, "who felt somebody walking beside him and when he looked, he realized it was his own apparition. He was so frightened that he couldn't speak, for he knew the belief that this was a forerunner of death. A few months later he died."

I remembered then having heard of a Capt. McConnell of Port Medway who was said to have had a similar experience, only in his case his own apparition walked ahead of him and would not answer to his call. Instead, it left him and turned in at the gate of the cemetery with the result that the captain went home and said to his wife, "I'm not going to be long for this world." Soon after, he was stricken with pneumonia and died.

Returning to Seabright Mr. Deal recalled a man, named Henry Awalt, telling about being out on the back road when he met a tall man like himself. But, he said, he was so much taller than his own height of six feet that he could have walked between his legs. The apparition was carrying a lantern. Mr. Awalt recognized himself and in a few months he died, but not before telling his strange experience.

Here too a man named Pat is said to have learned his fate. Before his wife died he had promised that he would never marry again, but after a while he went courting. He was coming around the bend of the road at the top of the Seabright hill when he met himself. Knowing the belief, and looking upon it as punishment for breaking his word, he assumed this was his forerunner. He told the story before his death which happened three months later.

At Tancook Island in St. Margaret's Bay a man was going to the shore one day when he met himself. He told about it and said he was going to die. He did soon afterwards, with diphtheria as the cause.

It is comforting to know however that death is not

always immediate, at least according to this story from Tangier on our eastern shore, that is, east of Halifax.

"Mother lived on Tangier Island before I was born, and her sister, my Aunt Maime, was with her, a young girl at that time. One night Aunt Maime was looking out the window. The moon was bright. There was a little outbuilding nearby with a window in it, and she said to my mother, 'There's a woman looking out that window. It's myself, and I have a baby in my arms.' Mother went to the window and looked, and she could see it too. It was too far away for it to be a reflection, and anyway Aunt Maime wasn't holding a baby at that time. But fifteen years later when she died she had a baby in her arms, and my mother recalled the incident."

Usually with a ghost story or a forerunner you can find a reason for the happening, but there is one story that puzzled me for several years. I went back a number of times and made casual references to it, always hoping that a chance word might throw some light upon it. I was finally rewarded although the interpretation is still open to question. I will tell you the story and let you decide for yourself.

In the summer of 1947 I stayed at Victoria Beach where I was collecting folklore for the National Museum of Canada. I was told that I should see Mr. A. B. Thorne for an experience that no other member of his family would talk about. My companion was the author and poet, Martha Banning Thomas. The evening of our call was fine and pleasant, with a warm summer breeze drifting in our car windows. We drove the narrow, hilly road in the spirit of sweet companionship, little realizing that our return trip would be far from serene, or that our thoughts for many a night afterwards would be in a turmoil.

The Thorne house is at Karsdale, a white frame cottage with a garden that is always filled in summer with beautiful flowers. Mrs. Thorne is the gardener, and she knows

the botanical name of everything she grows. The interior
of the house shows the care of loving hands with its
hooked and braided mats, antimacassars, cloths with
crocheted edges, and embroidered cushion covers. She
also has treasures of old china handed down in her family
and cherished through the years. It is a dainty, pleasant
house, and she and her husband are a gracious host and
hostess, making their visitors feel at home immediately.

Mr. Thorne is a man of medium height with blue eyes,
an aquiline nose, and a rather sensitive mouth. Now
probably in his sixties, he can still dig garden or ditch in
a way that would shame many a younger man. Yet with
work to occupy him, and an excellent wife to care for all
his needs, he appears to be a singularly nervous man. This
is little wonder, considering the experience of his youth
which we had come to hear.

We had a short period of conversation until the proper
atmosphere was established, and then we asked Mr.
Thorne if he would tell his story. After a little hesitation
he began.

"I hope I'll never have to go through that racket
again," he said. "Well I'll tell you. I had just come
home from the States and I had a friend whose name was
Joe Holmes. We were always together when I was home,
but Joe wasn't very strong. We were young men then,
about twenty, and one evening we were together and I
had a letter to mail. We hadn't been drinking. I don't
want you to think we had because we hadn't, and we didn't
imagine what we saw. About ten o'clock we took the
letter to the post office. It was in the Riordens' house, the
way people often have them in the country. I lived at
Thorne's Cove this side of it, and Joe lived two houses
away on the other side.

"Well, we mailed the letter, and then we sat alongside
the road opposite the house and talked. It was a bright
night with a full moon, and it was too nice to separate
and go home so early. The Riordens' grass was about

three feet high at that time, and there was a turnip field behind it. We heard a hoe strike against a rock and it attracted our attention. We sat forward then and looked and, to our surprise, we saw a Thing come crawling on its hands and feet from the southeast corner of the house. Then it stood up and we could see that it was a man. We were on the lower or south side of the road, and it was on the upper or north side. Then it went out of sight.

"In the country we often think a lot without saying anything, and anyway there's often no need of words between friends. So we just sat there and didn't say anything, and before long it came out again. We didn't move an inch, but we watched, and this time it came half-way across the road. The time for keeping quiet was over now, so I said, 'Joe, did you see that?' He said yes, he did, and by this time it had gone back again. You might think we'd had enough, but we kept still and it didn't keep us waiting very long.

"The third time was like the others. It came out and went back. We still sat there and in a second's time it was back and it went under the cherry tree. There were more apple trees on our side of the road then than now, and they took to shaking and the apples fell to the ground. I was frightened by this time and I said, 'Joe, I've got to go home.' That would have been all right if we'd both lived in the same direction. Probably we'd have left even before that, but we were braver together. We decided to go to Joe's house and we started to run. Joe wasn't very strong as I said, but he always thought he could run, and he could, and I was afraid I couldn't keep up with him. I guess the fear got into my feet because I ran just as fast as he did.

"When we got to his house we stood in the road and talked. We were young men and curious, and we didn't like to leave it there because it would always pester us and we'd never know what we'd seen. It didn't seem like a prank, but if it was, we wanted to settle it. Finally

I said, 'Let's go back; I'm not afraid.' I wasn't either, so long as Joe was with me. Nothing was going to hurt the two of us and besides, it's easy to be brave when you have company. 'We'll see what it is,' I said. So we walked back and pretty soon we saw it and it was coming to meet us. It was half way between the Riordens and the Cronins, and that's the next house, the one in between. I said, 'There it is; don't leave me.' As I said, I figured that with two of us it couldn't do much harm and I wanted to find out what it was. I meant to touch it and then I'd know for sure if it was real. When we were within twenty feet of it I said again, 'Joe, don't leave me,' and then I walked up till my face was close beside it. I'll never forget that moment as long as I live.

"It had on black pants, a white shirt with a hard bosom front, and black braces. Its head was bare and he was of medium size. It looked as though its eyes were deeply sunk in, and they were very bright and penetrating, and the only thing it looked like was a skeleton. I didn't touch it, although I would have even then, but Joe gave a scream and ran, and I was scared. I wasn't long overtaking him, and from that time Joe had a hard time to keep up with me. It followed and kept twenty feet behind us. There were bars on the Holmes fence. We jumped them, and the Thing cut across the field to head us off, but we got there first. We stood in the doorway and watched it for half an hour. There was a stone wall with a rotten pole on top of it, and it stood on this pole. In the morning I went out and felt that pole and, do you know, it was so rotten it just crumbled up in my hands. Why that pole was so rotten it couldn't have held a bird.

"As I said, I'll never forget that racket as long as I live, and as for Joe, he would never talk of it except to his mother and to me A year later he was taken sick and a while later he died, and he always claimed this was a forerunner for him. We were both sure it couldn't

have been anybody playing tricks because the moon was
full and we could see everything as plain as in the day.

"Then a strange thing happened. Joe died of a tuber-
cular throat, and he died hard, but he never rambled in
his mind. It was always clear right to the end. But one
day not long before his death Joe said to his mother, 'My
throat won't hurt me any more. He (the apparition)
was here and rubbed it.' The pain had been almost more
than he could bear, but from that moment it stopped and
he never felt it in his throat again. I sat up with him
every night, and do you know what he looked like when
he died? He looked just like that man, for he was pretty
well wasted away."

Was this then the explanation, and had Joe seen his
own apparition as he was to appear in death? Was that
the meaning of it all?

When Mr. Thorne was through we sat quietly and,
after a while, I said jokingly that he would be telling me
soon what colour the man's eyes were. To my surprise
he took this seriously and pondered the matter. Finally
he said, "No I can't quite do that," but his hesitation
showed how vivid the experience was even to that day
which would be forty or more years after the event.

When the story was over Mrs. Thorne gave us a hot
drink and some cookies and we started back to Victoria
Beach. The country road was very dark that night and
there was no moon to comfort us—nor to show us this
unwelcome figure either. As we came to the Riorden
house Miss Thomas said, "Now that is where they sat,"
pointing to the bank on the south side of the road," and
that is where they saw it," pointing north

"Yes, Martha," I said, pressing the accelerator a little
harder.

"And this," as we approached the Cronin house, "is
where it stood in the road and they saw it clearly."

"Yes, Martha," driving faster still.

"And that is where it must have stood on the wall," she said as we reached the Holmes property. I relaxed a little then glad enough to be away from that district, for I wanted no more of the supernatural that night.

A year later I attended a service in the Karsdale church and the Thornes stood almost opposite me as we sang that lovely hymn, "Unto the Hills." When we came to the line, "No moon shall harm thee in the silent night," I looked at Mr. Thorne who has been a nervous man since this incident and thought, "But the moon did harm him." Or at least it revealed what the ghost was like, and the effect has never worn off. Would his nervousness be due only to the fright of a moonlit night in his youth, or does he fear that when his time comes the apparition will appear as his forerunner too? It is a question I have never liked to ask him.

Let us turn now to another kind of forerunner, and for this we will leave the Annapolis Basin and go to Clarke's Harbour on the southwestern shore, a settlement peopled largely from Cape Cod. Here in the old days, as in many other places, they used to have boards to lay people out on when they died. "A woman's mother-in-law had been sick, and one day as she was sitting in her kitchen she heard the sound of boards at her window. She got up and looked all around but she couldn't find anything to account for the disturbance. When the older woman died, her daughter-in-law heard the boards being put in the window, as sometimes happened when the main entrance was too small for them. She recalled her forerunner then and said, 'There's my boards.' "

Clarke's Harbour reported another event that was heard before it happened In Miss Evelyn Swim's home a sick boy was sleeping in the front room downstairs. "He was not thought sick enough to die," she said. "Mother was stitching, and Aunt Julie had just come from her room when they heard a little knock. Mother said, 'You go see who that is.' Aunt Julie went, but she came back and said, 'Levie, there's nobody there.' Then came another knock. She looked out and still there was nobody there. She went back to the child's room then and everything seemed in order. The knock came then for the third time. They couldn't understand it unless it was somebody playing a prank, but there was no sign of anybody anywhere. In a few days the baby passed away, and shortly afterwards the coffin maker came to get measurements. He put the child's body in the coffin and he used a hammer to drive little brads into the coffin. This happened three times and was so exactly like the sounds they had heard that they realized it had been a forerunner."

Another story came from the same house. It was told by a woman who had grown up here, then had married and lived in the United States and now was returning as a widow to settle in her childhood island home. This island, Cape Sable, is exposed to all the vagaries of weather from the Atlantic Ocean. The coniferous trees are small, and the island has a wind-swept look. Weather is a factor that can never be forgotten because fishing is the main industry, and most island men spend the greater part of their lives upon the sea. Now that a causeway has been built to connect it to the mainland it seems slightly less remote, but until very recently it could be reached only by boats which struggled against strong currents and pulling tides.

This is the widow's story told as she, Miss Evelyn Swim, Miss Beth McNintch and I sat together one evening.

"Father used to go to sea in the winters. When he left this time there were two little boys in our house. They were perfectly healthy and beautiful children. Mother didn't like staying in the house alone, so a cousin used to come and stay all night with her, and they slept together in the corner room. One night at twelve o'clock something woke them up and at first neither of them spoke. Finally my cousin said,

" 'Aunt Isabel, do you hear anything?' She said yes, she did. It was a frosty night, and what they heard was a rumbling coming down the road, rumble, rumble, rumble, rumble. It rumbled by the house like a wagon going over a frosty road. They were frozen in bed because it seemed to be coming straight towards our house, and that's what it did. It came rumbling around the house and stopped by the front door. They clung together in terror. Then they heard a knock like somebody pounding on something that was frozen. Then it sounded like something being thrown away. By and by it started again and turned around and rumbled back over the road until the sound was lost in the distance. They couldn't figure it out because they knew the sound of every wagon and who owned it, and who would that be driving up the road and turning off and stopping at their very door?

"They were up then, and they were afraid to go back to bed. Ma said, 'I'm going to get Maurice.' He was their neighbour, but Serena was afraid to go out. At the same time she wouldn't stay in the house alone, so both of them went and they woke Mr. Nickerson up and he came and stayed all night. He looked around but he couldn't see the track of any horse or wagon, so they thought it must be a forerunner and that my father was going to die. Ma cried and took on something awful, but the forerunner wasn't for my father. It was for one of the little boys who was taken sick and in a week was dead from diphtheria.

"The day he was buried was frosty and cold, just as it had been that night. He had been prepared in the house for burial. Then the hearse started up the road for the funeral, and it made exactly the same noise they had heard. All the people in the house could hear it coming over the frosty ground, and it came rumbling up the frozen road and rumbled right up to the house. Then it stopped before the door just the way they'd heard it. Ma and my aunt couldn't speak. They were listening for the next thing to happen. The hearse had a door at the back with a lock, and the undertaker couldn't get the lock open, so he picked up a rock and hit it. Then he threw the rock away exactly as they'd heard it that night. Everything was repeated in detail, and it happened about sixty years ago."

Miss Swim nodded her head in agreement, for she too knew the story well. It had often been told on the island.

At Marion Bridge on Cape Breton Island, they told of a child's death and of the tapping noise of the coffin maker being heard before the fatal brain fever had even begun. Another story came from a Mrs. McGillivray who had spent most of her life in this pleasant village.

"Father was a builder and was working away from home, and mother was expecting him to finish his work and come back. She would not have been surprised if he came at any minute. One bright moonlight night she was sitting in her rocking chair with one ear cocked expectantly when she heard wagon wheels outside. Then everything was quiet until she heard him take the butt of the whip and give three strokes on the door, but he didn't come in. She went to the door to open it for him, supposing he might be carrying a load and didn't have a free hand, but there was no one there. She went out to the barn then, but the horse and wagon were not there, and apparently had not come into the yard at all. She was very alarmed then, thinking something must have happened to my father. Everybody knew what three knocks meant and nobody at the door when it was opened, so it was with a feeling of great relief that she heard his wagon wheels very soon afterwards, and saw him in the flesh as he appeared in his usual good health and spirits.

"My mother puzzled over this and wondered what it meant, and later it was explained to her. At that time the body of a man was found up the Salmon River Road. The men who found it stopped at our house to change horses. They arrived at night, and at the very hour when she had heard them before, and they came to the kitchen door and knocked with the butt of the whip three times. Everything was repeated."

Forerunners come sometimes as a kindly form of preparation where the shock of sudden death might be too great. An Amherst couple, for instance, lived happily together, and both were in excellent health. There was no reason to suppose any change would come to alter their unruffled lives. The house they lived in was very old and had bolts to fasten the doors. One night Rachel and her husband went to their room and he bolted the door as he always did. They were no sooner settled than she asked him to shut the door. He said, "I did." She said, "It's open," so he got up and closed it a second time. Once more they prepared themselves for sleep when again Rachel pointed out that the door was open. This time after closing it he got back in bed, but crawled in beside her and shivered and shook. She said, "What did you see?" but he refused to tell her. Finding him so greatly upset, and not being able to discover the reason, she appealed to her brother for help. "No," her husband said, "I won't tell you now, but if it ever comes to pass I'll tell you then." The next day Rachel took sick and a few days later she died and it was all very sudden and distressing. She was laid out in a white dress and, when her husband saw her like this, he said,

"There, that's what I saw. Yes, I saw her laid out in her grave clothes."

Sometimes it is puzzling to know why a man will not try to avoid his fate, and some stories leave us with many questions unanswered. A young man in Caledonia was going down the Brookfield mine one day, and he came to say good-bye to his mother and aunt. He said, "I'll never see you again. I know I'm not coming out of the mine alive." They told him not to be silly, but that day he was killed. Nobody knew what form his warning had taken.

There are other forerunners however that have actually prevented disaster, particularly with men going to sea. At Jordan Falls the story is told of a vessel that was supposed to sail out of Shelburne with a crew of eighteen or twenty men. One Ephraim Doane was lying in his berth when he heard the mainmast fall. He got up to investigate and found the mainmast intact, so he took this as a warning, and the vessel sailed to Boston without him. It was December of 1888 and there was a great gale. The ship was lost off the New England coast with all hands, but the man who had heard the mainmast fall was spared.

At Liverpool Captain Godfrey's wife told me a strange story. "My husband was in his bunk ready to go to sea when first thing a bundle of papers came flying across the room and hit him. He thought his mate was having some fun, but he turned over and there was a blaze of fire the size of a man in the centre of the floor. A voice said, 'Don't go in this ship or you'll be lost. If you don't go you'll live to be an old man and you'll die at home,' so the next day he packed up and left the ship, but of course nobody knew why. They got a new captain and the ship sailed and was never heard of again. After that he sailed on ships all over the world and it was just as the voice said. When he died he.was an old man, and he died at home in his bed."

A warning told to me at Paddy's Head, a fishing village on the south shore, has a less dramatic ending because there is no telling whether it was really a warning or not. "At Aspatogan there were two fellows trying to get squid for bait, and there was a boat there from

Tancook Island. They are great fishermen at Tancook. They asked the Tancookers if they had been out in the big summer storm and they said no, they hadn't. They said the reason they didn't go was that their father had seen a man who had been drowned before that walking on the water, and the next day his brother had seen him too. They took this as a warning and stayed home."

Pubnico is an Acadian French settlement farther down the southwestern shore. One time a Pubniconian was on a ship in Shelburne and was planning to sail. A vision of his mother appeared and told him not to sail. It was so vivid that he jumped overboard and swam to shore. On that trip the ship was lost and all hands perished.

It seems unfortunate that warnings may come and not be recognized as such. The argument against this might well be that if we were looking for them all the time we would always be imagining them. But the following story would have had a different ending if the significance of the startling events had been realized.

Mrs. Ethel Morris of West Gore told me that an antimony mine used to be worked there. A Mr. and Mrs. Wallace had a boarding house at the top of Antimony Hill, and there were twelve or fifteen men living there. At two o'clock one morning there was a loud knock at the front door, an unusual circumstance in this quiet, peaceful inland village. A miner, Tom Weatherhead, said he would answer it so the Wallaces would not be disturbed but, when he got to the door, there was no one there. The knock had awakened the whole household. He went back to bed and a second knock came, and again he opened the door and found no one there. This time he walked all around the house and called, but nobody answered him. It happened a third time. His brother Jim took this one, but with the same result. The next night at two a.m. the mine caved in. Tom was killed and Jim was injured. Talking it over afterwards, nobody could account for the knocks unless they were a warning.

It is quite apparent that some people are more sensitive to impressions than others, although people who have little belief in the supernatural confess to experiences that are nothing less. A friend of mine when in New York went to a drug store for medicine for her dying father, and suddenly felt his handclasp on her arm. At the same time her watch stopped. This proved to be the very moment of his death. Communications from loved ones who are dying or in great trouble may therefore come in the centre of a city's traffic, or on a remote country road.

"Rod and Hector were brothers who lived in Scotsburn, Pictou County. One day Rod was working on a bridge when a big timber slipped and the supports came down. When he realized how seriously he was injured he said to himself, 'We'll have to get Hector for this.' At that identical moment Hector was driving to Pictou which meant that he was going in the opposite direction, and away from Scotsburn. Suddenly he felt a wall ahead of him, and he said to himself, 'Rod needs me.' The feeling was so strong that he turned back and on the way he picked up a friend. The friend could see his anxiety and said, 'What's the matter?' Hector said, 'I don't know,' and told him his feeling. Neither questioned what he was doing, nor were they greatly surprised to arrive at the house just as Rod was being carried in."

Another story where the family tie was very strong came from the same county. "A man and his wife arose one morning and set out for the house of their daughter Mary without the slightest idea of why they were going. As they approached her house they met a friend who said, 'I'm so glad you've come. Isn't it too bad about Mary.' 'What happened?' they asked. 'Didn't you know? She went to bed last night as well as we are and died in her sleep.' "

You may wonder how people recognize a phenomenon. It is difficult to explain and I suppose it needs to be experienced to be fully comprehended. I expect that in most cases it comes as it does to me, not as a telling by a voice that is heard, nor as a sign by anything that is seen. I can only describe it as a knowing. It is conveyed by some strange means of communication or transference of thought, and is so strong that the recipient has no doubt of its veracity.

People of Celtic descent, like those in our last two stories, seem to have an understanding of the occult that is denied to the rest of us and, because of this, we have a warm and tender story from Marion Bridge.

Mrs. Allen Morrison was deeply attached to a neighbour's baby, particularly as she had always felt it had been born blind. One evening between six and seven she was milking and had the milk pail in her lap. While the milk was flowing into the pail, encouraged by her gentle, competent fingers she saw a round red ball of fire coming in the barn door. She watched it and it came towards her and finally lodged in her lap. She freed her hand to push it to one side but at that moment it floated away. She waited, recognizing it as a forerunner, but for whom was it meant? She expected to see it go to her own old home where her elderly parents lived, but it changed its course and went to the Munroe house where the baby lived.

She finished milking and went home. She put on a clean dress and then went to the Munroe's house. They were accustomed to having her come in like this, particularly then because the baby had been ailing. She said nothing of the forerunner, but picked the child up and held it in her lap, ready to do anything that was required. The little one's short life was closing in, and in an hour the child stopped breathing. Who can say that in her loving kindness Mrs. Morrison was not guided to that house to care for that baby in its last moments? The mother, not realizing the seriousness of the illness might well have let it die unattended in its crib. Surely some higher power must have directed the course of the red ball to the one person who would recognize its purpose and would have the courage and greatness of heart to do its bidding.

If the young man in our next story had been of Scottish instead of German descent, he might have been better prepared for the following tragedy. He was coming from Petite Rivière to his home at Broad Cove one foggy night when he saw a woman alongside the road and, as he described it, she was a mass of fire. One night shortly after that, when his mother was going to bed, he heard her scream. He hastily flung open her door and found her a mass of flame. He tried to save her and was badly burned, but his help was too late. The lamp she was carrying must have overturned and set fire to her night clothes.

An incident from an Irish source came to me on my first visit to Devil's Island at the mouth of Halifax Harbour where I had gone looking for folk songs. The teller was old "Aunt Jane" Henneberry, and she repeated it on every possible occasion, sitting in her rocking-chair beside the kitchen window, looking out to sea.

"What I'm going to tell you now happened as true as I'm a-settin' here, and it happened just two weeks before the accident. (You will notice that this fore-runner is of an accident, and not of death). I looked up and there, standing in the doorway I seen the figure of a man. Not a man I'd ever seen before. No, no, he wasn't anybody I'd ever seen, but there he was just as plain as could be, and I knew that as long as ever I'd live I'd never forget the look of him. And besides, I thought to myself as soon as I'd seen him, 'There now, that man is a doctor.' I told th' island people about it, and I says, 'There's going to be an accident. It's a forerunner, that's what it is,' and do you know, it wasn't two weeks later that my Jim had his leg broken off in an ice jam.

"What a day it was. The ice never was in like that before nor since, not since the world first began. It was mountains high and it was blue right through. He was brought home and the doctors were sent for right away. It was a bad case, so not only one doctor came, but there was three of them. One was Dr. Cunningham from Dartmouth, the second man I'd seen before, but the third —now this is the truth I'm tellin' you. As soon as I seen the third I almost screamed. He was the very man I'd seen in this very room just two short weeks before. That is what we call a forerunner."

Another story from Devil's Island, also from an Irish source, came from Mr. Ben Henneberry, one of the best folk singers I have ever found. He said he was coming home from fishing one day when he saw a log in the water ahead of his boat. As he drew nearer it seemed to sink deeper in the water and, as he came along beside it, the log seemed to change to a plaid shawl. He was going to gaff it when it went pffff and disappeared. His son Edmund was with him at the time, and both were very much frightened. I had known Mr. Henneberry many years before he shared this strange experience with me. Three days later his wife died in childbirth.

The Acadian French at West Pubnico have their fore-runners too, although experiences of this kind are far less common here. During the Second World War one of their young men was serving overseas and his mother at home was a semi-invalid. One night a soldier came to her bedroom and she saw him only from the waist up. She was sure she was not sleeping, but she kept the vision to herself and slept fitfully, awakening with a lump in her throat, for she realized its meaning. The family could see that she was worrying about something but they could not think what was on her mind. Less than a fortnight later the news of her boy's death arrived by telegram. It was a great shock to the rest of the family, but she was prepared. It was then that she told the priest. The story has been related in the village in hushed tones ever since.

Here, too, a priest heard three knocks at three a.m. shortly before being called to a deathbed. More unusual however, was this event.

"One night my father was seeing a girl home. Her name was La Belle Frances. They saw a light in the marshes and she said to him, 'That light is for me,' meaning that it was her forerunner. He paid little attention at the time for she seemed perfectly well, but in three weeks that girl was dead."

A story came to me by way of Pubnico that has nothing to do with the French; it just happened to be known there. The people involved are probably of English extraction. They said that the girl in the story belonged to a very good-living family, and that they lived in Halifax. At the time, her brother Willie was serving overseas. She was awakened one night by the sound of the doorbell ringing, and she went downstairs to answer it. Her brother was standing in the doorway and he said, "My work is done. I've done what I have to do." Then he was gone.

Meanwhile her father had heard the sound of the door being opened and, when he saw his daughter he was angry. What was she thinking of to open the door to whatever stranger might be there at three a.m.? She surprised him by saying, "Willie was just here. I've been talking to him and he said his work was done." Her father thought she must have been dreaming and had walked in her sleep, but the next morning a telegram arrived telling of the boy's death. The story had been told to a Pubnico girl who was working in Halifax. My informants did not know the name of the girl in Halifax.

A story from an English source goes like this. Many years ago when people used to travel by ox team many miles to Halifax, a couple and their child broke their journey and put up for the night at Three Mile Plains. The mother developed toothache during the night, and her husband got up and went to the team for a bottle of liniment. As he went through one room he saw a woman in white sitting nursing a baby and supposed it was his sister-in-law who lived there. Then he realized he could hear her breathing in her sleep in the next room, so he woke her and asked what it meant. She awoke the whole household then which consisted not only of themselves, but a number of men who were staying there for the night. Some of them saw this woman go into the black-smith's shop across the road. They followed her and discovered that the shop had only one entrance. They went through the door but the woman and child were not to be found then or at any other time. Within a week the baby in the house died. They concluded that this must have been the forerunner of that event.

Mrs. Bishop who lives on the Broom Road at West-phal is a dear, motherly woman to whom many people turn for comfort and encouragement. One of these was a bachelor who suffered from a heart ailment and high blood pressure. About five years ago Mrs. Bishop had retired for the night and was reading in bed when suddenly everything in the house became very quiet as it does sometimes just before something happens. She kept expecting a rap on the door or a telephone call, and the tension lasted a good fifteen minutes. At that time the young man was presumably on his way to see her, but was stricken on the ferry, lost his balance, fell in the harbour, and was drowned.

Occasionally a forerunner is heard at two places at the same time, although this is unusual. It happened at Clam Harbour when one of the Stoddard men died. A few of his friends were sitting in the Russell home when they heard a man open the porch door, start to come in, and stop. When Mr. Russell went to investigate there was no one there. The same thing happened at another house in the settlement at the same time. The victim had died in his car either from carbon monoxide poisoning or from a heart attack. Death was sudden.

More extraordinary is a report from Cornwall in Lunenburg County of three forerunners in one evening. "There was an old soldier who had not completed arrangements about his cemetery lot before he died, although he had been working on it. The night he died a man was seen coming to a house carrying a lantern but when he failed to enter, an examination was made and there were no footmarks on the soft earth outside. The same night a car drove to a neighbour's house and went away, and again there were no tracks. The third incident was a light which appeared to lumbermen in the woods at about the same time. Putting all these things together, these people concluded that the old soldier must have been very restless before his death, and had probably wanted to get in touch with his friends."

We all do things at times which seem to have little meaning and then are explained soon after. "A man in Ellershouse was looking over his ties the night before his nephew died, a thing he hadn't done for years. He picked out a black tie and, for no reason at all, put it to one side. The following day he got word of the child's death which was totally unexpected." Similarly a cousin of mine was looking through some trinkets one night when she found a ring given her by an old sweetheart some sixty years before. She slipped it on her finger and her mind drifted back to those far off, happy days. Shortly after, she went to a friend's house and picked up a magazine and there she saw the photograph and read of the death of this same man.

At Cape Mabou they used to see an old man standing alongside the road. Sometimes in his place they would see a fine-looking rig, horse and carriage, but it went only one way, and it never left any track. That went on until one time an old school inspector was driving over the bridge and fell out of his carriage and off the bridge and was drowned. After that they were never seen again.

One November day I went to the supermarket where I met Rev. Grant MacDonald, minister of the United Church in Dartmouth. I had addressed a group in his church hall one evening, and had found him one of my most attentive listeners, particularly on the subject of ghosts. On Hallowe'en night he had heard me again on this subject, this time by way of television. He began to ask questions, and I thought how surprised other shoppers would be if they could hear our conversation. Being of Cape Breton birth he had heard stories of the supernatural all his life and had learned to discard those that were mere superstition or the result of overwrought imagination. Two stories, however, could not be dismissed, and these he very kindly recounted as we stood at one side of a busy aisle.

He had been born at Fourchu on the southern coast of the island. Not far from there the land jutted out into the sea and formed what was known as Winging Point. A man named Fred came there to live many years ago and settled in one of the small fishing shacks beside the water, but he could not remain there. Sounds came to disturb him, and these were so noisy that it was impossible for him to rest. He used to go to the nearest village and tell how he heard the voices of men shrieking as though in agony. His stories were not taken too seriously because he was an outsider and little was known of his background, but people encouraged him because he would be almost beside himself as he talked, and they were greatly entertained. Finally he could take it no longer and he moved away and nobody knew what became of him.

In former days there used to be many wrecks along this rocky shore, and in the spring of 1924 a trawler named *Mikado* foundered a few hundred yards from the place where he had lived. The sea was too rough for any of the crew to be rescued, and the people on shore looked helplessly on as sailors and all dropped one by one from the masts to which they had been clinging, shrieking with despair. It was thought some may even have gone insane before they finally lost hold.

The fishing shack had been unoccupied for five years, ever since Fred had left it. Now it was opened up and, as soon as weather permitted, the bodies were brought in and placed upon the floor. As they were going about their sorry business the men recalled the sounds that Fred had reported. Ever since then the people roundabout have concluded that he had heard the forerunner of this event.

Another incident came from Mr. MacDonald's grandmother, an upright realistic woman who was not given to fancies nor to making up tales for her own or other people's entertainment. She had five daughters, and one evening as she and her husband were driving home by horse and carriage they came in sight of their house and were surprised to see it all lighted up.

"The girls must be home," they said but, when they turned the final bend in the road there were no more lights and, when they arrived, there was no one in the house. They were at a loss to account for it. There was no moon that night, and it was long before the days of automobiles when there might be a reflection.

A year later one of the daughters died and people came from far and near to the funeral. The house was filled and all the rooms were occupied. Therefore anyone approaching the house as they had done the previous year would see it exactly as they had done. The question then arose. Had they seen a forerunner of this sad event? It was generally supposed that they had.

A man and his son in Oakland had the same experience of seeing their house on fire as they approached it, but they were never given an explanation. Or if anything happened to account for it, they failed to recognize it as such.

Mrs. McGillivray of Marion Bridge, whom we have already met in this chapter, told of another strange occurrence.

"One evening many years ago Uncle Neil was visiting us and I went to the window to draw the blinds. I stood there for a moment looking out at the night, when I saw a light moving up by the apple trees. I said, 'I think you're having a visitor. It must be someone carrying a lantern.' He said, 'I must go.' (Cape Bretoners are always considerate of visitors and would not dream of being away when a call was made). I said, 'No, don't go. I'm making the tea.' (That too is a Cape Breton custom; they always make tea for their guests.) But he felt he should return home.

"The next time we met he looked at me strangely and said, 'Was that a trick you played on me the other night when you saw a light going up my place?' I said, 'No, I wouldn't do such a thing when you were out ceilidhing (visiting). Mother and I were so glad to have you.' When he had arrived home that night he found no visitor there, nor had any of the neighbours called. That was October. In December his daughter died. It was probably a forerunner of her casket, for it had looked like a light carried by a person on a wagon."

The sound of a horse galloping got Willie out of his bed at Elton, P.E.I. It came right up to his door and he jumped to see who was there. He found no person and no tracks. The next night at the same time the sound was heard again, but this time in reality, and the rider brought a message that Willie's uncle had died during the day.

If this Clam Harbour man had known the meaning of

various signs he might have saved a life although in all probability the man would have died anyway.

"Some years ago another man and I went to pick our crews and afterwards I was eating my supper when outside my window I heard the awfullest noise of a man gasping for breath. It faded away and I looked and there was no one there. The next Sunday the man who had picked his crew when I picked mine died of a heart attack and he gasped for breath just as I heard him. I never guessed it was a forerunner for him."

Many people think that birds are forerunners of death and if one beats against the window pane or comes into the house they are sure bad news will follow. I would have thought so too if my father had died on a day in May when he was stricken, but the swooping of a bird against our window seemed to startle him so that his weary heart revived again, and he lived until the following October. It could still have been a forerunner although death was delayed. A friend of mine had a similar experience before her husband died, but I was in her house at a later date and twice heard birds beating against the window. I do not take birds too seriously. However other people do, and we get stories like these from Middle Musquodoboit.

"One time when dad was away from home a dove came into the house and flew around it. My mother said, 'Someone is going to die,' and my father had no sooner come back than a call came to tell him his mother had died."

"In Ship Harbour two young men were returning home one cold icy night. After the driver let his friend out he drove on alone and must have gone off the road. At that time his mother was walking down the road when a huge bird that was more like an owl than anything else swooped out of a tree and nearly knocked her down. It was an odd time of year for a strange bird to appear, so this was supposed to be a forerunner.

Many people are deaf to forerunners. Of six people sitting in a room with the body of a man who had just died, only three heard him call the name of his wife. Similarly when Indian sisters, Mary Ann and Kate, were sitting together making baskets at Mooseland and a friend of Kate's died in another village, only she heard a sound as of gravel rolling off the roof.

This reminds me of a tape recording I made of a Micmac Indian from Middleton. I expected it to be a moose call such as hunters make, but that was only part of it. "If the moose start to answer the call, then stop and fight and go away from you," Mr. Peter Michaels said, "it means there is trouble at home. It happened when my father died and this is the Indian's 'telegram'."

CHAPTER TWO

Leave 'em Lay

THE SUMMER of 1950 was spent largely along the shores of St. Margaret's Bay and I often used to drop in at the Boutilier home at French Village. Mrs. Boutilier kept the post office and had a number of supernatural experiences to recount. Her husband, known locally as Sydey Pete, was a man in his late eighties who sat for long hours every day beside the kitchen window, his crutch by his side, and an expression on his face that was dour and forbidding. I learned later that this was caused by continuous pain, and that he was a man highly spoken of by all his friends. It was a further surprise when they said that he had been a fine singer in his day. I wondered then if I could break through his barrier of silence.

On my next visit I therefore turned my attention to the old man, only to discover that he was stone deaf. This meant that everything I said had to be shouted at the top of my voice but he was willing to talk and soon seemed to be enjoying it. I gradually brought the conversation around to songs and told him about visits I had made to his friends in that community. It occurred to me that if I could get him to hum a tune this time, he would sing for me on my next visit. It took time and patience, but he did it without being asked.

I waited a few days before returning and upon the next visit carried my tape recorder into the house and set it on the kitchen table. No longer was I given a disgruntled nod as my only greeting. He spoke, and his words might have dismayed me if the foundation of our friendship had not been firmly laid. He pointed to the machine and said, "I'm not going to sing in that thing."

I said, "You don't have to, but you'd like to hear your old friend John Smith, wouldn't you?" At that he nodded happily, for Mr. Smith was also aged and infirm and it was some years since they had been together. We chatted away as I got the tape recorder ready, and then I played Mr. Smith's repertoire. These were familiar to Mr. Boutilier and he was happier than he had been for a long time, just sitting and listening. When we came to the end I said, "You're not going to let Mr. Smith get ahead of you are you? And besides, think how pleased he'd be if he could hear your voice." These thoughts evidently appealed to him and, to my great delight, he began to sing. I had to manipulate the machine quickly to catch him in time and my hands trembled because, in spite of his great age and infirmity, his voice was incredibly sweet.

At the end of the first verse he had to stop and cough and I took that opportunity to play his voice back to him. It was clearer than any of us had expected and he was delighted. He went on then from one song to another until his limited strength rebelled but, from that time, he bent every effort to record all the songs he could remember. When I left after my final visit he thought of all he had sung after his unwilling start. He then laughed heartily in a way that was good to hear from one who laughed so seldom now and said, "You've got a way with you, you'd bewitch the devil." I looked at Mrs. Boutilier doubtfully, not knowing quite how to take this, but she was smiling and assured me this was a great compliment. This singing and story-telling were probably the last real pleasure he knew. A few months later I learned with genuine sorrow that I would see my old friend no more.

With an old man like this there are many lapses between songs when I guide the conversation into channels that will be fruitful. It was on one of these occasions as he sat in his chair by the window that he recalled an experience of his youth. It embraced an old belief that there are those among the dead who will not tolerate any indignity to their mortal remains and that upon occasions some will even come back to protest actively.

"One time a friend of mine, named Henry, and I were digging a grave and we dug up some old bones. I brought home a piece like a rib bone, and Henry took some pieces home too. In the morning it was pouring rain and I looked out this window and saw a woman going past the house. She was a tall woman in a long black coat. I turned to stir the fire to make the room more comfortable, intending to ask her to come in out of the weather but, when I went to the door to call her, she had disappeared. We can see a long distance from here, and I couldn't think where she had gone. I told Henry about it, and he said she had walked past his house, too. In fact three of us had seen her.

"We got talking about her and the more we thought about it, the more we didn't like it, so we decided the bones might have something to do with it and we'd better throw them away. We wondered if they might have belonged to a woman pedlar who went around here years ago and, while she was missing, nobody could give an account of her. There were Indians a few miles out the road and it was claimed they had killed her. We calculated that was the woman. After we put the bones back, she was never seen again."

Another story of protest came a few years later from a fisherman at Spry Bay on our eastern shore.

"What I did see, brother Uriah and I. When my mother came to Mushaboom there was a place called Black de Cove and she dreamed there was money buried there. One foggy evening Uriah said to me, 'We're going to hunt for this money,' so he took a hoe and I took a shovel and we dug. The tide was low and we wasn't to speak to one another. After we got so far down we got a bone a foot long like a man's bone from the wrist to the elbow. The minute we got to it Uriah said, 'We're getting close to the money,' and I out the hole. You dassn't speak, you know, when you're digging for treasure. (The reason for this will be explained in the next chapter.) In five minutes the hole was full of water.

"Uriah should have thrown the bone back, but he didn't. He took it with him and, when we got home, he showed it to an old man we had in the house to teach school to the family. He was scared to death of it and told Uriah to take it back, but he didn't. That night it was dark and foggy and when he went out in the yard something chased him and it was as big as a puncheon. He claimed that after he went to bed he saw it come into the kitchen and he looked and saw it setting on a chair. He decided then that he wouldn't fool with it any longer and the next morning he took the bone and put it back in the hole. We never went digging again for the treasure, and the owner of the bone never troubled us any more."

From East Ship Harbour which lies along this same shore, Mr. Bert Power had this to tell.

"I lived on the west side of the harbour one time in Wes O'Brien's house. I was working up at the head of Ship Harbour and the missus was home. I used to come home weekends. One foggy night in winter time when I came home she said, 'Bert, I saw a ghost.' I said, 'Go away, what did you see?' and she described it. She said it was a light like a candle and first it was on one side of the screen and then on the other. I talked her out of it, and then didn't I see it myself.

"The very next night I went to the spring for water and there was this very light on the gatepost, and it was about the size of a candle. I kept thinking about it and expecting something to happen like it was a forerunner, but nothing did. Not any more than a trunk belonging to Wes O'Brien's boy who had been drowned in the harbour. It was here in the house and had his watch and some of his clothes in it and we had shifted it. I put it back, and that was the last we saw of the light, but that wouldn't be it, would it? It makes you think, that's all. With things belonging to the dead, whether it's their bones or their belongings, you should leave 'em lay. They don't like what they've left behind being disturbed."

We go inland from the Bay of Fundy now to Bear River, whose verdant hills and gently flowing waters make this one of the most idyllic villages in this Province. In these tranquil surroundings it seemed strange to talk to a Micmac Indian about fearsome things like ghosts and witches, but he said the Indians believed in them and that when old Jim Muise was their governor, he had a strange and frightening experience.

"A man at Weymouth wanted to buy a canoe and asked Muise to bring it to him. Jim got a boy to go with him, and told him he could have all the trout he could catch. He kept going and going as far as he could and, when it was coming dark, he saw an opening and turned his canoe in to the shore. After they had taken their gear out of the canoe, they turned it over for the night. They were both tired, the boy especially, and soon he was snoring.

"Jim had made a fire and he was dozing beside it

when he heard somebody coming. You can't fool an Indian in the woods you know, and he could easily tell the difference between a human's steps and an animal's. This was a person all right, but it was different and didn't ever get anywhere. When it got too close and he still couldn't see anything he woke the boy for company and said, 'Make some more fire.' They could both hear the thing all night making just enough noise to keep them awake but never coming in sight.

"In the morning when it got light enough to see, there were two feet sticking up out of the ground in front of them. They belonged to a fellow named Black who had been drowned and was buried with his feet sticking out. When they realized there was a dead man right beside them they packed up and got out of there in a hurry, because by this time Jim was sure it must have been this man's ghost that had given them the fright.

"I've thought quite a lot about that ghost. They say the dead don't come back unless they want something. It was a nice point of land to be buried on, but I guess he didn't like his feet sticking out that way. Mebbe Jim should have stayed long enough to tuck him in; cover them up with earth. I wonder if he ever did get that message across to anybody."

As you have seen, the disposal of the body and one's effects may be disturbing to the dead. It is therefore a rash and unimaginative person who will deliberately disobey their wishes, particularly if they have been expressed in words or on paper. We might go further and say even if they are only surmised. Not only must they be buried according to their desire, but they also expect to have any trinket they have specifically mentioned buried with them. The most hair-raising story in proof of this comes from Lunenburg.

"A woman was buried here with a diamond ring on her finger. Three young men at the funeral saw the ring and decided to go and dig the remains up and take the ring for themselves, and nobody would be any the wiser. It was a daring scheme but not too dangerous if there had been only the living to contend with.

"They went to the grave and it was a simple matter to remove the earth and open the coffin. They then proceeded to extract the ring but at that moment the dead woman sat up and spoke. One man died there and then. The second only lived for a short time, but the third survived the shock. By this time, however, the woman was so revived that she got up out of her grave and went home. When she knocked at the door and announced her presence her family could not believe she had actually returned. She remained there for some years with all the attributes of a living person except that she neither smiled nor spoke in all that time." Stories similar to this have been reported from Germany, Scandinavia, Finland, Africa and other countries where the person wandered about until a second death followed by complete disintegration in the grave.

We go now to Seabright, a little further down the road from the home of Mr. Boutilier who introduced this chapter. Here we meet Mr. Oliver Hubley whom I visited many times for both songs and stories. I often think of his remark when he first heard his voice returned to him from the magic recording tape. His face got very red and he said with a mixture of delight and shyness, "You know, I'm just a little proud of myself." His singing voice was responsible for that. Here is one of his recorded stories, but only first names are given as some of the descendants are still living.

"Nearly ninety years ago there was a young man named Allie who was a very wicked fellow and he contracted a disease that was incurable at that time. His sister Lillian used to tend him. He had a ring that she would a liked to had, and he also had a pack of cards he used every night, along with four or five other young men. As he was getting pretty low and his sister knew he wouldn't last much longer, she asked him if he would give her the ring and also the pack of cards. She said, 'I could wear the ring, and the cards would be nice to get my friends together with.' He says, 'No, that ring stays with me and when I'm gone, I don't want that ring taken off my finger. And as far as the cards are concerned, I want you to open the stove and throw them in and burn them up. I don't want you to use those things.' She said that she wouldn't bother just then, but she had made up her mind that she was going to take that ring off his finger. The day came that he passed away and she took charge of the cards and also the ring.

"Ten days after Allie died Lillian was at my mother's house where she and my aunt often spent their evenings. They were all good friends together. So she said, 'Barbery, what say if I bring down my cards next time and we have a little social game before we go to bed at night?' Mother says, 'I never play cards, but it would be all right for an hour or so. Bring them down, Lil.' So she did. They had just played two or three games when first thing they heard a knock on the side of the house. It started in the corner and went round about a foot at a time, right around till it came to the door. Then it was just like it struck the latch and jingled it. Mother says, 'That's somebody trying to play a trick. Don't bother noticing that.' So they kept on playing and the knocking got louder and it got up around the eaves of the house. It was so beautiful moonlight, and mother was never afraid of anything, so she said, 'Look, I'm going to open the door. You and Lil run one way and I'll run the other.' There were the three of them, you see, so they bolted out the door and round the house and it was nobody. She says, 'Are you sure you didn't see anybody run and hide?' 'No, I didn't see anybody,' So mother says, 'It's only somebody playing us a trick anyhow.' So they went in and started to play again.

This time the noise come down round the door latch and it shook the door latch so that you'd swear the door was going to go to pieces. At last she said, 'It's time for us to go to bed anyhow,' so they stopped playing.

"The next night they started to play again and until then everything was quiet, and you know how quiet it can be away out in the country on a still night. Then first thing the noise started in again but, instead of going round the eaves of the building, it took the door and shook it hard. Mother said, 'Whatever fool that is will tear the door right off the hinges,' and she went out and she opened the door and she said, 'You coward, whoever you are get out of there,' because she couldn't see a sign of anyone outside. As soon as she closed the door the noise came back and this time it hit the door three or four times in succession. Mother says, 'The devil, we'll close up and go to bed.' My father was away and they were all sleeping there together.

"The next morning she says to Lil, 'Lil, where did you get that pack of cards?'

'Why,' she says, 'they were Allie's,' and then she said, 'He told me not to use them but to burn them but I wouldn't listen to him.'

" 'You open that stove and put them in,' my mother said, so she got the cards and they all watched while she put them in the fire.

" 'Now,' my mother said, 'have you anything else belonging to him he didn't want you to have?'

" 'Yes,' she said, 'his ring.'

" 'Well,' she says, 'you'll have to make away with that ring.'

" 'No,' she says, 'he wouldn't like that. The last words he said was that he wanted that ring to remain on his finger.'

" 'Then he's got to have it,' my mother says, and do you know what Lil had to do? She had to go to the graveyard at twelve o'clock at night and punch a hole in his grave until she struck the coffin and drop that ring down to him and that's all they ever heard of him. That ended it."

A story on these same lines, but told in considerably less detail, comes from Glen Margaret, just a little further down this same shore.

"Uncle McDonald lived at French Village. When he died he was wearing his mother's wedding ring. He had said that he wished to be buried with it, and the people in the house knew this very well. Nevertheless they decided to keep the ring, and it was taken off his finger and he was buried without it.

"After his burial things began to happen in his house. For one thing his big rocking-chair rocked in the night and doors opened and shut and there was no peace for any one. They realized then that there was only one thing to do, so they dug him up and put the ring back on his finger. After that nothing happened any more."

Still on this shore, but nearer the main road, this story comes from Glen Haven.

"A man named John had a sister who wanted to be buried in the Methodist burying ground and they buried her in the Church of England cemetery instead. She used to come back and shake the whole house. It got so bad they had to dig her up and put her in the Methodist burying ground and then there was no more trouble."

Sometimes the stories take a ludicrous twist like this one from the Negro settlement of Preston.

"People passing the cemetery years ago were troubled by the appearance of the ghost of a man who was buried there. They decided he wanted a drink, so they got some rum, bored a hole through the ground to the coffin, and poured the rum down the hole. After that they were not afraid to pass the cemetery and they were never troubled again."

On a more serious note, there is a story from our

neighbouring Province of New Brunswick about a nun who appeared to a man on a bridge at Morrison's Cove. Her home must have been in France, for she wished her body to be taken there. She told him that if he would obey her wishes he would make so much money, and he must take a pick and shovel and dig up her remains, and he would have to do that alone. He promised to do it, but failed to carry out the task. Whether it was from conscience, fear, or the touch of her fingers upon his head we will never know, but soon grey streaks appeared in his hair like five finger marks.

For a reason that was never determined, a nun also appeared on the old highway between Chester and East Chester, according to my friend Mr. Earl Morash. Later it was seen at Zinck's Road on the same night. "There would just be time for her to get from one place to the other. She was first seen by a man on horseback, and then by a father and his two boys." It may be that in both of these cases their burial wishes were not carried out.

Some of the dead go so far as to disapprove of changes in their old homes. A fisherman at Victoria Beach said, "When Mr. Walters bought his house and was making repairs, a carpenter dressed in a pepper-and-salt suit would appear and say, 'Don't do that. Why are you doing it this way?' He was supposed to be the original builder who wanted his house left as it was."

At Victoria Beach Mr. Sam McGrath was building a house and was half finished when he would hear a noise like a wall being ripped down. It bothered him so much that he made inquiries about the lot and found that an Indian had been killed and was buried on that site. He knew the old belief that the dead do not like anything built over their resting place and, if I remember rightly, he told me that he moved to another location.

Mr. Archie McMaster is an elderly Scot who lives at Port Hastings. It is a joy to visit his house and to listen

while he and his wife sing Gaelic songs together, sitting
with their finger tips touching, and their arms moving
back and forth with the rhythm of the music. In his
younger days he used to go to the lumber woods of
Maine and there the men would sit around of an evening
spinning yarns and singing songs. A good story-teller
and a good singer were great assets in any lumber camp
and competition in both of these arts was keen.

The following story which he picked up there, may
have originated upon this continent although it has an
old sound and may have come over with early settlers
who handed it down. It is a good example of the theme
we have been following. Much of the charm of the
narration is lost in the printed word. I only wish I could
bring you his pleasant Scots accent along with this tale.
The house he tells about must have been a very desirable
dwelling judging by the trouble the son went to after his
father's death to make it habitable. Of the happenings
that took place after they moved to the paternal roof
Mr. McMaster said—

"They didn't get no rest at all, at all. They moved
out as quick as they moved in. It was so bad that he
twice hired a man to sleep there and see if they could
discover what was wrong, for nothing had ever caused
a disturbance in his father's day. In both cases when
morning came and he went to see what kind of a night
they had put in, he found that a man was dead. He
offered a large amount of money then to anybody who
would sleep in that house and about that time a soldier
came along.

"That feller, the soldier, went in and stayed all night.
He heard a little noise about eleven o'clock at night from
the other side of the house and there was a skeleton
come down and he started playing around on the floor.
He watched him for a while, but he got tired of looking
at him and he walked down to the other end of the house
and went to bed, leaving the skeleton rolling around on

the floor. The next morning the son who owned the house but couldn't live in it came to see if the soldier was still alive. When he saw that he was living he said, 'What did you see last night?'

" 'I didn't see nothing or hear nothing that would scare me,' he said. 'I want to stay here for a couple more nights before I have anything I can tell you.'

"The second night was pretty much the same as the first but, on the third night when the skeleton was dancing and tearing around, the soldier said, 'What in the name of God kind of man are you?' So the skeleton said, 'I'm glad you spoke to me like that. I wouldn't touch you. I didn't touch the other fellows who were here but they got frightened. I could tell the first time I seen you that I could get you to speak. (Many people think the ghost can speak only if the human opens the conversation.) You're not a coward at all.'

"Then he told him that he was the man who had owned the place, and that his son was scared his funeral would cost him money, so he hadn't buried him right. He'd made a cheap funeral. He said, 'You talk to my son, and tell him to dig into the graveyard and take my remains up and make a wake for me and notify all the neighbours around. Then when he notifies all the neighbours he is to make a good funeral for me and, if he does that, no one will hear nothing from me any more.' So the son did as his father wished, and the family lived peacefully in the house forever after."

There is no doubt about the locale of the next story, for it happened in the north end of Halifax. One day my furnace was being serviced by a man with the appropriate name of Burns. This included checking the thermostat. I had been working on this book and did not wish my train of thought disturbed and besides, upon this subject, anybody is grist to the mill. He must have been surprised therefore when he came to my sitting room and, instead of the usual form of conversation I said, "Do you know any good ghost stories?"

"Ghost stories?" He hesitated while he made sure that I was serious, and then said, "You should have been around when my father was living. He was full of them." Seeing my interest he went on, "He used to tell about a house on Windsor Street where they couldn't keep the doors closed. They even put nails in them and the doors would still open." In this story he was feeling his way along, getting his mind in order for the following tale, and trying to assemble the facts. He finished his work on the thermostat and then hesitantly continued his story.

"There was one thing happened that my father always thought was queer. My brother could tell you about it better than I can." He then told the story as he remembered it and later, his brother filled in the missing parts. All, including the brother's wife, had often heard the incident discussed and they assured me their father had always insisted it really happened. It is a different kind of "leave 'em lay," with a ghost having a proprietary attachment to a bed you would think he would be only too glad to forget.

Many years ago Mr. Burns' great-aunt and uncle kept a boarding-house in the north end of Halifax. Their name was McLaughlin. They bought what appeared to be a very handsome bed at an auction sale, but nobody could sleep in it peacefully. The disturbance took the form of hair-pulling and turning down the bedclothes. One of the boarders who used the bed had heard of such things happening and decided there must be a ghost in the room. He therefore asked the spirit what he wanted. The answer came that the ghost had been murdered in that bed and his body had been thrown in Halifax Harbour at Deep Water; that is, just off of Pier 2. This seems to have been the full conversation, and the Burnses were sure he had made no request.

In those days beds were often made of the finest wood, and the McLaughlins wondered if this might be mahogany. If it were, they could not understand why it had been painted over, so they decided to scrape the paint off and see for themselves. I would have thought this had happened before the ghost disturbed the sleepers, and that this might have accounted for his activity, but the elder Mr. Burns was sure it came later. At all events the mystery was soon solved for, upon one side of the wooden frame, they discovered human blood stains. Try as they would by rubbing and scraping they could not get those stains off and they decided then they were better off without the bed. They therefore consigned it to the flames and were glad to be rid of it. The incident has never been forgotten, however, and the story has come down through the family. The owners died about twenty-five years ago, and we presume the ghost rests peacefully, now that the bed that saw his death and retained his blood stains can no longer be used by others.

CHAPTER THREE

Ghosts Guard Buried Treasure

WHEN NOVA SCOTIANS tell their stories of buried treasure they assume you know the legend of the ghost that guards it. Treasure is a favourite topic, especially in rural districts. As you know, we are almost an island here and all along our shore line there are sheltered coves, bays, and beaches, with woodland growth coming close to the water's edge. These would all make excellent hiding places for pirates of the early days or others who may have wanted to dispose of their booty for a time. So, too, would the islands within the bays. A sea captain with a quantity of gold and silver in his possession may well have favoured hiding it until some future date, rather than risk being robbed of it upon the high seas. Or pirates may have preferred to commit it to the ground for a while and come back for it later on, marking the spot with great care by map and chart. Then again there were the Acadians who left their homes hastily. Some had time to confine their possessions to the good earth until they could return. There were others later who mistrusted banks and hid money on their property secretly, intending to reveal its whereabouts before death, but being stricken suddenly without having done so. This was said to have happened at Port Mouton, but the son was fortunate in finding the $2,700 his father had buried. It was in a three-legged, iron pot and lay two feet under ground.

The greatest inspiration however stems from the fact of Captain Kidd's fabulous treasure, and many people think that it lies in Nova Scotia. Some say it is buried in a bay that has three hundred and sixty-five islands and that both Mahone and Argyle Bays answer to these requirements. Rocks have been found bearing the name of the famous pirate. At Glen Margaret in St. Margaret's Bay there is a rock bearing the words "Kapt Kit." Oak Island in Mahone Bay, made internationally famous by the many unsuccessful attempts to find treasure there, has another. It bears the letters "200" and the word "Kidd." When first discovered it was in a field but was later dragged by ox team to the shore. Another lies at Marion Bridge. It is shaped like a tombstone but is not so large. It is not near any highway or waterway, and is set upright in the woods. It gives the year and date of his death chiselled in the rock, and these words, "Captain Kidd died without mercy." It was discovered by a man who was hunting and trapping and it was covered with moss, showing that it has been there for a great many years. A rock on White Island on the eastern shore has letters and a hand pointing to the tip of the island. Just why this name appears with its different spellings in such widely separated parts of the Province we will never know, for there is little likelihood that Captain Kidd was ever here.

We may speculate upon the source of treasure, but there is no doubt that money and other wealth have been extricated from the ground and washed up on our shores. People known to be poor have suddenly grown rich like a couple at Clarke's Harbour who were seen through a window drying bills on the oven door.

Another man there found a bag on the shore in the eel grass, kicked it, then opened it, and hastened to get his wheelbarrow to take it home. He and his family have prospered ever since. At Clam Harbour a woman dreamed of buried treasure and a man went with her and found it with a mineral rod. They unearthed a copper bake pan full of English sovereigns. It must have been a sizable amount for they divided it and the man was able to buy horses and also to send his sons to college. A transport struck off Egg Island loaded with soldiers for Halifax, and the payroll was on board. The captain and mate got the money chest and made off with it but nobody knew where they went. Fifty years later a small steamer went into a cove at Laybold Island. In the morning fishermen went out and saw the skids where an iron box had been taken from the ground. They have wondered ever since if this was the missing payroll or some other treasure.

At Indian Cove a man and woman went to get treasure revealed in a dream, but a ship's boat with ten men, each rowing a single oar, arrived at the same time. When these had left, there was nothing there but the hole and the skids. In a similar case at East Chezzetcook a man and his wife were just starting to dig and had actually got as far as striking the chest with their pick when they heard a boat coming. They did not want to shed blood to get their treasure, nor were they prepared to risk their own lives by claiming it for themselves. They hid in the woods and, when this boatload of men went away, there was nothing left but the imprint in the ground where the chest had rested and an empty three-legged iron kettle which they had left behind.

A man at Sambro picked up a gold statue from the ground; another at Ball Rock who never did anything but dig suddenly became prosperous with no rich relation to account for his changed circumstances.

This also happened at Blandford. Just a few years

ago two powder horns full of gold coins were found by two children playing in a quarry at Yarmouth. A chest filled with coins was taken from a stone wall when the Imperial Oil Refinery at Dartmouth was about to be built, and the owners of that property have prospered ever since. A Mochelle field is supposed to have given its pot of gold, and three silver spoons hidden by the Acadians, were dug up at East Pubnico. Men came to Victoria Beach and asked permission to dig on a certain property. They left before daylight, but not before placing two twenty dollar gold pieces on the owner's gatepost. How much had they taken away that they could afford to be so generous? At Berwick a story is told of a family who came to the eastern end of the Province soon after the Acadians left. They hired a yoke of oxen and a French plough from a neighbour. They were brought up with a jerk as the plough caught in the bail of a huge iron pot. The farmer suddenly realized what it was and sat on the ground to hide it. He said to the boy working with him, "Unhook the oxen and take them home. You can leave the plough where it is. I have a violent cramp in my stomach and when I recover I'll let you know." As soon as the boy left he unearthed the pot and with its contents, he and his wife bought a fine house. When they died they left a property worth $12,000. The pot was about two feet across and was kept in the family for many years. The story was told me by the descendants. Other French money was supposed to have been found on Goat Island by men named Delap and Holliday.

These are just a few instances to show that stories have some basis of fact and are not mere imagination and desire. We would know more if people were not so secretive about their financial affairs. They regard the finding of buried treasure as a personal matter and of course, in the days before there were banks to safeguard our wealth, it was dangerous to tell that one had it.

In the preceding stories the extrication of treasure was not fraught with any danger because presumably it had been buried in the normal way. Pirates, however, were not content with this and, to make sure that their booty would have an added safeguard, they turned to the supernatural for aid. Stories in support of this come from all races throughout the whole Province, and are so much an accepted part of their thinking that they deserve considerable attention. Because we have this deep-rooted belief, and because eye-witness stories have been handed down and do not vary, we must acknowledge a custom which could have originated only in a diabolical mind. The following story in explanation of this came from an Indian and had descended through several generations of Micmacs from one of their members whose name was Glode.

"There used to be pirates around on the south shore of Nova Scotia and one day this Indian named Glode was out in his canoe. He had his little girl with him and when they got to a place where there is a point of land, he saw a ship sailing towards them. They were scared of strangers in those days, so he paddled into a cove and hid his canoe away in the woods. Then he climbed a tree. From there he could see everything that went on, and he watched that ship. It stopped and the pirates on board took down the sails, lowered a rowboat, and four or five of them came ashore. They came straight to that point, chose a spot and started digging. The captain gave the orders. After they got a trench dug big enough, he sent two of the men to the boat for a big chest. After they had brought it up and put it down beside the hole he lined them all up and said, 'Have you got everything ready? Who's going to keep this money?' One of them says, 'Well, the other fellers don't say much. I'll look after it.'

" 'All right,' said the captain, 'You're to guard it for a hundred and fifty years,' and before the man realized what he had got himself into, the others grabbed him. They cut off his head then and they put him in the hole with the chest. After that they drew a map, covered up the hole, and went away.

"When the ship was out of sight Glode came down from the tree. He didn't know what the dead man was supposed to do, so he wasn't afraid to dig him up. He wanted to see what was in that chest. It was mostly gold. In those times Indians used to wear a sort of gown with no sleeves, so he took that off and piled in all that he could carry. Then he covered the place up again and got his little girl and the canoe. As they paddled towards the open water he got thinking that it wasn't safe for an Indian to have money and he'd be better off without it. By this time he'd reached a great big ledge two or three feet wide, and he'd made up his mind. He poured that money down in the split of the rock, and he never went back for it. For all I know, that money is there yet."

Mr. Enos Hartlan of South East Passage had been the first to tell me about the pirates' custom, but he varied his story in one point. He said that when the man volunteered to stay with the treasure "they had a party and they soused him (made him drunk) and buried him alive with the treasure."

At East Petpeswick a man named Stingles lived to tell of his narrow escape in one of these episodes. He was new to pirates' ways and was just about to offer, "but a darkie said it first and they off his head an' fired him down the hole." And at Port Hastings a story has been handed down, through three generations, of a woman who was in her barn when she saw a coloured man running down over the hill. He told men in the village that he had heard the pirates planning to kill him and bury him with a treasure and he had made his escape. He told them they had killed another coloured man the day before.

The burial of a human being with the treasure has

led to many strange beliefs and there are countless stories of his obedience to his orders. Whether he ever actually functioned as a guardian is an open question, but the fact that he might do so had an extraordinary psychological effect. Many a time a group of men have got as far as finding the chest, and one of them has spoken, thus breaking an inviolable rule. Without waiting to see what would happen they have simply dropped their shovels and fled, confident that the whole expedition was ruined by the indiscretion of one spoken word. For with human speech the guardian ghost was given power which, until then, it could not use. After this power was released anything could happen and, if our tales are to be believed, things often did.

The stories can be sifted fairly easily, taking into account the natural temerity of the informant and the extent of his superstitious belief. We know of many cases in which the digging has been interrupted by pranksters who could not resist the temptation to howl from a nearby bush or throw a pebble and sit back laughing as they saw the treasure-seekers flee in terror. As all digging must be done at night, any least sound would be heard by listening ears. It would take very little to frighten away anybody brought up on the potentialities of the guardian ghost.

As a result of these beliefs stories like this occur, the first one coming from French Village, by way of Mr. Boutilier.

"Every Sunday a man named Dauphinee, a friend of ours, would come down here, and one Sunday a storm blew up, and father and mother wouldn't let him leave. About twelve o'clock it cleared and he started for home. The wind had gone down and it had stopped raining. When he got between Clam Island and the main (mainland) he kept close to the island and he heard somebody hollering and he turned and looked and by and by the man told him to 'come ashore and take me off this island.'

He got frightened and took to rowing hard but the ghost came abreast of him and said, 'Come ashore and take me off this.' The third time the man said, 'You're not going to take me off this island? Do you mean to say I've got to stay here for another hundred years?'

"Another time three other fellows went to this same island and they started digging and one fellow was in the hole and he saw something and he was struck paralysed. The two others had to drag him to the shore and put him in the boat. He didn't know what he saw. It seemed to have struck him."

They said at Glen Haven, "If you talked while you were digging for treasure the money would sink down, or the devil would come with his head bare, or the man buried with the treasure would come with his sword in his hand to kill you." These are all fearful things to contemplate, so it is little wonder that at the snapping of a twig or the rustle of a leaf the stoutest-hearted men might scamper.

Because blood was shed in the burial of a treasure, there are those who believe that it must also be shed to get the treasure out. Also it would seem that the guardian ghost is not always a man. There are instances where a woman has been reported in that role.

"On Red Island at Chezzetcook Mr. Roast went out for his cows and a woman chased him around the island three or four times. He stopped for breath and she sung the pitifullest song he ever heard. She said, 'I'm in trouble. There's money here and I want you to get it. You've got to draw blood from two twins.' He could have drawed it from two lambs but he never bothered." (The guardian ghost's existence seems to be a strange contradiction. It may plead with the human to remove the treasure and even explain how it can be done but, when the attempt is made, it will carry out its orders in all sorts of terrifying ways.) In similar cases of "not bothering," and there are many, I have wondered if the thought of the treasure did not in itself bring joy to the person. It would be a profound disappointment to dig and find nothing. Why not enjoy the illusion and drift along, knowing that if the need for money became too great, the experiment could then be made and the risks encountered. Why chance the spoiling of a pleasant dream?

There are a few people however who know how to dispel the power of the guardian ghost so that digging may be done in safety. This curious belief has turned up four times in Nova Scotia but the only other parts of the world where it has been reported to my knowledge are Finland and Estonia. Each of ours is a separate story, and they come from Dartmouth, South East Passage, West Jeddore, and Port Wade. The most complete one comes from South East Passage through a family of German descent.

"A poor man from Rose Bay in Lunenburg County was out getting firewood when he saw a treasure chest being buried. After they'd killed their man and buried him with the chest and covered up the hole the pirate threw down his shovel and hoe and said, 'Now devil, you take the keys until such time as a rooster will plough and a hen will harrow. Then deliver up the keys.'

"So the man went home and he told his wife what he was going to do and he made a little plough for his rooster and a harrow for a hen. He took them then to the place and made motions for the rooster to plough and the hen to harrow and what should appear at his feet but a shovel and a hoe. He knew then the ghost wouldn't trouble him, so he dug and he found a chest full of money and jewels and he never wanted again all the rest of his life."

The Port Wade version adds that he was to spill the blood of the rooster as a final act to dissipate the evil of blood having been spilled when the treasure was buried.

Another story where blood must be spilled comes from

Ship Harbour. "There's a flat rock between Musquodo-boit Harbour and Jeddore. A sailor with a bundle in a handkerchief tied to a stick carried over his shoulder used to be met there. If he liked you, he'd tell you how to get the treasure, but if he didn't like you he'd disappear. He said you had to kill a baby and let the blood spill on the rock to get the treasure, but people thought it didn't need to be a human baby."

It was fortunate that I had a good background of these stories before I met Mr. Isaac Doyle and his family at West Jeddore. I might explain here that all along our southern coast there are points of land jutting out into the sea and that these form separate bays and harbours. You get place names like East Jeddore on the eastern side of the harbour, West Jeddore, and Head Jeddore, the head being at the land-locked end of the waterway. Mr. Doyle is an elderly fisherman and, like many of his craft, he has a gentle, kindly manner and a quiet sense of humour. He also knows all the customs and beliefs so far related in this chapter except that of ploughing with a rooster and harrowing with a hen, and he is also a singer of folk songs. When our talk turned to the supernatural he told me so many stories about a place called Goose Island that I felt I ought to see it for myself. Consequently an expedition was planned with Mr. Doyle as guide and his son Arthur and grandson Sheldon as boatmen. There were eleven of us in all, seven of them children.

Goose Island is not more than 200 yards long and 100 wide, and it is six miles out in the Atlantic from our starting-place at West Jeddore. As we approached it from the distances of Egg Island and Duck Island it looked completely unapproachable. At the eastern end however an opening appeared in the rocky shore. It was large enough to take a small boat, but not the large fishing craft we were in. That meant that we must go ashore in relays, rowed in the small boat we had towed behind us for this purpose.

Before the use of engines made it so much easier and safer to move about on the sea, men used to go out to Goose Island for a whole summer, leaving it only to go home on Saturday night. There would be as many as eight or ten of them and they lived in wooden camps. The island is almost flat and it is covered with a low scrub of weeds and grass, and it is protected all around by a rocky cliff.

Strange things have happened on this island. For instance different men have heard a boat rowing but, upon investigation, there was no boat there.

"My father walked all around the island, looking for the boat," said Mr. Doyle, "and suddenly his cap was taken off his head and clapped back with the weight of lead. When he got back to camp he heard a noise like fifty wine bottles being broken against the clift on the western end of the island. He thought afterwards that he might be hearing the sound repeated of a boat burying silver in that hole, as it might have done in pirate days.

"Another time some of the men went out there and they had a boat with a capstan for hauling the smaller boats in. There were three little trees on the western end of the island at that time and on that day three birds came and perched on the only three spruce trees on the island. They were unknown birds. No one had ever seen their like before. One was blood red, one jet black, and the other snow white. From the trees they flew to the capstan but, when the men tried to catch them, they flew to Black Point and were never seen again. The men all saw them and talked about them a lot. They decided they were three pirates, and that they were trying to show where treasure was buried. There are initials carved on the clift on the eastern end of the island and all kinds of plans, and we've always supposed they were French. They are all over the clift."

We were all over it too, up and down, scrambling from one craggy rock to another, trying to make some sense out of all the markings. I took tracings and photographs and sent them to the National Museum but there they remain, as much a mystery to scholars as they are to our fishermen. Mr. Doyle continued his story as a gentle wind blew in from the quiet sea and the sun shone upon us from a cloudless summer sky.

"With all these marks on the eastern end of the island we were sure there must be marks on the western end to give us our direction, but they couldn't be found. But when I was a boy we were there one handsome day with a spring tide and at about half-tide I was on a clift. I see this pretty thing on the clift like a butterfly, only bigger. I went down and looked up at it. Its wings were opened but it never moved. I went in and told father and Uncle Joe to come and look. It was brown and was about two inches long. It had four wings and a looking-glass on each wing, and the wings were purple. It was the handsomest thing you'd ever want to see. I said, 'I'm going to get that,' but they said not to touch it. But later I thought, 'I am going to get that,' and I put my hat over it and where it rested were the letters no one had been able to find. I went into the camp and I said, 'I got him and I'm going to put him in an old cigar box. I'm going to get a pin and stick through it so it won't go away.' It just laid there and never moved. Uncle Joe took his pipe and just touched it. It flew to the eastern end of the island and I after it, and then it flew to Black Point where the birds had gone and that's the last we ever saw of it. We decided it must have come like the three birds to show us how to find the treasure.

"On the eastern rocks there were the numbers XIX, so we supposed that meant we should walk nineteen paces in a direct line from the eastern to the western clift. I was only eleven then but I'd been hearing treas-

ure stories all my life. I went out about sundown and
I took a long bolt with me. I measured off my nineteen
paces and then I stuck the bolt down in the ground. I
hit something, and it was half a grindstone. I dug away
and felt something else and by and by came to an old
French brogan, or shoe, and I got that up. The earth
was all red around it. I suppose the shoe belonged to
the man buried with the treasure. I dug a little spell
longer but it was getting dark by then so I took the
brogan and grindstone and showed them to the men. By
and by I saw something coming and I thought it was a
woman except that there wasn't any woman out there
and no way for one to get on the island without being
seen. I tied the door shut to keep her out. We had two
big Newfoundland dogs and two camps with turf all
around. From just above where I had dug we heard an
awful sound and the two dogs started and they'd drive
their paws into the ground betwixt the two camps and
they kept it up. It made a comical noise like a man or a
woman, but not comical enough to make us want to keep
it around any longer. It was either the dogs or the ghost
all night, and when one stopped the other began. The
next day they made me take the French brogan and the
grindstone and bury them both in the hole and, for all I
know, they're there yet."

As we scrambled again over the rough weather-beaten
rocks every detail of Mr. Doyle's story was in my mind.
I looked again at the numerals XIX and wondered if
the fishermens' interpretation had been right. The other
markings were all initials that formed no word and therefore seemed to serve no purpose. We wandered on to
the place where Mr. Doyle had dug and observed that
the earth had been freshly turned. Perhaps it would be
safe now, and the ghost's vigil over. On the western end
we saw where the butterfly had rested. I looked at the
peaceful scene about me on this glorious summer day,
and also at my companions. A friend, Mrs. Frank Mac-

Donald from Dartmouth, was with me. The rest were all close relatives of Mr. Doyle, people completely trustworthy and fine in every respect. I tried to picture the island in a storm with the wind shaking the low scrub and the rain beating furiously against the rocks. The night would be dark then and there were men in the world of a very different calibre from my good friends the Doyles. I shuddered and thought with pity of a ghost destined to stay in such a lonely exposed spot as this for as many years as the pirate captain chose to consign him. Or was this a woman ghost, since it was a woman Mr. Doyle had seen? Poor unfortunate soul.

The children scampered happily like mountain goats, jumping from rock to rock, caring little for such thoughts. I shook my mind free and looked instead upon Mr. Doyle as he stood tall and straight for all his eighty-two years. The wind caressed his white hair, almost with tenderness as he waited patiently for the children to finish their fun. As he turned his kindly blue eyes towards me to make some further remark I breathed a prayer of thankfulness that my visit to Goose Island had been made under such auspices, that there were people in the world, like the Doyles, and that I had been privileged to know them.

Let us turn now to the Micmacs whose stories follow a not dissimilar pattern. This was told by Louis Pictou's wife Evangeline as she twined the ash sheens into the basket she was making.

"Years ago there used to be people who buried treasure. My father had built a house in back of my grandmother's. There was a little porch and three doors to open before you could get into the bedroom. I was just a child and I slept in a corner of the bedroom that we all shared. This night the others were laying there talking and about twelve o'clock the door opened and in came a soldier with his head off. He says to my father, 'Andrew, I'm tired keeping the money for you. I'm not going to keep it any longer. My time for guarding it is up.' Daddy says, 'How am I going to find it?' The headless soldier he says, 'You follow southwest and you go twelve o'clock at noon and you got to take your wife and you got to take your daughter and when you get there, there'll be something strike you and where you fall, that's where you are to start digging.'

"So we went and he fell and there he started digging. He came to the pot that held the treasure and was just bending down to get it out of the hole when my mother said, 'Oh Andrew, look at the little monkeys on the fence,' and daddy went to look and the pot went down in the ground. So he said, 'I'll try tomorrow,' and he did, and he had the pot up in his hand. They claim you must either take money out or put money in before it is yours and he thought maybe if he took it out it might hurt me or my mother. He decided we were getting along all right as we were and, rather than run the risk of something happening, he let it go back in the ground. Every so often since then something comes back and tells him to go and get that money."

There are several interesting features about Evangeline's story. For instance the lack of a head did not prevent the ghost from speaking. A suggested explanation for this is given in the chapter on Headless Ghosts. Then there is the appearance of monkeys. In so many cases the diggers keep faithfully to the ban against speaking but, at the moment of finding their treasure and succeeding in their quest, they are startled by something so surprising that they speak without thinking. This happens over and over again in these tales, but this is the only instance I have of monkeys making an appearance. These animals would indeed be startling because monkeys are not indigenous to our Province and certainly would never be seen in our woods unless they had got loose from a travelling circus, a most unlikely event. Where the story varies from the usual pattern is in the treasure still being available the next day. Once it goes back to the earth it stays there as a rule for seven years, and it is useless to start digging before that time. The belief that in order to get treasure you must put something in the hole or take something out, is known in Sandy Cove and Victoria Beach.

The most famous spot in Nova Scotia for treasure digging is Oak Island on the southwestern shore. Immense sums of money have been spent in trying to solve the mystery of various wooden platforms placed beneath the sod by men of an earlier time. Digging always proceeds just so far when the sea comes in and the place cannot be kept dry. Various expeditions have arrived with the latest scientific equipment and men have dreams of great wealth hidden in the island's depths. For this island was covered with oak trees at one time, and there are supposed to be oaks where Captain Kidd buried his gold.

Having heard of an iron tackle being found on a branch of an oak tree years ago, one of the local men decided to go out and see what he could find. Friends went with him. They were digging and had just struck something when they saw a boat rowing in with eight oars, four on each side. Knowing by their dress that the men were not of this world one of them spoke, and the object their picks had touched vanished before they could see what it was.

One man said, "My brother was digging on Oak Island once and he got so far and had to quit. The next time he went back a man in a red coat came to meet him. He said, 'You're not digging in the right place,' and he disappeared down the very hole where he'd been digging."

Again, "On December first, twenty-two years ago a party of us went digging on Oak Island. We heard a noise like a heavy fence mallet hitting the ground with a hard thump. It began a hundred yards towards the

shore and kept coming nearer and nearer. One of the
men broke his shovel and spoke, so we had to leave.
We'd begun at twelve, so we went to bed till four and
went out again before daylight. We got five feet down
in hard pan and we found seven or eight live frogs. We
could never understand how they got there where the
earth is so hard and dry. As we dug, the treasure seemed
to go down further. We bore holes six or eight inches
but we couldn't seem to bore through the hard ground.
The last noise we heard was on the shore about six feet
away. There was thin ice there and it wasn't broken,
so that didn't account for it. The sounds followed the
line the pirates would have taken in burying their treasure. We had to give it up at daylight but coming home,
we saw something tall and white three-quarters of a mile
up the shore. It went up the field and disappeared. In
the middle of an afternoon in 1950 my wife saw it again
in the same place. It was like a tall white pillar.

"My brother wasn't the only one who has seen a man
in a red coat. A lightkeeper's daughter when she was a
little girl was supposed to have seen him and later, when
she was thirteen, she told her father she had seen two
men over the hill. He went down and looked, but there
were no men and no tracks in the snow. One time a boy
from Chester Basin borrowed a boat and went out and
when he came back his mother saw how white he was and
said, 'Did you see anything?' and he said, 'If you saw
what I saw!' for he too had seen the man in the red
coat."

Another story comes from East Chester. "Twenty
years ago a fellow named Mills came and asked me for
the loan of my boat to get some clay, and he wanted to
go to Oak Island for it. I said it wasn't clay he wanted,
but the treasure, and the man admitted he had a mineral
rod. After a while he came back, rowing for all he was
worth and as white as a sheet. He said, 'I went out there
and I had the mineral rod and first thing a man spoke

to me and here was a soldier with a musket on his shoulder and he said, "You're in the wrong place," and he took me to another place and disappeared.' But they went out again, Mills who had seen the soldier, and a man, and a boy. They started to dig and before very long, on the other side of the island, was a sound like a man with an anvil driving fence sticks. The boy quit and so did the man and last of all Mills and, when they got to the boat, something came down to the shore and it looked like a four-legged animal draped as though it had a sheet over it and it came to the water's edge and was still there when they rowed away."

At Wolfville I was told, "A big bright light comes up at Oak Island and they can see the men come up as though they were hiding the treasure (an example of "looking back into time" or hindsight). One family moved from the island on account of it and that was about 1921.

"Old man Joudrey lived on the island for years, but he moved away and it was supposed he went because it was haunted. He said when he was ploughing he would hear unexplainable noises."

The story of Oak Island has been written up many times and will continue to be a subject for speculation as long as its mystery remains unsolved. But if those who come here wonder why it is so difficult to find local men to take part in their excavations, the reason is not far to seek. Let visitors from other parts approach them with the most modern and costly equipment possible as they have often done and the local men will scarcely lift an eyebrow in response. But let them bring in addition some foolproof charm for quieting the guardian phantoms which so far they have failed to do, and they will show as adventurous a spirit as anybody. A man can pit his strength against the known but against the unknown he would rather keep a respectful distance.

There is a place at Pubnico with the odd name of

Dick's Noise, an unusual name in a French settlement. It came from a man called Dick being the first one to hear it and report it. The story was told by Benedict d'Entremont.

"Many years ago a dory was seen coming into Pubnico and there were four men in it. They were supposed to have buried a treasure there and also a man to stay with it. Their reason for thinking that was because when the boat went out again there were only three men in it. Since then there are sounds like loads of stones being dumped, chains rattling, big iron-heeled boots walking around, and horses and carts. Some men took dogs down there once and the dogs were scared. The sound is not heard all the time; only on the first of December."

Mr. Enos Hartlan said, a wistful look in his pale blue eyes, "My mother nearly had a treasure once, true as I'm a-settin' here. She dreamed a dream three nights runnin' that there was money in back of Cow Bay. (Such dreams usually come in cycles of three.) Yes, she dreamed this dream three nights. The next night after she had her work done she took her hoe and shovel and walked through the woods. She found the spot all right and then she started digging, and she had just dug a little bit of a hole when a groan came up out of it. She kept diggin' though and soon there was annuder groan, and she got timid. (This is little wonder for she had been brought up on the foregoing beliefs and this would be a lonely spot even in daylight, with low spruce trees all around her and the surf pounding heavily on the beach nearby.)

"Her little dog had come with her and, after the third groan my mother stopped because the dog took after the sheep. (Here again is that counter-attraction to make the seeker speak.) She told the dog to keep away from the sheep and then she heard a jingling in the hole. She remembered then that she had spoken and that the ghost could do anything to her it wanted now. She was almost too frightened to run, but she did run though. She run all the way home.

"Afterwards she got two men to go out and dig again. Not that same night, but some time afterwards but all they found was two sticks. The treasure had gone back in the hole and she said it wouldn't come up again for seven years. Yes, treasure comes up every seven years for a bath, you know." (This was said in all seriousness.) They did not return in seven years because rushes had grown all over that particular spot." It is odd that they were content to leave it there though, because they knew the formula of the rooster and hen. Perhaps they were not as ingenious as the man in our earlier story, and did not realize that a miniature plough and harrow would do. Like so many others, they were content to dream and to satisfy themselves with the thought that pirates' money is bad money, and no good can come of possessing it.

Mr. Horace Johnston, farmer and fisherman at Port Wade, used to say, "Some times I tell the truth and sometimes I don't." This is supposed to be one of his true stories (I think). The setting is beside the Annapolis Basin.

"When I was a young man, a Scotchman came here and claimed his father had sailed with Kidd. He had a chart and he supposed Kidd had hid his treasure at Hudson's Point. Four of us went with him to dig but, for all I know, the treasure is there yet. I saw the chart and went once to find it, but I'll never go again.

"These treasures are supposed to be dug at night, so we went at ten o'clock. We could tell exactly where it was by the chart. In those days when the treasure would have been buried a man was killed and buried with it to stand guard. The Scotchman had hunted up some pretty brave fellows to help him and he was a-digging on even shares. I was young then and I didn't fear the devil or anyone else. If he came along and I couldn't cope with him, I figgered I could run. We had a man named Corneil, Ike Fleet, the Scotchman, and me. That made four.

"Well sir, we hadn't been digging long before we had an extra man with us. We had five, and he was there all night. While we was a-digging in the hole with pick and shovel and throwing stones, we didn't notice the fifth man but, when one of the party crawled up out of the hole and looked back, there were still four below. He dassn't speak, but beckoned up us, all but this extry man. Then we went away and talked it over.

"Who's the fifth man?" he says. We went back and there he was all alone in the hole now and still digging. All at once there was the devilishest noise I ever heard. The ground trembled and the rocks shook. I began to get tender-footed and the rest were shaking some, but we had one brave man among us. That was Ike Fleet. When it got too tough for us and we mentioned leaving, Ike said,

" 'No, I'm not going to leave. We've come to dig a treasure. We heard a little noise, but that's thunder. Maybe it was this extry man digging deeper and rolling a big stone that made a noise like thunder. Anyhow I'm going back,' and, mind you, he did. It took a brave man to do that, and a foolish one. We were twenty feet from shore and the tide was a hundred feet out as it often gets in the Annapolis Basin. First thing we knew Ike was in the waters of the Basin to his neck, and none of us knew how he got there. He wasn't hurt, but we didn't have any trouble getting him home after that.

"What did the extry man look like? He looked like any of the rest of us working at night. He was a medium height and he was digging with pick and shovel just like we were doing. Whether he really put Ike in the Annapolis Basin or not I don't know but, if he didn't, how did he get there all of a sudden over 120 feet away? I'd like to know the answer to that, but I'm not going back to find out."

A story from Stillwater says, "Some men were digging at Port Hilford Beach in Guysborough County and they came to a box. One of the men spoke and the box went out of sight, but they dug again till they found it. Night came on, so they left it, planning to take it away with them in the morning but, when they went back, there were half a dozen men standing around it with no heads, so they couldn't touch it." In Mahone Bay when they dig for treasure in a certain place it thunders, no matter how fine the day.

A note with the next story says it was told with a twinkle in the teller's eye, so you may take it or leave it as you please. "At the old foundation at Port Royal there is supposed to be a treasure. One time we took our picks and shovels and a little to drink. About ten the moon came up. By the corner of the barn where they used to see things, we were digging and joking and by and by when we were down about three feet we came to a flat rock. It was as big as the top of a table and we figured that was the top of the box that held the treasure. We shoveled it off and one fellow up-ended it and said, 'There's something else down here!' It was one of those old iron cook pots. He was just going to tear the cover off when he looked up. He said, 'Look there,' and, as far as we could see was a big rock hanging above us by a rope as big as the Peggy's Cove rock that could have fallen down on the three of us, and a big hound of a man with black scraggly whiskers on him and he had a handkerchief knotted in four corners and a big loose shirt and a belt and a candle. He was holding the candle against the rock that held the rope up and the rope was burning. His feet were bare and the moon was bright. The three of us all saw the rock with the rope holding it, and we skedaddled. We went back three Sundays afterwards and we couldn't see where we had broken ground.

It looked just the same as all the ground around it." So said my informant from Tantallon. Was this an actual experience or a story that has been handed down? In one respect it reminds me of a story from Blue Rocks in which a woman asked a companion to help her dig. She said there was no need to be afraid because she would hang a stone overhead like a mill stone that would fall down and kill the ghost that was guarding the treasure. How you could kill something that was already dead, she did not explain.

An interesting story, but one with an unsatisfactory ending, comes from Parker's Cove on the Bay of Fundy shore. This is a remote spot, accessible now by car over a mountain road, but reached at the time of our story only by horse and carriage or by boat. Any stranger appearing unannounced would be well looked over and questioned, for they would be few and far between. A woman turning up alone would be almost unheard of.

"When my father lived at Parker's Cove he dreamt three nights in succession of money buried at Big Pond. He even dreamt how to go and get it. He was to drain the pond and dig. The dream used to ask him, 'Why don't you go?' Years later an old lady came in one day and said she was on her way to the poorhouse. She asked for something to eat, and then said to my mother, 'Would you like me to tell your fortune?' She was a complete stranger. She said, 'You're going to have one more child.' Then she said, 'Your husband dreamt three nights running where to find money and how to get it, and if he gets it he can make a chain to go twice around Nova Scotia.'

"After that they tried to dig but it was quite a job. They had to do it at night time unbeknownst to other people and that was hard, because the place was close to the road. It was odd that this woman appeared at all, and we could never find out who she was or where she came from. She said to my mother, 'If he doesn't get it, nobody else will.' Well he didn't try very hard, and I guess it's there yet."

Dreams of buried treasure are not confined to remote villages. "Over a hundred years ago a sea captain from Chester Basin sailed to Boston and went with a girl there. She dreamed three nights running there was a barn at Chester Bay with a big granite rock and a piece split off one side, and that it was on an island. The girl had never been here. The captain was going on a trip and hadn't time to look for it, but he told my grandfather and his brother about it. It wasn't hard to find and one night four of them went out. They worked quietly and, after a while, they heard a noise like a bird whistling three times and then a sound like a rock thrown three times against the barn.

"By the time they got to the flat rock they were supposed to find, they had to stop, but they cleared the ground above it for when they could come back. It was a little while before they returned. This time they put a crowbar down and they couldn't believe their eyes when there was nothing there. The rock had gone and there was nothing but an empty hole. But about that time a man named Cleveland at Blandford got rich and he seemed to have everything he wanted. They never asked him, but they thought he must have rowed out to the island, found the hole, and discovered the treasure just below where they'd finished off. That island answered the girl's description exactly."

Mr. Washington Harnish of Hubbards told of people from New York who hired a schooner many years ago as the result of a dream and took away a treasure from Shut In Island in St. Margaret's Bay.

Many years ago too, Mr. Albert Foley had met a man at Head Jeddore who told him about a treasure at Salmon River and said, "There will be enough there to make you and all this place rich, but you must follow instructions." Mr. Foley thought about it and decided not to take the risk. But one evening when he and his wife were having tea late in the fall a rap came to the door. They were surprised to see a stranger there. They asked him to come in and sit down. He said, "There's treasure buried on that island out there. You should go out and get it." At that point Mr. and Mrs. Foley both had a creepy feeling which they had not felt before he began to speak. This increased as he continued, although he was dressed in ordinary clothes and there was nothing about his appearance to frighten them. He said, "You have to go after twelve at night on the second Tuesday and there must be two people. One will land and he will find three steps and a lead pencil. There will be a woman in white come with no head. She will try to get in the boat but the other man must push the boat away and not let her in. She would try three times, and the third time it would be all right to take her in and then she would lead them to the treasure." After he had given his instructions, the stranger went away, but he left such an unearthly feeling behind him that the Foleys decided to leave the treasure where it lay. Yet at the same time they would see a light that came up the harbour to a spot just west of the Salmon River Bridge. It went from the west side to the east and back, and just a little up from the water and moving quickly. Different people saw it, and all thought it indicated buried treasure.

Years passed and the story became well known, for the Foleys had told their experience. Eventually their son and a friend went out, deciding the place was Mackerel Island. They found the pencil and steps as indicated, but no headless woman came to guide them so they gave it up. Would that prove that no treasure had ever existed, or had her vigil expired?

In another story from this district a woman in white

not only tries to stop the treasure-seekers but she swims after them and tries to take the oars. This is an unusual feat for a ghost, for it is an old belief that they cannot cross water.

At Victoria Beach a pall cloth such as those used for a funeral, has often been seen crossing a road. It comes up from beneath a rock, supposedly to convey the information that treasure is there. Another old belief is that you can secure a treasure for yourself by throwing your coat over it. A man tried this when he saw a chest crossing the road at the top of the Seabright hill, possibly the same chest mentioned earlier in this chapter. Immediately he was surrounded by a bodyguard of soldiers. He was so terrified that he shut his eyes and ran right through them, and never stopped running until he got home. The next morning he went back to the place. His coat was lying there but, alas, there was no sign of the chest.

You will recall the ghost earlier in this chapter who begged to be taken off Clam Island. One night two men were digging there and one of them said, "I believe we've got the chest." Immediately a whole army of soldiers appeared above them, dressed in the uniforms of pirates. (I was not aware that soldiers dressed as pirates, but let us not spoil a good story for the sake of a small detail.)

At East Petpeswick too a number of ghosts have been seen. "My grandfather and grandmother were roving up the Narrows one handsome moonlight night and they saw a man-o'-war jolly boat. There wasn't a sound. The crew were men-o'-war sailors. The boat kept on up the harbour and then turned in to the shore. They lost sight of them then." It was supposed they were on their way to their buried hoard.

These stories could go on indefinitely, so let us end our chapter with a final one on this subject from Mr.

Enos Hartlan. "Father was coming from Cow Bay one beautiful night and he picked up a collar in the sand at low tide. He was looking at it and he heard a sound, 'Put it down.' There was nobody in sight. He heard it a second time, and still he just stood there looking. But the third time the voice hollered and the whole earth shook, and that time he put it down in a hurry."

CHAPTER FOUR

Foresight and Hindsight

FORESIGHT

THE FORERUNNER, as you have read, usually deals with sounds. Foresight, on the other hand, is visual. On the island of Cape Breton it is known as double vision or double sight and people who have the gift are said to be double-sighted. It occurs here mostly among those of Scottish descent although there are isolated instances among other groups. On my field work for the National Museum of Canada in 1956 I visited many descendants of settlers who came originally from the highlands and islands of Scotland, and was amazed to find this strange faculty possessed by so many people. Perhaps the word gift as applied here is inappropriate, for a gift is a pleasurable attribute. This is not, for the vision is usually that of a funeral. Stories, of which there are a surprisingly large number, go like this. I quote from the words of Mr. Hughie Wilson of Glace Bay.

"There was a woman in Mira who could see a funeral ahead of time, even sometimes before the person had been taken sick, and she would know whose funeral it was. When it happened she would be walking along the road and would be pushed to one side by the crowd following the hearse. The experience would exhaust her because not only could she feel the passing procession, but also she could tell who were the people in it."

Another woman at Round Island had this same faculty and could describe the clothes the people would be wearing. Mr. Angus A. MacDonald of Loch Lomond, Mr. Peter McKeigan, Mr. Donald McPherson, Mr. Peter Morrison and Mr. John MacDonald of Marion Bridge have all reported being pushed off to the side of the road by a passing funeral and some, like Capt. Simon Lewis of Edwardsville, could distinguish the people in the carriages and tell where the horses would be placed for colour, John's horse being grey and Peter's brown. Similar stories have come from Big Bras d'Or, St. Anns, Boularderie, and Glace Bay; in fact from all over the island. In most of these cases everybody might feel what was passing, but only one could see it. That one would tell the others to step to one side as he did himself and, at the same time, he would bow his head and raise his hat in respect.

"A Mr. McNeil of Bras d'Or was down by the shore one day when two younger men came along looking for a boat. He said they must not go out in the boat that day. 'If you go one of you will not come back at all, and the other will almost not come.' They laughed at his foolish superstitions, launched the boat, and chugged away but, sure enough, it happened. Their boat capsized and one of the men went under and was never seen again. The other would have been lost too if another boat hadn't seen the accident and come to his rescue. He pulled him out of the water by the hair of his head as he was about to go down for the last time."

An amusing incident along these lines took place not far from Glace Bay. A man was on his way to kill a pig when he met a woman known to have second sight. She looked at him in distress and said she saw blood on him.

He felt very uncomfortable but decided to go on with the job. He killed the pig but his knife slipped and before he knew what was happening he was covered with blood. Pig's blood.

The ability to see ahead is not the prerogative of older people only. Peter Morrison was only twelve when he saw a coffin-shaped light pass him low to the ground and turn in at the cemetery just before a fatality at a mine, and the same thing happened to Mrs. Allen Morrison and a friend when they were young girls. A boy at Point Edward heard digging in a graveyard when the ground was frozen too hard to be dug, and in all these cases a death followed within the week.

On Cape Breton's north shore, tools have been heard rattling before a death just before they would be required to make the coffin and, in the Morrison House at Marion Bridge, the box where funeral clothes were kept would open by itself just before being used.

It is necessary to keep these manifestations in mind to comprehend fully the significance of the two following stories. The first comes from Mr. and Mrs. Bagnall, an elderly couple who live at Glace Bay.

"When we were young people it was the custom for us to make the coffins for our own dead, but you couldn't put the parts together without specially matched planes. My father was a contractor and had moved away to the States, but he had left his box of tools behind. They were in a chest with a cover and the box was bound with brass. Without the tools it would have weighed 150 pounds; it was heavy.

"One cold night in February when we were twenty-two we had been out and, when we came home, we didn't bother to make a fire but went upstairs to bed. Just after we got into bed we heard a noise. There was nothing downstairs to make a noise but the tool chest, and it was all packed up ready to be sent away. The crash sounded three times. Mrs. Bagnall said, 'What noise is that?' I said, 'Something slipped downstairs,' but I knew. I was familiar with it because I had heard it before and there is no other sound like it. I didn't like this happening in my house and I said to myself, 'This is one time that I trim it.' (Overcome it.)

"In the morning my uncle came across the street and told me that grandfather had died during the night. He said he was going to make the coffin, and would I let him have the planes? I said, 'No, you can't get them. The trunk is packed to go away.' He said, 'I'll go across to John Hardy's.' That was fifteen or twenty minutes away, but pretty soon he came back. John's planes were at the French Road twelve miles away. So he said, 'Now I'll go up to McKinnon's. That was three miles away and no cars to drive him in those days. I was ashamed all this time because in five minutes I could have had them out but I thought if we could get along without using them, they wouldn't make that noise the next time there was a death.

"Well, after a while he came back again and by now it was three o'clock in the afternoon. He said, 'We'll make it without the planes.' I said, 'You can't,' and I knew he couldn't, so I had to open the box and unpack the tools after all. Whether the tools ever jumped again at the time of a death I don't know. I shipped them off the moment they came back, and I hope that's the end of them as far as I'm concerned."

Next we have a story from Marion Bridge which contains most of the motifs already mentioned and a few more to boot. They follow one another in rapid succession, and each one is important in folklore. It was told by Mr. Alex Morrison, son of the blacksmith who plays such an important part in it.

"A strange thing happened just before Sandy Munro fell over the bridge and got drowned. At that time Neil McPherson was just a lad and he was walking over the Marion Bridge one night with his mother. He stopped for a moment and said, 'Come here mother and look at the little boy lying on the bottom of the river.' His mother couldn't see anything and told him to come along home. It was just after this that Sandy was drowned, but that wasn't all that happened.

"About that time they were seeing a light on a boat up the river at Grand Mira. The owner wanted to sell the boat but nobody would buy it, being suspicious that something must be wrong with it on account of the light. My father wanted it, light or not, so he bought it.

"They always thought foul play had caused Sandy's death. The night before he died the irons in the smith were making a great racket. You could hear them in the forge and they seemed to be jumping around. Sandy and the blacksmith were friends and the boy often did errands for him. Just before he died the blacksmith had asked him to take an axe across the bridge for him. He was doing this when he must have met two boys who were known to be bad and whose mother was said to be a witch. Someone saw the boys having a tussle on the bridge and, a while later, the body was discovered lying in the water as Neil McPherson had described him to his mother.

"They called on the blacksmith then to get the boy. The grappling irons he used to take him from the water were the ones that had jumped in the forge the night before, and the boat that he took to go out on the river was the one that had shown the strange lights and that nobody would buy but my father. After the body was recovered Sandy's mother had a dream. She thought the boy came to her and pointed to the blacksmith's axe as it stood in its place at the forge, and said, 'That's the axe that killed me.' And when Sandy's body was laid out on the bridge of the boat my father had bought, there were a lot of people from the village who came to look at him. One was the boy who was supposed to have murdered him. You know it's an old belief if a murderer passes by or touches the person he has murdered, that blood will issue from the wound, and that is exactly what happened. The wound that killed Sandy was in his temple and, as the suspected murderer walked past him, blood flowed from the wound and stopped as soon as he went by. The thing was hushed up and the boys and their mother moved away, but that's the way it all happened."

A story of another boat comes from Broad Cove in Inverness County. It was a good boat as far as the owners could see, and they had built it themselves. Soon after it was finished, however, people began seeing lights on it, and there was no accounting for them. Since no physical explanation could be found, the lights were taken as a warning and, one of the older men said, it must never be used again or it would drown its passengers. Consequently it was hauled up on the shore and left to rot until it was of no further use.

At this time a young man named McNeil was building another boat and he looked at this derelict lying idle. He thought he might as well remove the steering irons and use them in his boat. The older people, he thought, were pretty superstitious. Why listen to all their foolish talk? So he took the equipment and he and his brother set out for Prince Edward Island. They were sailing close to shore with everything well under control when a squall came up so suddenly and so unexpectedly that it capsized their boat and they were drowned. Was this mere coincidence? We shall never know.

When Donald McDougall saw a black boat sink in a vision, he and his friends all supposed a boat of that colour would be seen by him some day. When Archie Gillis bought a blue boat they concluded the old man had made a mistake and had seen black instead of blue. The blue boat, however, proceeded on its way without accident. What Mr. McDougall had seen was a black car, but he had the vision before automobiles were known.

In the place where he had foreseen it, a black car went through the ice.

Another Cape Breton story is perhaps more forerunner than foresight, and is very like the Fourchu story in that chapter told by Rev. Grant MacDonald. "One winter night the people of Boularderie were disturbed by the sound of noises on the shore. Drift ice was in, but this was a different sound. They invited their neighbours to come and listen, and they could all hear a murmur of talking and a rattling of ropes on boats. They were greatly puzzled.

"The following summer three men were out in a boat and they tried to land, but the sea was so high that they failed in their attempt and the boat capsized. Two of the men were drowned. It was at the exact spot where the sounds had been heard the winter before, and the noise made by the people who gathered there after the accident was exactly the same as they had heard then."

A man from Sydney Mines was coming home one night and was passing a house where the inside stairway was very narrow, too narrow for anything large to be taken outdoors that way. In such cases windows were sometimes used instead. A daughter of the house was lying at that time upon her deathbed and, as he looked towards the house, he distinctly saw her coffin coming out through the upstairs window. In a few days the girl died and her coffin did come out that way.

Rory was double-sighted. It happened that a young man died and, when people went to see him, they remarked that he hadn't lost his natural colour. It was also noted that his fingers were supple. At that time there was no such thing as embalming. One day Rory came to the lad's home and said to his father, "And you buried your boy alive." The father was most indignant. Rory said, "If you don't believe me, dig him up and you'll find him on his face." The mother was so distressed that somebody suggested they open up the grave and find out, but she replied, "If I did and I found Rory was right I'd never come out of the grave." So the doubt has always remained, but the benefit is given to Rory.

A woman in Sydney got up one morning and said to her husband, "I had a horrible dream last night. I dreamed your sister Martha was dead and you were summoned home. I dreamed I saw the funeral and, when the casket was being taken in the double doors, they couldn't get it through so they had to take it back, put it down, get a hatchet, and chop enough away to make room for it to go through. The horses were grey, not black as you would expect for a middle-aged person." That morning, shortly after the dream had been told, a telegram arrived saying, "Mother died, funeral Tuesday." Now the dream had said Martha, but the telegram said Mother.

The husband left at once for Yarmouth and, when he had gone as far as Windsor, he met his brother-in-law. Feeling that he might have further information he said, "John, what happened to mother? She was fine when I heard from her just the other day." John said, "It isn't your mother. It's Martha," and it turned out that the operator had made a mistake in transmitting the message.

They went on then to Yarmouth and the funeral was held on Tuesday. When they brought the casket in they couldn't get it through the double doors and they had to take it out again. In his haste, as John ran for something to open the door with, he picked up a hatchet and, as he began to use it, he thought of this dream. Then the funeral was held and sure enough, the horses that drew the carriage were grey.

Visions of the future do not always deal with death, and may have a happy significance. "At Framboise a man was living in a new house and he died of TB (tuberculosis.) His widow and one son moved away and the house was left empty for some time. We could see it

easily from our house and one night, when we happened
to look out, we could see a light. Yes, there was a light
in the house and there were people passing between us
and the light. We saw it again, and nobody living there
for a year and no way for anybody else to get in the
house. The lights meant the house would be occupied
again, and so it was. About five years later a family
bought it up and moved in and we saw everything
repeated exactly as we had seen it on those two occasions."

At Port Hood I talked to two women who had one
day seen a city and two churches on a site where there
was a later drilling for oil. To date the city has not
transpired, but it is expected to come some day. Train
headlights were seen long before there was any train.
At Wellington, Prince Edward Island, in December,
1885, a phantom train was seen by forty people.

Turning now to the peninsula of Nova Scotia, but still
with people of Scottish descent, we have two women
at Bridgeville in Pictou County. These sisters were
awakened one night by the sound of a train and they
got up and saw it running along the track. At that time
there were no trains there and, although they were not
far from Pictou, they had never seen a train in their
lives. They described their vision and the following year
surveyors arrived. Eventually the train ran where they
had seen it. At Eureka in Pictou County a child had
the gift of foresight and it came to her several times.
She would say, "Do you see that light down there?" but
nobody else could see it. At that time the railroad had
not even been planned, nor did it come until she was
grown up. She not only lived to see the train, but married one of the men who worked on it.

During my recent visit to Marion Bridge a huge piece
of road-repairing equipment used to glide up and down
the road like some great pre-historic monster. I never
saw it without wondering if the Scots ever had a vision

of its appearance in the community and if so, what a
great fright it would have given them.

Although the Scots in this Province are far more
double-sighted than other races, we also get stories like
this from a Mrs. Hirtle of German ancestry who lived
in Lunenburg County.

"We used to live at one time in Mahone Bay, and
then moved away. One night I knelt down to say my
prayers and the house in Mahone Bay came up in front
of me and, as I looked at it, I saw a funeral procession
leave the house and go through the field. I thought a
great deal about it, but didn't mention it to anybody.
The house was then occupied by people named Evans.
In the morning my father came in and said, 'Evans'
little girl died last night.' I said, 'What time?' He said,
'Half past nine.' I had taken note of the time and it
was at half past nine that I had seen my vision."

Mrs. Hirtle came honestly by her ability to see things.
Her mother had the same faculty for she had been lying
in bed one night when she felt a cold hand come down
and pass over her face. She sat up in bed greatly startled
to see her aunt standing over her. The aunt said, "Fare
thee well." Mrs. Hirtle's mother was not frightened
enough by the occurrence to call the family but, in the
morning when she came downstairs, she announced that
her aunt was dead. Word came later than this was so.

At Annapolis Royal a woman of English descent was
given a visual warning. She had an eleven-month-old
baby, to all appearances in perfect health. "One night
I was awakened from my sleep and saw a little white
coffin in front of the bed. I woke my husband and said,
'I'm afraid something's going to happen to my baby.'
He laughed at me, supposing I'd been dreaming. The
next day for no known reason my baby died in my arms."

A woman of French descent at Boutilier's Point had
this to tell. "My mother had been sent for to stay with
my grandmother who was dying. One night all of a

sudden the lamp shade at our house came apart and the crinkly part at the top flew up two feet and then came back and set on top of the shade. Grandmother died at Indian Point at that time."

A mother at Oyster Pond said, "The night my husband's father died there were several of us here. I went upstairs to see that my babies were all right and the three-year-old opened her eyes and said, 'Mama, was grandpa here because I saw him beside my bed and he looked right down on me but didn't say anything. He had on a white shirt.' He was very fond of the children but, as for being in a white shirt, that seemed very strange because he so seldom wore one. The child was sure she was awake when she saw him. That night he died and of course, he was laid out in a white shirt."

Tancook Island, where the people are largely of German descent, reported this amazing phenomenon. "When Sebastian died, when his last breath came, the whole shape of him came out of his mouth like he was a young man, no longer old and wrinkled, and it went out the door. Just before he died three little taps came to the door, just a couple of minutes before. He must have heard them because he looked to the door. Sebastian's mother was seen twice by two women after she died."

A young man at Jordan Falls had gone to sleep after walking home from Lockport and was wakened by a light in his room. A picture of a girl friend, though not the one he was engaged to marry, floated through his room. It was not a dream, but a vision, "and later he learned she had died at that time."

Two extraordinary stories were confided to me in the summer of 1956, both by rather shy, gentle ladies of more than usual intelligence. The first story I think had never been told to anyone before, but I was permitted to use it here as long as no names were mentioned.

"My husband had multiple sclerosis. He has always been a good-living man but has never been particularly religious. He is well educated, but not an intellectual. The doctors thought an operation might help him and he was sent to Montreal. He has always been perfectly clear in his mind. He has only once mentioned what happened, and has never referred to it again. I respect his silence because it must be a wonderfully precious memory. He said that one night Christ came and sat upon his bed. No word was spoken, but he felt a deep peace."

Think of it. A person like that does not make up such a story, nor did the next one, told by the second lady.

"When Rev. Mr. Hares was in Windsor I attended a Whitsunday celebration of holy communion in the Anglican church. He was a deeply spiritual man. As he was preparing the elements I looked up and was startled to see a brilliant tongue of flame that rested for a brief period on the top of his head and then vanished. It did not move nor flutter, but lay flat, just as it must have done on the heads of the disciples. I watched in fear and my knees trembled. Then I looked to see what the other parishioners were making of it but I realized they hadn't observed it. The vision seemed to be for my eyes alone and I was greatly upset. For a long while I kept it to myself, then finally told Mr. Hares. He was most disturbed. We discussed it and agreed it couldn't have been a shaft of light through a stained glass window, nor was there anything else to explain it. This took place about a year before he died."

The stories of Christ's appearance and the tongue of flame came to me by the merest chance, for I had never met either of these ladies before. I have wondered since how many people have seen or heard things which they have kept locked in their own hearts for fear that the telling of them might result in their being ridiculed or misunderstood. A vision is not a thing to be talked about lightly, so it is possible that there are others who have experienced equally extraordinary phenomena about which we will never hear.

HINDSIGHT

WE HAVE just seen how some people have visions of future events. There are others who have looked back and have seen before their astonished and unwilling eyes a scene from out of the past. Mr. Earl Morash of East Chester who has had one such experience, calls it looking back into time. This is far more unusual than the perception of things to come, and it can be terrifying. It is best explained by a life-long resident of Annapolis Royal who told it as a legend of her family.

"When my grandmother was a young girl about the year 1830 or 1835, there were soldiers here. One evening when the officers entertained as they so often did in those days, she met a young man and danced with him all evening. They jokingly made an engagement to go horseback riding the next morning and, although they had spoken in jest, my grandmother took the invitation seriously, as indeed was intended. She therefore got ready and waited with more than usual pleasure for the young man to appear. Time went on and he failed to come and she was very displeased. When he finally arrived he looked ashen and distressed. He was full of apologies and told a story that none of them believed. He said, 'I spent the night at the Inn and, after I had been asleep for a while, I woke up and heard somebody fumbling at my door. The door was bolted on the inside, so I knew nobody could get in. But they did get in, not only one man but two. I noticed particularly how they were dressed. They both wore top boots turned down, long military coats, and tricorn hats with plumes. (Uniforms of this kind might be French or English of the seventeenth or eighteenth centuries. Both were garrisoned at different times at Annapolis Royal.) They appeared to be very gallant gentlemen. Then without a word to me, or any sign that they were aware of my presence, they took off their coats, drew their swords, and had a duel right there in my room. I was in such a state of terror that I couldn't speak, and I could do nothing but watch in a horrid fascination. The duel went on until one man ran the other through with his sword, and then wiped the bloody blade on the counterpane. Then, as though that were not enough, he picked the body up and threw it out the window.'

"Well, how my grandmother laughed, for she supposed the young man had made the story up as a means of retreat from an embarrassing situation. Nothing would induce her to take it seriously although his white face and nervous demeanour should have been indication enough. The story has been told in our family ever since, and years later when the Royal Bank was built, the body of a man was found dressed as this officer had been described. The Inn where he spent the night, was near this spot."

It is questionable whether the body that was found was this man or another, for at this point the story becomes confused. There must have been two incidents, for this is what Miss Charlotte Perkins, historian of Annapolis Royal, and I concluded after talking together. In the story that she has written, the man glided into the room and came over to the bed, holding up the stump of a bleeding arm. Then he suddenly disappeared. Several people saw him, and their description is quite different from that in the first story, for he was dressed in a torn and defaced uniform of the Royal Engineers, and wore a helmet that was thrown back and was suspended by the chinstrap over the right shoulder. Spurs sounded as he approached the bed. Miss Perkins reports that "his face was deathly white and his eyes were bulging with pain. He seemed to be searching for some one and, in his left hand, he carried an unsheathed cavalry sword. He then raised his bleeding arm which was severed at the wrist."

Miss Perkins' account is that of an unhappy spirit who, was probably unable to rest until his body was found and given proper burial. The first story however is an illustration of the extraordinary faculty a few people possess of seeing the reenactment of an event that has actually taken place a great many years before. And, if we are to believe one story, the other is just as credible.

Another story in which a clash of arms may have played a part was told me by Mrs. Fred Redden of Middle Musquodoboit. I had been collecting folk songs from her husband for some time before she could bring herself to talk about it, because ever since it happened she has been trying to put it out of her mind. She realized however that I would be interested, and she finally gathered up enough courage to relate her experience. It took place in our own time, during the Second Great War.

"At that time accommodation was hard to find in Halifax, but it was necessary for me to spend a few nights there. I had a friend who was living in an apartment on Barrington Street towards the north end of the city. They occupied three small rooms on the ground floor that opened out from each other and were in a row. Frances and Alex slept in one room and I slept with their child in a bed that was placed so that my head was close to the wall nearest them. There was nothing between but a thin partition. A gentle tapping on the wall from my side would have awakened them. It was poor accommodation, but the best they could get at that time.

"I must have been asleep for some hours when I was wakened by the sound of bottles clinking, knives slashing, and men talking, and they were right there in the room with me. I was terrified but, after a little while, I forced myself to open one eye to see what was happening. To my surprise I saw four men sitting around a card table. I only looked long enough to get a vivid picture of one of them. He was probably the leader. I can still see him plainly today. He was a big man with an oily look about his face, and he had a dark moustache. He was a swarthy man. One thing that I distinctly noticed was either a bright red kerchief that he was wearing, or it might have been the sleeve of his shirt. He held a long knife in his hand and the blade was silver. It was the sound of cards and the whisky bottles that woke me up.

"I saw all this in one quick look. Then I closed my eyes and lay there, paralyzed with fright for the rest of the night. I was even too frightened to call my friends or knock on the wall to wake them up. When daybreak came the noise stopped, but I still didn't open my eyes until my friend's husband came through my room on his way to work. I kept saying to myself, 'You're not asleep, you're awake. It isn't a dream.' When Alex went through I looked up. Men, tables, and bottles were all gone, and there was nothing in the room that hadn't been there when I went to sleep, and there was no sign of any disturbance.

"When morning came I didn't say anything to my friend because I didn't want to frighten her. I'd never had an experience like that before, but I've had other things and I know I can see and hear things that don't happen to other people. I could tell that she hadn't been disturbed. I made an excuse to leave that morning, and I knew I would never sleep in that room again under any circumstance. After I got away I went to see another friend and there I told what I had seen. This friend knew the place well and said it had been a hotel at one time with a window that opened out on an alley way. At that time the apartment was all one room. One man would take it and let others in through the window and they would drink and play cards. At one time, he said, a lad of sixteen was stabbed there. Whether I would have seen the stabbing if I had kept my eyes open I don't know, but I must have looked back on an event that took place perhaps a hundred or more years before."

As we often say, nothing is stranger than people. Mrs. Redden has often since then seen the couple whose apartment she shared with such devestating results but, although they have moved from there long since, she has never asked them if they ever had a similar experience there. Perhaps it is not so strange though when her one thought has been to forget it. Yet she has promised to do it now and, if they have anything to report, I hope to have it before this book is finished.

Mrs. Redden's story came to me long after I had taken one down from French Village that might be related to it. There is no way of checking up on the address because the man who told it is no longer living. It will also be noted that while one incident took place upon the ground floor, the other came from the top of the house.

"I slept in the attic of a house in Halifax one night and I heard bottles being moved at the end of the room where I slept and later I heard leather boots coming towards me boom boom bang, and then I see him. He looked like a big man. When I told the woman of the house in the morning, she said I wasn't the only one who'd seen him. They told me there had been a murder in that room." Another house? Another murder? Well, possibly.

The experience of Mr. Earl Morash to which I have already referred, is of an entirely different nature, and it was shared by his charming wife. I sat in their pleasant home over-looking beautiful Mahone Bay and noticed particularly how convinced they were themselves about what they had seen. Before beginning the story I should mention that there are many islands in this bay and, in the days of sailing ships, there were many adventures experienced here.

"Years ago Indians came out of the woods and scalped the crew of an American fishing vessel. All the crew went ashore on one of the islands and the Indians killed them. The cook and the flunky were the only ones left aboard and they escaped by taking the boat and cutting the anchor rope and joining the other boats in the harbour.

"We saw the scene re-enacted. If it wasn't that, what was it? That would be about 1936 or 1937. It was September and we were going to Herman's Island in our yacht. When we left, the moon was out and we sailed out the Bay. We sailed in the moonlight until the wind dropped when we decided to anchor off Black Island and spend the night, proceeding to Herman's Island in the morning.

"There were just the two of us on our yacht and there were no other boats in sight. I was on deck furling sails when I looked up and there was an immense fire going up all of a sudden. It might have been fifteen or twenty feet in diameter. There were Indians dancing around the fire holding tomahawks in their right hands, and their right arms were held up and they were yelling. The Indians that weren't dancing were getting wood and throwing it on the fire. One second the fire wasn't there, and the next second it was. It came up too quick for it to be people out from Chester and, even if it had been human people, where would they have put their boat? There was nowhere to beach it that we could see. We watched for an hour or more and then we got tired and went below to sleep.

"The next winter some friends were here and they said, 'You gave us quite a fright that night you anchored off Black Island. We were hand-potting lobsters on the other side and didn't see you till the morning.'

" 'If you were there, you saw the fire then,' I said.

" 'No, we didn't see any fire.'

" 'Well then, tell me, could there have been a picnic on the island that night?'

" 'No, there was no picnic because there wasn't a boat.' So that settled any picnic, with both sides of the island being seen. We have often thought about it and talked it over. If the fire had been real, they would have seen it too, but with these supernatural things it isn't everyone who's able to see them. The only conclusion we've been able to come to is that we looked back that night into time." Mrs. Morash nodded her head in agreement.

On the road between Halifax and Chester there is a village called Boutilier's Point, and an unexplained story comes from there.

"My mother was teaching school at Oakland before she was married, and she started out one Saturday afternoon to walk to her home in Lunenburg. It was early in the day and, when she came to the short hill at Mader's Cove, she saw two army officers riding on white horses coming towards her. They rode so easily and so gracefully, and were so completely unaware of her, that she stood for some time and watched them. Who were these handsome strangers?

"When she got to Lunenburg she asked her father about them. He was a constable and would be sure to know but he had not seen them nor even heard of them. She asked everybody she saw after that, but nobody had seen them. She decided then that they must be known at Mahone Bay because there is only one road in that town and they would have to take it to go anywhere. But again she met nothing but negative replies. Nobody had seen them. Although she lived to be over eighty she was never able to discover who they were or where they had come from. She always wondered then if they had gone that way before. Had their spirits returned to ride once more over the familiar roads." Or was she seeing an event from out of the past?

You will find many stories in this book from Shelburne, which is largely a United Empire Loyalist town.

"A dwelling known as Shelburne House was erected at the time of the Loyalists but it was torn down many years ago. The sound of the front door opening and of an officer's sword clanking as he ascended the stairs was heard at times, but only by certain people.

"One time a lady who had never been in the town before was a supper guest at Shelburne House and, during the evening, she heard this same mysterious interruption. When her husband called for her later she asked if the house was supposed to be haunted. He asked her whatever made her think such a thing? 'What did you hear?' he said.

" 'I heard the front door open and it was followed by the clank of a sword on the stairway,' she said.

" 'I can't say you imagined it,' her husband said, 'for it's been heard before.' Nobody knew the reason for it, or whether this was a restless ghost or a scene re-enacted from the past."

There is little doubt in the next case, which comes from a man of Scotch-Dutch descent in Chester. "My wife's grandfather was a ship's carpenter, and he lived out on a point at a place called the Half Moon. It was a back harbour and formed a little cove. From this little cove, he said, different people have seen old-fashioned longboats row away on certain nights. They always claimed they were repeating either the burying of a treasure or the hunting of it. The last time it was seen would be about eighty-five years ago."

At Ballast Cove in Queen's County people used to be seen in old-fashioned clothes coming up from the beach, and it was thought they were carrying a corpse. They would always disappear in the woods. The people got used to seeing them, and presumed they were re-enacting a real event.

At Ditch Brook in the same county an engineer once plotted out the land. He has been seen making his survey and his chain is heard rattling.

At Seabright they used to see a chest of money crossing the road by itself, but nobody has attempted to stop it. Presumably a real chest had gone that way before.

At Hartlan's Point, now Devil's Battery, there used to be a flat rock and, according to my friend Enos Hartlan, they used to see two men as big as a thumb sitting on the rock playing cards. Could this ever have happened in the past?

A bit inland from Seabright two boys were coming along the railway track and, at a culvert, they saw a big black dog. (Ghosts often appear in the form of dogs.) One of them said, "I wonder who owns that dog?" and just then it brushed past them and they got a feeling of rushing wind. A man had shot himself at that culvert. Different ones have seen him at twelve o'clock as he must have been sitting that night with his gun across his knees planning his own destruction.

At Glen Margaret there is an old house with a brook running along beside it, and here the owner and his wife have seen a big man "rounded like he was hauling a chain down over the rocks by the brook," while at Victoria Beach an artist was sitting at his easel painting when he swore he saw forms on the cliff that looked like pirates. This happened more than once. Treasure is supposed to be buried there, and he thought he must have seen them as they put it there many years before.

In a fish house at New Harbour a light like a lamp has been seen many times on a table in the place where it must often have stood; and "one fellow came down to go fishing and a longboat rowed out and the stern fellow had a three-cornered hat on. There were four men on each side pulling their oars. Then the boat disappeared."

When Annapolis Royal was taken over by the English in 1710 a number of the people who came there to live brought slaves with them. Some of their descendants are there to this day and they are quite a superior strain. I visited one of the older women one day with the following result.

"When I was first married I lived in a house on the left hand side of the Granville road above the railway tracks. One day I was in my kitchen when I looked up and saw a man standing in the doorway with a chain around one leg and a dog sniffing at his heels, and I could hear the sound of the dog sniffing. That seemed so strange to me. I wasn't frightened, but I must have moved because suddenly they disappeared and I have never seen them since. He must have been trying to lift the wooden latch to come in. I didn't like to say anything about it to anybody until one day the rector's wife came to call. I thought she would laugh at me but I wanted to tell her and I did. But she didn't laugh. She knew the history of the houses in Annapolis and she said that years ago that house had belonged to a general and that he was known to have had a slave who was chained by the leg."

Finally, they used to say in Halifax that if you went to the Willow Tree after dark on Hallowe'en and had the gift, you would see a man hanging from a gallows.

CHAPTER FIVE

Devils and Angels

DEVILS

IT IS a risky business to challenge the devil or to call upon him in time of trouble. It would seem that he is always close at hand, ready to appear at your side to carry out your slightest wish, suave, handsome, and obliging, anxious to serve, but at a terrible price.

A few years ago there was a dance hall on the outskirts of Sydney. It may be there yet, for the events I am about to relate happened quite recently. The story was kept quiet at the time because it could conceivably injure the business of the hall, although the location had nothing to do with it. The incident could have happened anywhere under the particular circumstances.

On the evening in question a girl started off for the hall against her mother's wishes. The objection was based mainly upon the fact that she was young, and dancing had become almost an obsession with her. During the evening in a moment of complete abandon, she stood in the centre of the floor and said,

"I love to dance. I love to dance so much I'd dance with anyone, even the devil."

Then from the side of the room a fine looking stranger appeared and her invitation was accepted. He danced superbly. After a while however she happened to glance down and she caught sight of one foot. It was cloven. She stopped and screamed and in the ensuing confusion the stranger disappeared. Whether he went out through the side of the wall whence he apparently had come, nobody seemed to know. From all I could learn, the girl suffered no further ill effects than a very bad fright and I presume it was a salutary lesson. In a case very like this reported from our neighbouring Province of New Brunswick the girl did not get off so lightly. There the imprint of the devil's hand was burned into the flesh of her back and she was so disturbed by the dreadful experience that she died of shock.

Another story of the devil and a girl who loved to dance came from a former resident of Diligent River. My informant was a child when she heard it. This fearsome tale was one of the many ghost stories of the district, the type of bedtime fare which children of that time heard before going to sleep. She could not tell the actual location of the event except that it was in the Parrsboro area, probably between that town and Diligent River.

"Many years ago a girl was to have been taken to a dance but, at the last moment, the young man turned her down. She loved dancing and, in her disappointment and distress, she said petulantly, 'I'd go with anybody who would take me. I'd even go with the devil if he came.'

"Very shortly after this a fancy rig drove up and a charming dashing young man got out and came to the house and invited her to go to the party. She was delighted. What an impression she would make, not only upon the boy who had rejected her, but upon the whole gathering. She accepted readily, thinking of nothing but this fortunate turn of events.

"The evening went off happily and she enjoyed her handsome light-footed partner. But shortly after she came home the whole house was startled by a noise like thunder. It seemed to centre around the girl's room to which she had just retired. The family rushed in to investigate and found her lying dead upon her bed. Upon her forehead was the devil's mark, the imprint of a horse's hoof. They looked up then and saw a great hole torn in the roof and recalled her rash statement when she had said she would go to the dance with anybody, even the devil. It was presumed he had answered her challenge and then had exacted his price; that he had come for her soul and had taken it with him through the great rent in the roof."

In a Shelburne negro story told to Mr. Arthur Huff Fauset, the devil did not wait for the girl to go off from the dance floor, but removed her then and there. These places, Sydney, Diligent River, and Shelburne are widely separated, yet the incident is supposed to have happened in each place. You will notice that the devil is always handsome, and he is always recognized by his feet.

Many people connect dancing and card playing with sin, so it is not surprising to find him next as a gambler. The most famous story of his appearance in this role has a European origin, but people who know nothing of the story in its traditional form, report it as an incident from their own community. Mahone Bay insists that it happened at Fobo; Blandford says it was Dover, while Lunenburg town and East River Point tell the story without naming any specific place. At Mahone Bay I was taken to the site and shown where the building stood before it was abandoned as a result of the devil's appearance there. Upon consideration, if the devil went to one dance floor or sat in upon one card game, why might he not have done the same thing in other places? At all events the card playing story, except for a few minor details, is always the same, and it goes like this.

"At Fobo there used to be a little store and people would go there at night and play cards Sunday and Monday. It was a terrible place with drinking and gambling. One night when it was all filled up with card players a knock came to the door.

" 'Come in,' they said, and in walked a fine looking stranger. He said, 'Can I have a game?'

They said, 'Yes, sit down.' Before very long the cards started to fall to the floor and one or two men stooped to pick them up and they saw that the stranger had horse feet (or more often, a cloven foot.) You talk about getting out of that building. After that the shanty was boarded up and never used again. I heard my own father tell that, and he swore it was the truth."

An amusing story comes from St. John as a result of this belief being known by a visiting clergyman, and was told to me by Dr. R. C. Archibald of Brown University. The clergyman who had a club foot and wore a great heavy boot, was passing a place on Sunday evening when he looked down upon a basement room and saw a number of men playing cards. For the fun of it he went in, a stranger among them and, after a little while he lifted his foot quietly and placed it upon a chair. One look was enough and out they went. He waited until they had all disappeared and then went chuckling upon his way.

The devil does not make a physical appearance in the next story. Its meaning is that he was there to remind a sinner of a past event whenever he picked up the cards. It was told by Mr. Alex Morrison of Marion Bridge as a personal experience.

"Donald and I were out cutting timber and, when we finished our work the first day, we sat down and had a game of poker. The next day we cut a few props and hauled them to the gate. Then we sat down at the table and started playing again. It was just a nice friendly game. We hadn't gone on very long before we heard a noise like a bark at the door. Donald didn't move, so I went to answer it but there was nothing there. Next there came a racket and a screech from the room next to us, and then it was upstairs. I took the lantern and went up and there wasn't anyone there but, when I came down, Donald was lying on the bed and the cards were in the fireplace. He said, 'We're leaving here to-night.'

" 'Leaving here? Why?' It was a nice place and we hadn't finished our work.

" 'I'll tell you later,' he said and before we left, he did tell me. He said that he'd got in trouble once playing cards and he'd struck a fellow. I suppose the blow must have killed him, though I didn't like to ask. Anyhow ever since then whenever he played cards the same thing happened, noises in the house and rackets that weren't heard other times.

"After I'd heard that, I wasn't sorry to leave the place myself, so we packed up our gear and started for home. It was a very dark night. Suddenly there appeared before us three lights and they kept ahead of us all the way. If we tried to catch them they'd go faster and, if we slowed down, they slowed down too. The lights kept about a foot from the ground all the way but, when we got to the Sydney road—that's the main road—they separated. One took the road to Sydney and the other two kept on to the cross-roads at Marion Bridge and went off from there in different directions. I never want to play cards with that man again. I've often wondered whether it was the devil who got after him when he played, or would it be the man he may have killed when he struck him? And what was the meaning of the lights? I've tried to puzzle it out, but it's all beyond me."

Our next story has a nautical flavour. Mr. Horace Johnston of Port Wade crossed one long leg over the other, knocked the tobacco out of his pipe on the wharf where we were sitting, waited for a moment while a sea gull swooped gracefully before our admiring eyes, cleared his throat, and began.

"There was an old man named Capt. Gosse who settled in Maine and he went captain of ships in his earlier days. He rented a house and lived there all alone when he was ashore. He was sociable, but he didn't want any person in his house. He was known to be a great card player and at night people could look through his window and see him playing with the cards, but no other man was playing with him; only a hand of cards.

"One night when they were watching through the window they heard him betting. He had bet all the money he had at that time in his house, so it seemed as though the object they couldn't see would want to knock off. About that time the captain had just got a vessel by the name of *The Lively Nan* and had shipped three men as crew.

" 'Well,' he says, 'I'll bet my vessel, myself and my crew.'

"A short time after that he went aboard his ship, him and the three other men, and they went to sea. Then one day they took a very bad breeze and thick stormy weather. A man on the lookout reported a ship going to collide with them and called all hands on deck. No matter what they did, the other ship kept coming till it hit them and, when it did, their ship was dismasted. It made a real wreck of her. The men were pitched overboard and they had to grab on to anything afloat to save themselves and finally they got on to a spar. There should have been three of them with the captain but, when they counted up, there were five of them on that spar. They drifted about till the sea washed them ashore but, when they landed, there were only the three members, of the crew left. Capt. Gosse and the other man had disappeared. Looking around they found the old greasy pack of cards strewed over the beach. Capt. Gosse and the vessel were gone, and the man he had played cards with had won his bet. That man was the devil."

At Sangaree on the Mira River there used to be a resort where there was said to be "a lot of drinking and bad living." Here, according to people who live nearby, the devil was seen at the bar, mixing with the crowd, and was recognized by the cloven hoof. Word sped through the building and the rooms were abandoned with such speed that in no time not a living soul was left. It was sold soon afterwards and its existence as a resort was over.

When I was in Charlottetown, Prince Edward Island, I was advised to see the Minister of Industry, Mr. Dougald McKinnon. We talked of folk songs and legends, but we were interrupted many times by the ringing of the telephone as he was consulted about various important matters of state. As I sat there I wondered what the people at the other end of the line would think if they knew that the moment the receiver went down he was off on a story like this:

"There was an old man who had a dread of playing cards and he wouldn't allow them in his house. In his younger days he had gone to sea and he used to tell about it. He said he was a pretty godless man with his crew at one time and that, among other things, he played cards with them on Sunday, and he the captain of the ship. One Sunday when they were so employed they fought over the game and it got so bad that he took the cards away from the men. They were his own cards anyway, so he put them in his sea chest and locked them up.

"That night he was awakened from his sleep and was surprised to see a man sitting on his sea chest. He was dealing cards, and he dealt four hands. Then the stranger saw that the captain was awake and asked him to sit in and have a game with him. Before he could make up his mind he looked at the man's feet and saw the cloven hoof. He screamed and the stranger disappeared, and that was why he would have nothing more to do with playing cards."

So much for the devil as a card player. Let us see now how the Micmac Indians felt about him in a very different type of story. This was related by Louis Pictou, husband of Evangeline, whom we have met before.

"Once upon a time there was an Indian village with about seventy-five or a hundred families. This was a very long time ago, and the place was beside a lake back of Bear River. In English the name would mean the place where you get beads. They trapped and fished and traded with each other.

"There was a young couple like Vance (his wife) and I, just the two of them. No children. They got everything ready and lined up the traps, and the woman was just as good at that work as the man. First along they didn't have too good luck. The man would take his traps and be gone all day, and the woman just the same, only they didn't go together. They'd be gone all day and sometimes they'd come back with mink and otter and wild cat, so they went on like that, but they weren't making too big a progress at it.

"At last this woman got thinking some evil thoughts, and they claim she got in with the devil and she sinned this man. The devil told her that if she'd believe in him she could get all the game she wanted. Then the trouble started. She'd come home nights with all the fur she could carry, beaver and otter, and the man didn't get very much, and he was a good hunter. At last he wondered why she was getting so much more than him so he asked her. She said it was just her luck, but he kinda thought it was more than luck. It went on, but she wouldn't tell him.

"They got through with their hunting and went back and he got to telling the chief, and the chief said, 'If that's the way she's been acting there's something more than luck and it ain't good.' The old chief got kinda scared about it, so he sent for her to have a talk with him, but it didn't do any good. When she and her husband went back again trapping next fall they no sooner got their traps out than the same thing happened again. At last, as the time came for them to go home again, the man said to her, 'We only got a few more days and then we got to quit.' He talked and talked to her and coaxed her to tell him what made her have so much luck. Still she wouldn't tell him.

"At last one day it was dark and kinda rough weather and he told her not to go hunting, but she went, and that's the last anybody ever saw of her. She never returned. He went back to the village and told them, so they got up a party and they hunted for her over the hills and the lakes but with no success and from that day to this they couldn't imagine what had happened to her. But all the people thought that the devil had helped her with her trapping and then he had taken her. That happened before the French came to Nova Scotia, and it was told me by my old grandmother."

My appointment with Mr. John George Ferguson of Bay Head near Tatamagouche had been made for an early hour of the morning, or so it seemed to me. This is not my best time, but perhaps it was just as well that I got my story in the bright light of day. It was pleasant sitting on the verandah of his farmhouse, but the story that he told would not have induced a peaceful sleep if it had come late in the evening. I look upon it as a valuable addition to our devil lore; I cannot say that I enjoyed it, but then I do not relish any stories about the devil.

"The Ferguson family at the time of our story lived at Earltown. A man nicknamed Dumpy lived at Spiddle Hill nearby with his wife and child. He was big and fat as his name suggests and, although he had never murdered as far as anybody knew, he was thought of as a bad man chiefly on account of his thievery. About fifty-eight years ago Dumpy took the grippe, as influenza was called in those days, and he was very ill.

"My father, Joe McKay, and Sandy Ferguson, gathered at his house for the night to help his wife look after him, and he was so sick that they sent for the doctor who was John S. McKay. When they arrived, Dumpy was sitting cross-legged, tailor fashion, in his bed, and he asked for a bowl of crackers and milk. He was eating them and had half finished the bowl when he began staring at the wall. He kept staring for a full minute as though he saw something there and couldn't take his eyes off it but, if there was anything on the wall, none of the others saw it. Suddenly in a manner they could never understand, considering his weight and his cross-legged position, he rose up on his feet and gave a yell. His mouth was full of crackers and milk and they blew all over the room and, as he reached an upright position, he fell back dead.

"Just as that happened something struck upstairs like a ton of bricks and Mrs. Ferguson screeched. The upstairs of the house wasn't finished but they could go up, and there wasn't a sign of anything having been moved. It was February and frosty, and a sudden gust of wind blew so hard that the henhouse door blew off and the hens were blown out with such force that they struck the bedroom window. They had to go out and pick up the hens and put them back in the henhouse.

"Soon after all this happened the doctor came with

a horse and sleigh. He drove the horse in on the barn floor for shelter and came in. They told him about Dumpy so he looked him over and pronounced him dead. Then they told him all the things that had happened. After that the doctor didn't want to go out to the barn alone, so he said to my father.

" 'Come out with me while I rub the horse down.' They started out and had just gone a little way from the house when the doctor caught my father by the shoulder and turned him around and what they thought must be the devil was in the upstairs window, the figure was the full size of the window. He was a man with streaks of fire coming from his eyes and mouth. It was a dark night, but he himself provided enough light for them to see him clearly.

"Well, the horse was not rubbed down that night, and nobody went home because none of them wanted to be alone. The noises kept up all night and sounded like barrels rolling. They stopped when anybody went upstairs, but they couldn't stay up there because it was too cold. Dumpy's wife was home all this time, but she may not have heard anything and, if she did, she didn't seem to mind it. She was slightly under average mentality, to put it mildly. She and the child are both dead now.

"They laid Dumpy out in his cold downstairs bedroom, and there he lay for three days, but his body never stiffened. Looking back, my father thought he had probably gone into a trance and hadn't died at all. My father was a good story-teller, and so was the doctor, and sometimes they didn't mind stretching their stories for the sake of a good yarn. But Mrs. Ferguson was not like that, and she told it exactly as they did except for the part about seeing the devil. They didn't tell her that until a long time afterwards, but they always insisted this was a true story and that the devil was what they had seen. I know my father meant it when he said it like that."

We go again to Cape Breton for our next story which took place near Ingonish. Here the steep mountains slope down to one of the finest beaches in all the Province, and the sun smiles down upon village life which in its serenity would seem to be completely unsullied. Surely there is no room here for the devil or any evil thing. Yet even in this idyllic spot we have a story. It came by way of Mrs. Ruth Metcalfe who for some time had been writing to me about songs. Her home had been in the Louisburg and Gabarus area and it was there that she had heard this story. Later she moved to Ontario, but she had always cherished the songs and legends of her home. We met when she came back for a holiday, and I am indebted to her for a number of the excellent tales in this volume. Of this, she said,

"It happened to two men of the Roman Catholic faith at Lingan Bay, just off Ingonish Beach. One of them was a middle-aged man who wanted to get married. He had gone to sea and planned to return in the fall of the year. One thing and another detained the ship and he did not get back until early winter.

"In order to visit the lady of his choice he had to go across a bay that was fourteen miles in length, and he had expected to take this trip by boat. It being so late now, the bay was frozen over, and the only other way to get there was to take a horse. He had no horse of his own, but he knew a man who could lend him one if he could be persuaded. The difficulty was that they were rival fishermen, so the only way that he could get the horse would be by striking a bargain with him that would be a sufficiently worthy payment for the service. He therefore said, 'If you will let me have your horse to go and get married, I'll do a day for you in purgatory.' His rival said, 'All right, you can have the horse, but how will I know that you do the day in purgatory?'

"So he said, 'I'll make a bargain with the devil and he'll see that I keep it.' The rival then loaned him the horse and the prospective bridegroom rode triumphantly, away. But when morning came the owner of the horse was greatly taken aback to find the animal standing beside the barn door. There was no sign of his rider. He became alarmed then for his safety, and made inquiries. He had never arrived at the home of his intended bride. Evidently in crossing the bay on the ice, horse and man had gone through, but the horse, having no part in the bargain, had got out. The man had drowned and his body was washed ashore in the spring. The owner of the horse stood over the drowned man and shook his head. He was heard to remark, 'That's what happens when you make a bargain with the devil. He collects first.' "

Still in Cape Breton we turn now to Marion Bridge for a story of a family named MacDonald. None connected with this unpleasant tale is still living. It was told by Mr. Alex Morrison of Marion Bridge who lived a mile and a half from the MacDonald home.

"There were two boys in the family and they were tough, and there was also a girl who was deformed. The boys used to beat their father and their mother and every evening a dog used to circle the field, only it wasn't a real dog. The MacDonald boys used to go down the road and fire shots to frighten people and it was thought that the dog was the devil. We didn't know whether the boys were in league with him, or whether he was waiting around to get them. Perhaps they were possessed of evil spirits that we read about in the Bible. It was always just about dark when the dog would be seen.

"In the house where they lived there was a fireplace and a backlog three feet long and heavy. People used to go to the house at night to see what would happen. After they got in, this backlog would be placed against the door but, no matter how securely they fixed it, the door would open just enough for a foot to be seen, like a hoof coming in the door. That was all that anybody ever saw when the door opened. As far as we knew the foot never came inside. This went on for a full year, and nobody could understand how any live animal could have moved that door. After that the boys were taken away and the dog was never seen again. That ended it."

Although the devil himself does not appear in our next story, it tells of an evil man and what happened to him as the result of a cruel deed. It comes from Clarke's Harbour.

"There was a man at The Hawk (a village on Cape Sable Island) who was very bad. He was at the shore in the store (fish house) and when he went outside a sea gull flew very low. He reached out and grabbed it. He had been slitting fish and had his sharp knife in his hand, so he took his knife and slashed both its feet off. He swore an oath and said, 'God damn you, get out and get your living the same way I have to.' He never saw the bird again but from that day his hands began to take on the appearance of claws. Years went by and at last he died. The day he was buried was overcast with drifting clouds, a weird sort of day. The man's hands were crossed over his breast, and everybody could see very plainly that they were no longer hands, but claws.

"As the coffin was resting on the ground and the minister was about to commit the body to the earth, he looked up and saw a black cat coming towards them fast. There are no houses nearby and therefore no cats wandering about the cemetery. There were about twelve people standing beside the grave. The minister went on, and the cat made its way between them and ran right over the casket. They brushed it hastily away, but afterwards none of them could tell where it went or if it just vanished.

"When they were returning from the funeral the undertaker said to the minister, 'Did you ever see anything happen like that?' The minister said no, he never had and, to himself, hoped he never would again. The undertaker said, 'I wonder if that was the cat that caught that poor bird?' Everybody knew the story, for the man had told it himself. They inquired all around, but nobody was ever able to place that cat and that was the only time it was seen on the island. Perhaps, they thought, it might be the sea gull in the form of a cat or it might even have been the devil."

Another bad man story used to be told at Tiverton in Digby County to frighten children.

"There was a man whose name was Bramber, and this happened a very long time ago. He lived to be an old man but a very bad one, and everybody knew that he had an evil reputation. He went out of his house one night and disappeared. His shoes were on the steps when he went out and they were all that was ever found. People used to say that the devil had got him."

Occasionally we hear of two men having been seen in a boat when, upon closer inspection, there was only one. "Tom McDonald used to live at Moser's River and he was supposed to have been very wicked although it was so long ago that nobody remembers just what it was that he did. He was a fisherman and fished alone. The other men could see two men in the boat when they were at a distance but the second one was never there when they got close to him. They always thought it was the devil."

According to a story from Middle Musquodoboit, Ike Foley was responsible for his own death although he did not anticipate it when he spoke. "He was an awful man to swear. There was a hussock, a rock in the stream that bothered them when they were river-driving.

He got mad and said if the devil would come he would go out and help him, and together they would take the rock out of that stream. The boys laughed at him and said if the devil's voice came he'd be too scared to go out, but that evening they heard it. Ike wouldn't go, but they all got after him and dared him, not thinking it was really the devil that they heard. It came three times, but still Ike wouldn't go. Next morning when they went out the rock was gone, and nobody knew who moved it. Shortly after that, Ike was walking on thin ice at that place and he fell through and got drowned. We always felt the devil got him and, after that, you could hear the devil's chains rattling whenever you went by."

Another story of a rock that jammed logs in the centre of a river was told of a man named Cruikshanks and a logger in his employ. The place was Moser's River on our eastern shore. Here too the man said, "If the devil comes himself to move that rock I'll go and help him." In this story Mr. Cruikshanks forced the man to go, never dreaming it was really the devil who called from outside. The logger was never seen again and, as in the previous case, the rock had been removed while the other men had slept. It is said that Mr. Cruikshanks regretted for the rest of his life that he had sent his man to his death.

The appearance of a second man in a boat may not always have a bad effect, according to a man from Tantallon.

"A man here was a pilot and an awful drinker and he used to go across to the Head of St. Margaret's Bay. This time he had been at the Prince of Wales Hotel and as usual had spent some time at the bar. As he was going home his engine stopped. He got mad and swore and said, 'If the devil will come and help me it will be all right,' and he looked up and there was a fine-looking man beside him with a beaver hat and a frock coat. He wasn't too far gone in drink to recognize him for what he was, and he turned religious. Yes, he was a good man after that. A lot of people have told the story, and everybody knew about it at the time."

From the preceding story it appears that people sometimes get a second chance. I am reminded now of an incident from French Village. "My father and Uncle Steve and Uncle Albert were fishing and had only a couple of fish, so Uncle Steve said, just for fun, 'If we meet the devil we'll give them to him.' When they got to the road there was a great big animal larger than a dog. They all said it was an awful ugly thing, and different from any animal they'd ever seen or heard of. But they didn't give it the fish. They were scared to death and I guess they never said they'd give the devil anything again."

Mr. Edward Gallagher of Chebucto Head had this to tell. "Ten people saw the devil when the *Mary B. Grier* was tied up one year at the Commercial Wharf at Boston. It was a cold frosty night and, if there had been anybody coming afoot, they would have heard him. Three times he came and peered around the foremast, and twice he went away without making any sound. The third time a bean crock was thrown at him. He had red eyes like a blaze of fire. It was thought he was a former owner, probably because that year they'd got the best catch ever, and he was jealous."

Beans play a part in the next story which comes from Clarke's Harbour. In this case it was not the devil, but the Almighty who was challenged. The story was told me by the daughter of the man who had the experience. "Than Swim was cook on a boat. He used to swear a lot and he had a temper. One night he had a pot of beans in the oven and the pot came out and spilled. He got in a temper and put them back again. They came out a second time. This time he told God not to dare send those beans out again and to make

sure he wired the oven door so they couldn't get out.
But out they came.

"By this time he was so angry he went on deck and
told God to come half-way down the mast and he'd
meet Him and have it out. Nothing happened on deck
but, no matter what he did with the beans that night,
they kept coming out of the oven, and finally he had
to give it up."

Here now is what happens to a man who breaks the
Sabbath day as told by a Negro at Sackville. "Two men
went into the woods to shoot on Sunday and they had
to stay in a camp. About ten o'clock that night they
heard a ghost man hauling timber and a saw going,
and trees going crash, and he was calling, 'Timber!
Timber!' all night till morning. He did that till the sun
riz, driving horses and logging all night. That was his
punishment for logging on a Sunday. He had to keep it
up long after he died.

"My grandfather's brother kept on working after he
died, too, because he didn't get the wood cut up that
he was supposed to do. After he died you could hear
the saw going squak squak squak, and the wood going
blump blump. One moonlight night my father and his
brother saw the man sawing, and the next day there was
no wood sawed. What they seen looked like a big pile.

"Another man died without shingling his roof, and
they used to see him pounding and pounding, but there
was never any sound."

Conscience is such a strong force that a wrongdoer
may suffer the tortures of the damned before he leaves
this earth. "About eighty years ago a young girl had
finished a visit with friends and, when it was time for
her to leave, they got a ride for her with a young man
who was going to her home at Marion Bridge. It is unlikely anything was known to his discredit or they would
not have entrusted her to his care. This was the horse
and buggy era and the night was dark. A light appeared

upon the hillside and it came down the hill, crossed in front of the team, and disappeared on the other side. The girl was astonished and very frightened when her companion got down on his knees on the floor of the carriage and prayed fervently. He was so upset that he forgot all about the horse. It was necessary for her to take the reins until the light disappeared and the driver came to his senses.

"When he finally felt it was safe for him to raise his head he made a terse explanation. 'That light was for me because I'm a bad man.' In what way he had erred she never knew, but he must have thought the devil was in that light and had come to get him."

Only a man who believed that the devil was sometimes heard rattling his chains could have told the following anecdote upon himself. "One time I went to see my girl and as I was walking through the woods I heard the devil's chain following me. The faster I went, the faster he went, so I ran all the way home and was done out by the time I got there. The next week when I put my best pants on again I discovered a hole in the pocket and realized it was the change slipping down that had made the noise. But I'd heard so much in the lumber woods that I thought this must be a devil's warning, and I never went to see that girl again."

With so many horrible stories told about the devil it is not surprising to hear of incidents in which the more courageous have impersonated him in order to make sport of the timid. This was told by Mr. Horace Johnston.

"When I was twenty I went up to Kentville to visit a friend who was married. He was building a house and he was getting plaster from a man who said he'd have to knock off because he was afraid the plaster pit was going to cave in underneath his barn. This put him in a jam, so I said, 'Harness up your horse and we'll go tonight and get a load. He'll never know.' He had to have that plaster and it seemed like a good idea so away we went. We hitched the horse a little to one side where it couldn't be seen from the road.

"It was always claimed this place was haunted. While we were digging a crowd of men came along this way from Kentville and they were feeling pretty good. They'd had some Adam's wine or something. When they got abreast of the pit we kept quiet, and then we heard one fellow say, 'They say this place is haunted. Let's go see if the devil's there.' They looked down and we could see them but they couldn't see us. He said, 'Mr. Devil, if you're down there let's hear from you.' I was a stranger so they wouldn't recognize my voice, so I did the talking, and I says, 'I'm down here, and if you don't come down I'm coming up to get you.' Well sir they started in to run, and they were that frightened they fell down and left two bottles of rum behind and they probably tell to this day. how they heard the devil himself speaking from that pit."

Devil's Island has been mentioned earlier, and you may wonder how it got its name. Enos Hartlan gives this explanation. "One night there was a party out there on th' island. There was drinkin' and dancin' and old Caspar Henneberry was there. About one a.m. he went outside and when he came back he was all white and shakin'. 'Boys,' he say, 'my time is finished. 'Why?' they asked. 'How do you know?'

" 'I know because I seen the devil on the bankin' (of the house) and he come in the form of a halibut.'

"The very next day he was comin' from Halifax when his boat was picked up. Yes sir, his boat was picked up just off th' island, and there was old Caspar with his head and shoulders overboard drownded. That's as true as I'm a-settin' here. The funny part of it was that there didn't seem to be no reason for him being drownded that way, so the people called it Devil's

Island from that day." In another telling of this story there were signs of a tussle and one of the men in the fight had a cloven foot, for its imprint was on the sand. This had taken place on the beach, so that Caspar would have been in a weakened condition when he got into his boat.

The afternoon spent in the home of Mr. and Mrs. Alex McLeod of New Aberdeen was a happy and profitable one. Mr. McLeod and his friend Mr. Charlie Weeks of Glace Bay were old friends who had not met for some time, and each tried to outdo the other. As a result I got this explanation of a light that has often been seen in country places and that bobs up and down as though someone is carrying a lantern. The light is called a Jack o' Lantern and this, according to Mr. McLeod, is how it came into being.

"There was a fellow who was in the habit of going down the road to a bar-room, but he was always short of money and would do anything to get it. Once he looked in at the place but his purse was empty so he went unhappily away. Before long he met a strange fellow who spoke to him.

" 'Where did you come from?'

" 'I went to the bar-room.'

" 'Did you get in?'

" 'Yes, but I had no money so I didn't even have a drink.'

" 'You're a blacksmith,' said the stranger. 'What would you do for me if I'd give you a purse that would be always full?'

" 'I'd do anything.'

" 'Would you give yourself away?'

" 'Yes, I would.'

" 'When would you be ready to go with me?'

" 'In about a year's time.' So the strange fellow gave him the purse and he put it in his pocket and it was always full and he had a good time. He set himself

up in business and had people working for him and was
getting along so well that when the year was up he
decided he wouldn't go. He knew well enough of course
that the stranger was the devil.

"When the year was up the devil came and said,
'Your time is up. You must come with me.'

" 'Well yes, that is what I promised. But when I
pass the bar-room I never go by without going in to
have one. I'd like one more drink before I go.'

"The devil agreed, so the blacksmith said, 'They say
you can go around in any shape at all.'

" 'Yes.'

" 'Well, suppose I take you in the bar-room in the
shape of a dollar bill and pay you for my drink?' The
devil, being an obliging fellow agreed. But the blacksmith decided he wouldn't go to the bar-room. Instead
he put the dollar bill in his pocket and hurried back to
the forge. Then he put the purse in the fire and put
it on the anvil and pounded it to pieces and that, he
thought, was the end of the devil.

"Well, time went on and at last the blacksmith died.
There was no place for him to go but the bad place
and when he arrived the devil asked, 'Who's that?'
Attendants told him it was the blacksmith who had
played such a trick on him, and the devil said, 'Send him
back.' So the blacksmith picked up the lantern that was
at the gate and he took it with him and he's been all
over the world ever since always travelling. That's what's
meant by a Jack o' Lantern."

So you see, trying to outsmart the devil does not
work.

ANGELS

It is with a sign of relief that I say farewell to the
devil and turn now to the second part of this chapter.
Stories of angelic visitations are unfortunately less frequent, possibly because people are bashful about telling

them. Let us begin with heavenly music as it was told about at Victoria Beach.

"When my brother died, my sister heard the singing of "A Perfect Day," as if sung by a choir of voices. They sang the whole song and it seemed to come from our corner of the bedroom. She was sitting by his sick bed at the time and it was before there was such a thing as a radio. It happened one evening in March at Parker's Cove on the other side of the mountain."

One evening a couple were sitting together at Sambro. The husband's mother was at the point of death. His wife suddenly looked at him in surprise and said, "Listen to the birds sing. Don't they sing sweet?"

"I don't hear anything," he said. A few minutes later she heard them again, but they were for her ears only. Although he strained to listen, he could hear nothing at all.

At Middleton, a farming community in Colchester County, the people are largely of Scottish descent. Nearly forty years ago the daughter of a house was dying and people who passed the house heard sounds of beautiful music. No one could understand where it came from, and it has been talked about in the surrounding countryside ever since.

A woman at Ship Harbour said, "When my husband was dying he got up on his feet and said, 'Poor McDonald.' I said 'Who is he?' and he said, 'McDonald's one of the best violin players I ever heard.' He heard it and so did I, as plain as could be. I said, 'Where's the music coming from?' but he didn't answer, and I never knew who this McDonald was. It was violin music that we heard, but I didn't recognize any particular tune; just the sound of music and nobody anywhere near to be making it."

From violin music and heavenly choirs we go next to organ music and for this we return to Sambro Head where a woman had an organ in her house that belonged to a friend. "We were keeping it for him. One time there were a lot of people in the house including the school teacher, and she asked me why I was looking so hard at the organ as though I couldn't take my eyes off it. I told her the organ was playing. She thought I was crazy because she couldn't hear anything, but my son heard it as well as me. The teacher had heard about it and how it sometimes played before a death and she asked me to let her know if anything happened. In two hours a very close friend died. But that wasn't nearly so strange as what happened when the owner died. That time it played two lines of his favourite hymn, 'Softly fades the twilight ray of the holy Sabbath day.' It wasn't my son and I that heard it that time, but me and my daughter."

Two stories from Lunenburg County tell of the actual appearance of an angel as a warning or preparation for death. On Tancook Island a man told his wife that he had seen an angel and that he wouldn't be long in this world now. In ten minutes he was gone. The other angel appeared to a man at Simpson's Corner in a dream. He told his wife about it and said that the angel came to him holding an open book and showed him his own name in it. He was perfectly well at the time. Nevertheless he put all his affairs in order and a few weeks later he was murdered—an end even he would scarcely have anticipated.

Mrs. A. B. Thorne's beautiful garden at Karsdale has been mentioned in our chapter on forerunners, and flowers play a very important part in her life. The night that her brother died there was a knock at her door and, when she opened it, she was surprised to see a stranger there. It was a lady with a beautiful cross of white lilies in her hand. She gave this to Mrs. Thorne who thought, "how strange to bring it here, and no funeral." The next day word came that her brother had died suddenly. Presumably this was an angel in ordinary clothes which would not frighten her, and she conveyed her message in flowers, the language which Mrs. Thorne would know best.

In the heyday of sailing ships, Port Greville and Advocate on the Bay of Fundy shore were busy ports. One of the ships that sailed from here was the brig *Zebenia*. At the time of our story Capt. Hatfield who told it to me, was one of the crew.

"Bill Parsons was the captain. We had put new rigging, new sails, and new masts on her. We went then to Hantsport to finish fixing her up and then to Hillsboro to finish loading. After that we went to Port Greville to hunt up a crew and it came on a heavy gale and she went ashore. There were four men aboard her including me. The other three drowned. She covered over with water and went up to Fox Point and these other fellows floated out and around the rock. She had been so near the shore that her sails wouldn't draw and she rolled so her spars were lying right over.

"The three who were drowned were in the cabin. I got out of the skylight and let myself over the sharp end of the stern. It was December and the sea was ten or twelve feet high, but the beach was level and I was able to crawl ashore on the sand, gripping the bottom to keep going. It was half a mile to the first house and my socks were cut through before I got there. That was in 1883. After that Capt. Parsons couldn't get a ship although he was a good captain. People were afraid he was bad luck and the antics of the *Zebenia* on the day the three fellows were buried didn't help any. That day she didn't drift up and down the Bay of Fundy but lay outside of Port Greville for three hours. The fear was not only for the captain being bad luck then, but of the ship as well, for Port Greville was where the funeral was.

"A funny thing happened to me the night the *Zebenia* went ashore. I started out the cabin when something went flying by me and it seemed like an angel. It was a very dark night but I could see it plainly. It all happened quickly, but I could see it come right down through the galley doors. I thought it was coming for me and I put my hand up to stop it, for it had slanted right down towards me. An hour afterwards the other three fellows were dead."

It seems strange that the appearance of an angel should engender fear. I heard of this next event at Granville Ferry. A guest had arrived at a house for a visit some fifty years ago and she told her hostess that she could never leave her own home without having a terrifying experience. She said that after being away for a few days an angel in white always appeared before her. The story was not taken very seriously until she ran down the stairs one day screaming and said she had seen her again. Apart from the fact that the angel appeared only when she travelled, there seemed to be no other significance to the vision. It was never known why this occurred.

So far our stories of angels have not been particularly happy ones, so I am pleased to have a very heart-warming event to relate. Many years ago several little children were lost in the woods near Sambro and they had to sleep out all night in the dark. Their parents and friends were nearly frantic as they thought of the terrors that would beset them. The shore is very rocky here and the waves pounding in the darkness would frighten much older and stouter hearts. Imagine the astonishment of the searchers then when they found the children looking perfectly happy and untroubled. Afraid? They looked surprised at such a question. Why would they be afraid? They were all right, they said, because an angel had sat up with them all night.

Upon a visit to Tatamagouche I was fortunate in meeting Mrs. Norman McLennan who had a story to tell me of Port Arthur. Although that city is far from our Province it was related here and is too interesting not to be included. "A family in Port Arthur lost their daughter Edith and her newborn baby. The husband later enlisted upon the declaration of war and, being very despondent, he hoped he would not come back. His wish was granted. Upon the night of his death his sister-in-law was working a ouija board and it stopped. Then it said she alone was wanted and that there was a message for her. Her friends had taken it all as a joke until then, but she persuaded them to take it seriously and the message read, 'Will has gone; he's with Edith.'

"At the same time another sister who had so many strange revelations that her husband had grown used to them sat straight up in bed that same night and gasped. Her husband said, 'What's happened?'

" 'It's Edith,' she said. 'She was here and I can't be sad any more. She was dressed in white and she looked so happy and she said to me, 'Will is here now and we're all together and we're very happy. Tell mother!' "

There are countless stories of other people appearing after death, but coming in ordinary clothes. These will be told about in other chapters.

Phantom Ships and Sea Mysteries

ONE DAY I was sitting in my car at Victoria Beach on a high point of land overlooking the entrance to the Annapolis Basin. I looked up from my book and said to myself, "The *Princess*!" for it looked at that moment as though the boat that runs from Saint John to Digby were coming in through the Gut. I could see the black hull, the white superstructure, and even the smoke from her funnels. But it was not this ship at all, nor was there any supernatural explanation. It was merely a fog bank between me and the opposite shore which at that particular moment gave the impression of a moving ship. The land with the lighthouse and its adjacent buildings had formed what seemed to be the main body of the ship. In a moment it was gone.

Many ghost ships may be nothing more than this. I was reminded then of a young man from Chester who had been brought up on stories of the *Teazer*, and one night he saw it. It looked exactly like a sailing ship afire. He and his friends watched it from Borgal's Point for about two minutes and then it sank before their eyes. The scepticism he had felt all the preceding

years was over now for he had seen with his own eyes
what he had never believed before. They shook their
heads wonderingly and went inside. About fifteen minutes later they went out again and there, in exactly the
same place, the moon was coming up. It was at the full,
and they knew its location by its relation to Tancook
Island. It struck him then that there must have been
a bank of fog in front of the moon as it first came over
the horizon that caused it to appear like a ship on fire,
and he now thinks this is what the Mahone Bay people
have been seeing all these years. If the fog had not
cleared away that night he would always have thought,
like all the other people, that he had seen the *Teazer*.

I hate to spoil a good story by such a logical explanation, but this probably accounts for many of the *Teazer's*
appearances. It is usually seen before a storm, and
fishermen tell that there is nearly always a storm within
three days of the full of the moon.

However all stories of the *Teazer* are not dismissed
that easily. We must go back now to the twenty-sixth
of June, 1813, when a privateer, the *Young Teazer,*
was trapped by British warships in Mahone Bay on our
southwestern shore. She would have been captured if
a young officer had not set her afire rather than swing
at the yardarm. I have talked to people whose parents
witnessed the event when they saw a huge explosion as
she went up in a blaze of fire. Windows were broken
at Blandford, so strong was the blast. From that time,
and never before, her apparition has been reported.
The old people would tell about having her sail to
within a couple of yards of their boat and filling them
with fear because they were sure they would be run
down. In one case a fisherman told how she stood
directly in his way and he could hear the ropes creak
in the blocks. From Boutilier's Point it was reported
that the ropes were all on fire. It was seen then
coming to East Chester from Quaker Island at two

o'clock in the morning. Again some St. Margaret's Bay men were in a boat near Clam Island when they had to get out of the *Teazer's* way, and they said they could see the crew in the rigging. I have never heard of any calamity following the appearance of this burning ship, but it often seems to have had a frightening effect.

One day I went to call on Mr. Joseph Hyson of Mahone Bay, a kindly old retired sailor of eighty-eight who had sung me several sea chanties. Our conversation turned to the *Teazer* and he said, "My mother was a Mader from Mader's Cove and she saw it different times, and I've seen it too. One Christmas Eve we were coming from Halifax in a southeast wind. It was dark and a storm was coming up. There was a man up forward looking out, and the skipper had to go forward, too. I had the wheel and one of the men said, 'What's that?' and here was a big red light coming up. It looked like an explosion. Could it have been the moon? No, it couldn't possibly have been the moon, not on a night like that and seeing it as we did. The moon!" (Great disgust in that last word.)

As one man said, "I have seen the *Teazer* light as often as I have fingers and toes," and I could say that I have heard that many stories about it. Its last appearance to my knowledge was in 1935. They tell me it must not be confused with a ship that used to take oil to an island off Westhaver's Point where it caught fire and sank. When they see a phantom of a burning ship there they do not think of the *Teazer,* but of this other ship.

I have often been told of old-fashioned boats and their crews being seen, relics of an earlier day. This happened to a pilot who was accustomed to being on the water at all hours. He was rowing home one day from Steel's Pond to Bear Cove in Halifax County when a four-oared gig rowed with him. The Bear Covers all talked about it, and many of them saw it.

The row took about two hours, and the other boat was so close that sometimes their oars tangled. The boat rowed stroke for stroke with him. No further description of the event was given.

As late as the turn of the century a man from Schwartz Settlement was passing Red Bank when he saw a boat coming towards him with eight men rowing and one in the bow and one in the stern. They had big hats on with turned-up brims, and they followed closely along beside him. When they came to shore they went ahead of him and moored their boat and then stood in front of him but never spoke. He said they were large men and looked like pirates, so it was thought they had buried treasure there. He rushed past them, for he knew they were not human, and he would never go that way again.

At Tangier they told of a phantom ship that used to sail in the shoal at Pleasant Harbour. She had often been heard before on clear moonlight nights coming in and dropping her anchor, but she had never been approached. One calm evening she was seen so clearly, and with her sails apparently filled with wind, that some of the braver fishermen went out to meet her. When they arrived they reported all hands on deck and they said the men were drinking and talking in a foreign language. As they watched, she went right up to the shore and disappeared in the woods, and they concluded her appearance had something to do with treasure buried there. From that time she was never seen again.

Wise men do not tempt the fates as you will see by the testimony of a man from Seabright. "There were a lot of vessels fishing off the Banks and it was all shoal water. A big sou-easter came and they all turned back but one vessel and the captain said he'd go on no matter what happened. He said he'd stay there if it was the last thing he did, and he dared the

Lord to stop him. The vessel was lost in the storm. After that its light was often seen by the other vessels and it would disappear at daylight. When a vessel would tack, it would tack, and you'd see it first on the port and then on the starboard side. You couldn't see the vessel, only the light, but you'd know it was the vessel by the feel of it." (I suppose a sailor could feel a vessel, just as we sometimes feel a person nearby.)

A fisherman at Port Medway had this experience. "One time I took a load of fish to Lunenburg in September. We left in the middle of the night. When we got down to Hell Point my boy was asleep in the cuddy. It was as pretty a morning as you could see. Here come a boat, no spars, just a hull. It looked to be all sparklin' like there were little sparks all over it. I put my head in the cuddy to wake my son to tell him it was going to run us down and when I looked back it was gone. Next day in Lunenburg I mentioned it and the Dutchmen laughed at me. They said they'd seen it lots of times, but they didn't say what it was, and that's all I ever knew about it."

An Ostrea Lake man had what he interpreted as a forerunner in the shape of a phantom ship, although at the time he could not explain it. "One September day I was laying to my mooring when I saw a vessel coming straight towards me. I was so sure I'd be rammed that I untied my mooring so I could get clear of it, but I had no sooner done that than the vessel disappeared. It happened I had a brother at that time on a vessel that had sailed to Turk's Island for salt. Lots of them did that at one time, you know. I puzzled over it for quite a while until word came that my brother's vessel had gone down in a September gale. As far as I was ever able to tell, it must have been lost just at the time when I saw it coming towards me."

Most phantom ships are presumed to be connected with buried treasure. A man from Spry Bay said, "I had an uncle at Mushaboom, and one winter the water froze over and there was a foot of ice. Over the bay he heard a noise and he looked and saw a full-rigged ship coming across the ice. It was the fourth day of February. You can still hear the anchor being dropped at times and the same ship has been seen by lots of people. My brother Henry lived on the west side of Mushaboom. He used to see a ball of fire come up past his place from the same direction as the full-rigged ship. They 'lowed there was pirates' money on the island. They've seen people there with their heads off. On Blackmore's Island on the western shore of Mushaboom there are marks on the rocks, and they think pirate money is buried there." This reminds me of a boat that was said to have landed at Ballast Cove near Port Medway. The crew, who had no heads, left the boat and walked across the beach and vanished in the woods. There were people who would never pass that way at night again.

It must be about eighty years ago that a strange sight was witnessed in Halifax Harbour by two residents of that city. Mrs. King told me that when she was a young girl she was in a boat with a number of other people returning from a picnic. Fog was rolling in and there was a light breeze. Suddenly she saw a boat with square sails set which passed close beside their boat and they could see a crew at work as it passed them. Mrs. Turnbull, sitting beside her, turned to her and said, "Did you see that?"

"Yes," she said, "but I thought it must be a mistake." On talking this extraordinary experience over, they concluded this must be one of the boats of d'Anville's ill-fated expedition. It had suffered death and destruction, and the pay-ship was supposed to have been sunk in Bedford Basin. Others had told of seeing it in the vicinity of Navy Island.

It is a custom for vessels to speak each other as they

pass, just as we on our city streets greet one another with a nod of the head. On a long cruise a vessel might go well out of its way to dip its flag to another ship, just for the pleasure of its company on the mighty deep. Some Tancook men were on the Banks off Newfoundland one night when they saw a ship bearing down on them with masthead lights showing. She was full-rigged and had all the lights she was required to carry, and no more and no less. The captain and his watchmen stood uncertainly as she approached, waiting to see what she would do. They were tacking at the time, and the ship passed them like a ball of fire. They knew then that this was no friendly gesture, but that they had seen a ghost ship. They feared it was a forerunner of disaster and they were nervous until they got back to their home port.

Similarly a Seabright man was on a vessel off the Gaspé coast when another vessel showed up ahead. Then the Seabright boat passed it. Telling of it later the captain said, "I was going to speak it because it was so close and I could see the lights and the sails. Something told me to wait till morning and I did. It stayed in sight of us all night and, just before daybreak, one of the crew said, 'Where's the vessel?' It wasn't there. We learned later that we weren't the only ones who had seen it, for it had often been reported there. It was a good thing we didn't speak it, for that would have been the end of us. You see, if we had spoken it, not realizing she was a ghost ship, that would have been our doom." That, as a Lunenburg fisherman once expressed it, was the fairy of the time—the belief.

Bringing our stories up to date, a small ship whose name I had better not mention on account of the implications in the story, was lost off the eastern shore. To this day people often look out at ten o'clock at night and see a white light. It is about the size of a car light, but not as bright, they say. There was supposed to have been a mutiny on board and the cook was murdered. Hence the light.

A Norwegian barque once lost its way in Petpeswick Harbour and was sunk. Since then it has often been seen before a storm entering the harbour either as a vessel, or as a huge light like a big star. It has been seen as recently as twenty years ago. Like the vessel at Pleasant Harbour, it comes in and disappears in the woods.

A Spanish ship used to be seen about once a year. It came up the eastern side of St. Margaret's Bay from Peggy's Cove, across from Croucher's Island, then to Red Bank, and from there to North West Cove and out the Bay. Two men told that when they were out fishing and saw it, the ship was on fire, and they could see men going up the rigging. Suddenly it vanished and they had just got over that astonishment when it came up on the other side. People at Cape Negro used to see a full-rigged ship with lights on and nobody aboard, but they have no explanation for its presence. And from Hall's Harbour there is a story of a ship's lights going up the Bay of Fundy every seven years in winter. No voices are heard, nor is there any known reason for its appearance, although in these turbulent waters many a ship has foundered in days gone by.

"When I was eighteen years old," said Mr. Stanislas Pothier of Pubnico, "I was in a boat and, coming along Canso way it was dark and there was no moon. By and by we saw a ray of fire but no blaze. We looked at it and the engineer said, 'That's the burning ship they see all the time.' This same ship is seen at Port Hood where the masts and sails are seen through the fire. A woman watched it one dark hazy night not long ago, and she said she could distinctly see the masts and sails burning. There was a mutiny on board and it is seen on a certain date. I don't know what its name was."

Years ago a vessel was built at Diligent River between

Parrsboro and Port Greville and she soon became known as a bad luck vessel. "Once a ship gets a name like that," said Captain Hatfield, "there are not many men willing to ship on her as crew. She was owned and sailed by Capt. Roberts, and two of my sailors went aboard. She was loaded in Jacksonville and when found, the double reef mizzen sail and the fore staysail were laying with their sails set. Boats and men were gone and were never heard of again. She was taken ashore and then sent out again and of course this time she had an entirely different crew. What do you suppose happened then? She took on a load of salt and must have been sailing home when the whole of this second crew abandoned her. We never could figure it out but it was always supposed they had seen something aboard so terrible that they didn't dare remain. Maybe a ghost, we thought, or a crew of ghosts. Who knows?"

Oyster Pond had its full-rigged ship that used to be seen coming up the harbour. "One beautiful calm night without a ripple on the water a woman saw it from the road and stopped to watch it. It was coming up so quickly and the sails were so pretty, you'd think they were in full breeze. She met Mr. Nelson Webber on the road and he saw it too. He thought it was a handsome ship, but he wondered as he watched if it was real. The woman went into the barn and milked her cow and when she came out she expected to see the beautiful ship again." Here in the soft light of early evening with its white sails billowing it would be something to look forward to but, though she looked over the full length and breadth of the harbour, it was no longer there.

This was not the only occasion of this ship being seen. "It used to tack across the channel to Salmon River and then come across to Mitchell's Point. She must have known her route and had some purpose in mind, we always thought. The old timers could hear people talking on board, but it was always in some outlandish

tongue they couldn't understand. They could see and
hear her drop her anchor, but in the morning she'd be
gone. They thought she must be a pirate ship that had
buried treasure here. The last time she was seen was
in 1904."

There are many stories of ships being haunted. The
reason for the spirit presence is usually known, and is
an important part of the tale, as in this one from
Chebucto Head. "A Portuguese ship was fishing and
the captain told the crew to go in their dories when the
weather wasn't fit. The crew didn't want to go because
they knew it was going to squall, but the captain
insisted. They put the dories over the side and went
off as he ordered, then sure enough the squalls they had
been expecting came up, and he lost the whole crew.
He and the cook brought the vessel in to port, and the
cook told that when the squall came and some of the
fishermen tried to get back aboard, the captain let the
painter (the rope) go and left them to the storm, so
they were drowned. After that whenever this same ship
went out on the fishing bank they could hear the old
crew below cutting up the bait for their trawls but, when
they went down to look, there'd be nobody there. At
last they were frightened to go down. No matter what
skipper or what crew were aboard, the same thing
happened.

"As I said, the crew were Portuguese, and they'd
had a fashion of sitting on the rail in the night after
fishing, and smoking their cigarettes. All captains and
crews who went out on this ship after that drowning
said they saw the crew sitting on the rails smoking their
cigarettes. They took her to different fishing grounds
but the crew were always there. They were never seen
during the day, but always at night. The ship was the
Clara Sylvia, and the year was 1910. Gloucester was
her home port."

One of the best known stories of haunted ships is

that of the sailing vessel, the *Charles Haskell.* Its
strange story made such an impression at the time that
a song was made up about it and to this day it is sung
in many ports all over the maritime provinces and the
New England states. Two men from Lockeport, Nova
Scotia, and one from Lunenburg, were in her crew; the
rest were Gloucester men. This is her story according
to an account from the *Boston Globe* of that time and
shown to me in a scrap book at Annapolis Royal where
the vessel was well known later on.

The *Charles Haskell,* a fine new vessel, sailed out of
Boston and was one of three hundred anchored on
Georges on March 7, 1866. A hurricane and blinding
storm set in. Vessels were huddled together and were
torn from their anchorage. During the hurricane all
hands were on deck. At one o'clock at night one of the
other ships, a schooner, got adrift and out of control. She
was like a runaway and was being hurled by the storm
directly towards the *Haskell.* In order to save herself,
the *Haskell's* rope was cut, but she was then so storm-
driven that she was completely at the mercy of the wind.
Another craft lay in her path and she ran through it
like a cheese, standing the shock herself without losing a
rope yarn. Thus the *Charles Haskell* unwittingly transferred to the *Andrew Jackson* of Salem what would have
been her fate.

In time the *Charles Haskell* returned to the same
fishing grounds. Then a strange thing happened and all
the crew testified that it was true, for when they sailed
over the place where they had rammed the *Andrew
Jackson,* the crew of that schooner came up over the
sides in their oilskins and manned the *Haskell.* After
that the *Haskell* became known as the *Ghost Vessel,* and
the owners were unable to obtain a crew. She was
finally purchased by Captain David Hayden of Port
Wade, Nova Scotia, for whom she sailed out of Digby,
transporting wood along our coast. As far as I can

gather, she never went to Georges again, and therefore had only the one visitation. I have talked to men who had heard the story personally from the crew, and I too heard it confirmed from one who saw it happen, Captain Ammon Zinck of Lunenburg. The song however is perhaps the best source of information. This was my introduction to the story, and it is still the way that fishermen prefer to tell it. I first heard it in 1928 from the lips of Mr. Gordon Young. He sang sitting on a log on the Devil's Island beach with his friends around him nodding sympathetic approval as the theme unfolded. The evening light was growing dim and men and women moved about quietly in the late twilight, intent upon the words they knew so well. His voice was soft and musical, and his only accompaniment came from the waves lapping gently against the shore and the small fishing boats rocking at their moorings. Here are three of the verses:

Last night as we were sailing, we were off shore a ways,
    I never will forget it in all my mortal days,
It was in the grand dog watches I felt a thrilling dread
    Come over me as if I heard one calling from the dead.

Right over our rail there clambered all silent one by one
    A dozen dripping sailors, just wait till I am done,
Their faces were pale and sea wan, shone through the ghostly night,
    Each fellow took his station as if he had a right.

They moved about before us till land was most in sight,
    Or rather I should say so, the lighthouse shone its light,
And then those ghostly sailors moved to the rail again
    And vanished in an instant before the sons of men.

This is not the only instance of a sunken crew taking over. North Port Mouton also has a story of a man who was at sea when his ship rammed a vessel, but only the captain's ghost of that sunken craft appeared. Digby Neck tells of a freighter that rammed a dory with the result that her sailors came aboard and took over when the freighter returned to that spot.

Occasionally a single ghost turns up on a ship. This story from Glen Haven is one of my favourites. I would like to think it really happened, and perhaps it did. Ben Smeltzer was a West Dover man and one of the crew of a vessel fishing off Georges in winter. It was snowing and there were no fish, and they were getting all iced up and the captain had decided to take the ship to Boston. At this time Mr. Smeltzer went down below and, when he went into the cabin, there was a strange man sitting at the chart-table writing on a slate —a large, healthy looking sea-faring man.

For readers who are not accustomed to the sea and its ways, I might mention that it would be impossible in the limited space of a sailing vessel for a person to stow away for any length of time, if at all, and this vessel had been at sea for some weeks.

"Who can this be?" Mr. Smeltzer thought. "What does it mean?" He had heard of strange events at sea, and he scratched his head as he went up the companion-way to talk it over with his captain.

"There's a strange man down below," he said. "Never see him before."

"You're crazy," said the captain. Then observing that Mr. Smeltzer was serious about it he decided to humour him and added in a voice that had in it more than a hint of sarcasm, "What did you say to him?"

"I didn't say anything," Mr. Smeltzer declared. "He can't be human."

"Well," said the captain, who began to have misgivings himself, "you come down with me and show me your man." So down they went and there was no one there. However the captain was a thorough man and Mr. Smeltzer had stated specifically that the stranger had been sitting at the chart table writing on a slate. He therefore strode over to the table and picked up the slate. The top side was clean, just as he had left it. Without really thinking what he was doing he turned the slate over and there he was amazed to see a message. It read: "Change your course to nor'nor'west and steer so many hours and you'll come to a vessel turned on its side and the crew hanging to it."

He put the slate down and snorted.

"Tricks. Sailors must always be at their tricks," but Mr. Smeltzer insisted it was not a trick and he grew even more serious as he too read the message. More to satisfy him than anything, the captain called his crew down one by one and had each one write something on that slate. No script resembled the mysterious handwriting. By this time the crew all knew the story and they were as one in concluding that they should follow the slate's directions. Against his own wishes and judgment the captain changed his course. And sure enough, they had not gone far on their way when they came upon an upturned vessel. Men were still clinging to the hull, and they were in time to save them. They supposed then that the stranger who had appeared in the cabin had been one of the first to succumb and that he had taken this means of saving his fellow seamen.

No reader will doubt the next story although why should it be more credible than the last? If a message could be conveyed in one way, why not in another? And would the first captain, a stubborn man, have paid attention to anything less startling than a physical appearance? Well, here is the story of a dream, told to me in the 1930's by Capt. Joe-Boyd of Yarmouth, a man many of my readers will remember.

"I was mate and my brother was captain on a trip from London to New York and it was blowing a heavy gale. There were terrible seas running and we were

under lower topsails. We had been that way for nearly
a week.

"At breakfast one morning my brother, the captain,
said, 'I had a peculiar dream last night. It was so vivid
I couldn't sleep.' I just laughed and said, 'Didn't you
ever have a dream before that you couldn't get rid of?
One like that keeps coming back all night.' But he wasn't
being put off like that and so he told me his dream. It
bothered him. He had seen a ship with only one mast
light and he could even see the faces of people lashed
to the deck. He was a quiet chap and not given to any
funny stories.

"Well, you know, I couldn't get rid of it either and
it pestered me so that after a while I went up in the
mizzen rigging, a thing I wouldn't have thought of doing
without the dream on my mind, because there wasn't
any reason for going up. I looked over the stormy water
and I saw the wreck. I called for the marine glasses
and there was the ship, exactly as he had told of it.
This was a couple of hours after I'd heard his dream
and I sighted her a long way off.

"We changed our course and, when we reached the
wreck, hove our ship to and we found sixteen men in
the last stages of exhaustion lashed to the rigging. They
had put ropes from one side of the vessel to the other
and they were in a network of ropes to keep them out
of the water. This kept them up some twenty feet. All
the masts were gone but this short one.

"I manned one boat and the second mate the other.
There was an awful high sea, but we managed to get
them down without hurting anybody. The ship had capsized and filled with water and, as soon the the deckload
of heavy timber went, she righted. Four or five of the
crew were swept off and, when the timber went, it took
the deck house and everything with it.

"Getting them off the wreck was awful because we
had to tie them in a boatswain's chair and let them

swing when there was a roll. We made four or five trips. It took an hour to get up to her, and we were the whole afternoon till dark getting them off. All they wanted was water, but we wouldn't let them have it except a little at a time. Then we gave them a little in canned milk and fed each one like a baby. After that we fed them on gruel for about three days.

"Later I was talking with Rev. Mr. Gibson and I said, 'Can you give me any good reason why a man should dream such a thing?' and he said it was part of God's will that the thought should be put in his head. Anyhow the men said they had prayed for help with hands held out just as the captain had seen them. When we reached New York, reporters came aboard and I gave them the story. Cleveland was President at the time, and my brother received an inscribed gold watch for saving the lives of the men, and the crew all got medals from the life-saving society."

Our next story embraces features of the two preceding ones. It happened to Captain George Albert Hatfield of Fox River, and was brought to my attention by his grand-nephew, Mr. G. D. H. Hatfield of Halifax.

It happened in March, 1874, that Captain Hatfield was sailing from Cuba to New York when his ship ran into very bad weather. When he felt that he could safely leave the bridge and get some rest he went to his cabin, keeping his clothes on in case of a sudden call. He was no sooner asleep than he was awakened by someone tapping his shoulder and he heard a voice saying, "Keep her off half a point." He supposed it was his mate and went back on deck to ask what he meant by such presumption. The mate gazed at him in astonishment and said, "Why sir, I haven't left the deck since you went below." Captain Hatfield was embarrassed then, and surprised that a dream should be so vivid.

For the second time he fell asleep but not for long. Again he felt a tapping on his shoulder and heard the same voice saying, "Keep her off half a point." This time he was doubly annoyed, but the mate assured him neither he nor anybody else had gone to his cabin. Too tired to argue he made a third attempt to sleep but his head had no sooner touched the pillow than the hand on his shoulder went tap, tap, tap. This time it was not a request that he heard but a command. The captain opened his eyes and saw distinctly a strange man walk out of his cabin and go up the companionway to the deck. He particularly noticed his clothes because they were different from any of those on board. This time when he approached the mate he had a different question. He said,

"Did you see a man go out of my cabin just now?" The mate said no, and began to wonder if the captain were losing his reason. The captain then gave the order to keep her off half a point and once more went below, this time to sleep the night through peacefully. He said afterwards that he had acted like a man in a dream or one who was sailing under sealed orders. The mate kept the altered course and, when the captain returned to the deck in the morning, he ordered a strict lookout to be kept. It was no great surprise to him when a wreck was sighted and, of course, his ship went at once to the rescue. Captain Amesbury of the United States schooner D. Talbot, his wife, child, and all of his crew, were transferred safely over the stormy seas. Just one hour after she was sighted the wreck went down.

Later when they were sitting together Captain Hatfield told why he had altered his course and, when he was through, Mrs. Amesbury asked him to describe the stranger who had left his cabin. As she listened she was obviously shaken with emotion and, when she could trust herself to speak she said, "That was my father; he's been dead for ten years."

When they reached New York the rescue was reported by Captain Amesbury with the result that the Hatfield family still has in its possession the gold watch presented to the gallant captain by the United States government. The inscription reads in part, "for humanity and courage in the rescue."

These three stories of rescue came, as you have seen, from different parts of the Province, and two of them directly from the families concerned. They must actually have happened as they have been related, and they are entirely separate incidents. The first is the only one that I cannot be sure about because I have never talked to any of the Smeltzer family. It is conceivable that it is true like the others.

We have had several stories already from Mr. Horace Johnston of Port Wade, so let us visit him again. He was a tall lean man who loved the sea until the day he died. When I met him with another retired fisherman, Mr. Norman McGrath, they were spending part of their summer in a shack on the shore of Victoria Beach. They spent their time fishing and recalling events from their adventurous younger days. They were delighted when I came along because mine was a new ear to listen to the yarns they loved to spin. Some were very funny, some were folk tales from out of a far distant past, and others were personal experiences, true or concocted. The trick was to distinguish between them. This one about the *Vesta Pearl* was given in all seriousness by Mr. Johnston, and he assured me it was true. Again we have brothers sailing together.

"About fifty years ago when my brother was captain of the *Vesta Pearl* I sailed with him as mate. The captain takes care of the after end of the ship and the mate the forward end. Well, this vessel was built in St. John, and that's where we bought her and, after we got her, they said she was a hanted vessel. One old fellow said,

" 'You can't run her, she hanted.' So I said, 'If she's hanted now she's hanted so bad she's got to keep moving.' (The word hant is often used here for haunt.) The crew didn't want to stay aboard after the word got around. Someone told them the last captain had been knocked overboard when she was new and on her first trip and that he'd been drowned, but none of us knew the whole story. All we knew was that he was always around. He'd be there in a gale of wind when we were reefing the sails. If four men were reefing and one was at the wheel, there would be one man at the wheel and five men reefing, but you had to be at the wheel to see him.

"He didn't bother us until we'd been out four months. We got caught in an easterly wind going to Boston and we were bobbing in the sea and when we went to reef, here was Mr. Extry Man. My brother called me to come and take the wheel. He said, 'I'd rather go and help reef,' but he didn't tell me why. It was then I found out about the extry man. I saw him for myself.

"One time when we were in Annapolis we got rigged up (dressed up) and went ashore. It didn't take much to dress you up in those days. On account of the tide the boat was high up in the water and we figured out the tide to see what time we should come back. Tides are mighty high here and when it was out we could walk right up to the boat, but it would be muddy going. Then you could climb up the ladder and on to the ship's deck. If we stayed ashore too long we couldn't walk back to her. I had my rubber boots waiting on the shore and, when I got back I put 'em on, and made my way to the ship. The tide was getting pretty well up to the vessel when I got there, and I figured that the other men wouldn't be able to get back without a boat till the next tide. I shook my feet to get the mud knocked off my boots, and scraped them on every rung of the ladder.

"It seems that anybody going to sea, it makes no odds whether they've had their supper or not, because when they come aboard they always have to have a mug-up, hot or cold. This night I was the only one aboard

and I was having a mugup. Tea, it was. They had a
lot of salt horse (salt beef) aboard this vessel and I was
quite hungry because I'd gone without eating from six
to eleven. Well, I was having my mugup and salt horse
when I heard another fellow coming stomping same as I
did and, when he reached the deck, he seemed to go forward. So I says, 'My gracious, he just made it,' because
the tide was pretty well around the vessel. I could tell
because while I was setting there the ship riz and I
could feel her come up out of the mud. I said to myself,
'Who's that come aboard?' because after I heard him
stomping I didn't see no more nor hear nothin', but I'd
heard him all right because he'd scraped his boots off
the same as I done. So I took the lantern to see where
he walked, because I knew the mud would show his tracks,
but nothing showed.

"Well, the watch had gone off when I come aboard,
and I knew I was alone and I don't know whether I was
frightened or not, but it was a little bit of a strange kind
of feeling. I thought somebody might have gone overboard, but I couldn't see nothin' with the lantern and,
when the others came back, I asked and it hadn't been
them. So it must a been him—The Extry Man."

"The strangest things happened on that vessel. One
time we got into a little river and it was blowing hard
and a-raining bad. All those vessels have two anchors
and, if you let one go, you have the next one ready.
Well, we had the big anchor in, and when it goes out
the iron windlass with the chain going over it makes an
awful noise, and there's no mistaking it. Croquinole
had just come in then and everybody was crazy about it.
I wanted to play but I had a sore finger, so I said, 'If
I can play the same as checkers I'll play,' and I did.
We was settin' there playing when away went the anchor
and it made an awful noise. My brother says, 'That
anchor should have been made fast. The only thing we
can do now is to heave it up again.' He was pretty cross

but, when we went to look, the anchor had never moved.

"Later we were told the reason for it all. It seems that when the company was building this vessel they didn't know which of two fellows to give it to and, after they finally made up their minds, the fellow who lost went as mate. He was steering the wheel when the captain went over. He was probably working on the deck when the wheelsman gave it a sudden turn and sent the captain over the side. It was always thought he done it a-purpose."

One day I left the two old friends at Victoria Beach and went in to Granville Ferry. There I met a man who was vacationing along this peaceful shore, but who had a tale to tell that was the antithesis of peace. He gave it to me because he had heard of my interests in ghosts and thought I might like to add it to my collection. Actually it has nothing to do with Nova Scotia beyond the fact that I collected it here. I am not sure whether the ship sailed from Boston or New York, but it was one of those cities. This is what he said.

The *City of Rome* was a passenger ship that sailed until about sixty years ago. As it was leaving on one of its trips a passenger came aboard at the last minute and wanted a berth. The purser said it was impossible as everything was taken. The man insisted that his business was urgent, and he cared little where he slept. He was so anxious to go that the purser consulted the captain with the result that he was told one cabin was available. But, the purser took pains to explain, the stateroom had not been occupied for some years because the last three persons who had slept there had gone over the side. This man brushed off any such suggestion as nonsense and said he had no fear of anything supernatural. So, since he had been told the facts and knew what he was facing, he was finally permitted to use the stateroom, but only on condition that the ship would be absolved of any responsibility if anything happened. To this he readily agreed.

In the morning the purser asked him how he had slept. He said he had slept very well, but he thought he was to have had that room to himself.

"Well," the purser said, "you did."

"No," he said, "the upper berth was slept in. It's a strange thing, though, because before I went to sleep I bolted the door and fastened the porthole down. In the morning the porthole was open and the bed had been used."

The captain was told about this strange occurrence and his curiosity was aroused. He said he would go with the passenger that night and see what happened. So the passenger slept again in the lower berth and the captain took the settee. This left the upper berth empty as before.

Whether the passenger stayed awake to see what occurred my informant did not say, but the captain kept his vigil and, sure enough, after a while the porthole opened. A man came through it all covered with slime and seaweed and prepared to occupy it as before. Hoping to lay the ghost for all time, the captain grabbed him and they had a terrible tussle, and all he got out of it was a broken arm. As for the passenger, like the previous occupants he went over the side before anyone realized what he was doing. After that the door was locked and bolted and as long as the ship sailed it was never opened again.

Whether the man in our next story came up out of the sea or appeared as the more usual ghosts do, I do not know, but a Seabright man told of a boat called the *Sonora* from whose deck a man. had been drowned. Afterwards he used to be heard jumping on the deck. Nothing more was reported, just the jumping which was so characteristic of him that it could not be mistaken for anything or anybody else.

It is an old belief that a ghost cannot cross water, as we have mentioned before. You will also recall that a house built of wood from a wreck is likely to be haunted. A house at Cooper's Head was a case in point. I heard about it at Salmon River.

"My mother lived there and one time she was in bed and she heard four men talking and she couldn't understand them. They all took a turn speaking different languages. An old Mr. Dolby was there and he heard it too, and somebody said to him, 'Are you afraid?' and he said, 'No, but I'm very uncomfortable.' Various sounds were heard and they became so bad that it was decided to bring the house across the water to Oyster Pond." (I have seen the house and it seemed like a sizable structure to be floated over the water.) "It was the right thing to do, because from that time the sounds were never heard again."

Ragged Islands and Lockeport tell about a British troop ship, the *Billow*, that was lost with all hands. There was a snowstorm about 1830 when she struck off Ram Island and was lost. Residents at Little Harbour could hear the band playing as the ship went down. They claim that when the wind is in a certain direction in a storm you can still hear the band playing the same selection. It was "The Gay Cockade."

If we go now to The Pond past Mr. Charlie Taylor's store at Victoria Beach we may see a place where a ship is heard landing, but nothing has ever been seen of it. One morning, however, at an early hour a man was walking down that road to go fishing when he met a sailor and remarked to himself that his coat was of a particularly good piece of serge. He looked at the stranger more closely then and realized that he was not a living man at all. By this time he had seen more than enough, and left with all the speed he could muster.

Clarke's Harbour has a strange story about a wrecked ship and the use that was made of it. "There was a ship wrecked here many years ago. In the cabin there were knives lying around and things upset which showed signs of a fight. A man who lived near the wreck took timber from it and anything he could lay his hands on, and he built a house with that timber. From the first there was a knocking that he couldn't find any reason for. He looked everywhere but it never did any good. No good at all, and the funny part of it was that it always came at a certain time of the night when the house was still. It was more of a tapping than a knocking. People would move in and then move out very soon afterwards and he found it impossible to get a family to stay there. Well now I tell you it got pretty bad. So the old timers got together to "get" the ghost. They all congregated there together and had prayers, but it wasn't any use. They said among other things, "In the name of the Father and the Son and the Holy Ghost," the three highest words in the Bible. That's always supposed to lay them but the tapping still persisted and it does to this day.

"You want to know what a ghost sounds like? It sounds like somethin' soft knockin' on nawthin'. That's what it sounds like."

At Port Hastings the old people used to help one another with their haymaking and then, in the pleasant hours that followed a well earned meal, they would tell one another stories. One of these was about cattle being shipped to Newfoundland. The man in charge of the cattle was called the supercargo. In one vessel that went from here the only person saved when she was wrecked was the supercargo and for some years after that a schooner used to be seen in the swamp. It had never been seen before, so it became quite a subject of speculation, with the final conclusion that it was this cattle-boat.

One day when I was talking to a fisherman at Moser's River he told me an amazing experience that had come to his friends Albert Mosher and Will Lowe. They had gone to Toby Island in the lobster fishing season and had, as they thought, taken ample provisions for two weeks. Before the time elapsed they ran short of food, so Mr. Mosher said he would go ashore and get a fresh supply. He would then return in the morning. Mr. Lowe was therefore left alone and, after a while, he fell asleep. Some time later he was wakened by the sound of the door rattling. He supposed Mr. Mosher must have changed his mind and come back that night but, although the door was open, there was no one there. He settled down, thinking he must have imagined it, having first made sure that the door was securely shut. Again he was wakened by the rattling of the latch and again there was no one there. He went outside then, and there he saw a man all covered with eel grass. He laughed heartily, supposing Mr. Mosher had fixed himself up to frighten him, and thinking it a very smart trick he said, "You can't fool me Albert." Then the incredible happened and he stood dazed and terrified as the figure dissolved before his eyes, and in a moment there was nothing left of his visitor but a pool of water and some eel grass.

Another story along these lines came to me at Victoria Beach, where they told of a house along the Bay of Fundy shore where the son who was lost at sea used to come back at night and stand beside the mantel. In the morning a pool of sea water and seaweed would be there. This ghost apparently resented other people using his bed, for one guest reported his bedclothes had been pulled off in the night and he also said there were matches in his bed and on his pillows which certainly were not there when he retired.

The town of Lunenburg is noted for its seafaring men and many a rousing yarn has died with the old-timers. However there are still those who have adventures to recall and a reminiscent mood has a result like this: "Dad was in a four-master going to Quebec and at that time he was sailing as first mate. When they reached Quebec the crew were paid off and then they started to drink. The second mate was coming back to the ship for his clothes after being ashore awhile, and also to get money for the cook who had told him where to find it. He was too drunk to see where he was going and he fell between the boat and the water. He was seen, but even so they were several hours finding him. At last they got him out of the water and by this time everybody was sober enough. They gave him decent burial and informed his family and we supposed that was the end of it. It wasn't.

"That winter the ship was laid up in Quebec and dad stayed on it all alone. One night he was sitting reading when he saw a seaman come down the after-companionway, and then he came through the cabin. He went right on from there to the cook's room. Dad looked at him pretty hard, and it struck him that he was dressed exactly as the second mate had been the last time he'd been seen alive. He sat quietly and waited but nothing else happened so he left the ship and went ashore to see the captain.

" 'I saw the second mate last night,' he said.

" 'Don't be foolish mister,' the captain said. Mister was always the name used for mate. The captain wouldn't believe him so he went back, but several nights later the same thing happened again, so dad went ashore a second time. My dad was a reliable man or he wouldn't have been left in charge, so the captain began to think he'd better look into the matter. He went back to the ship and prepared to stay there a few days. Then sure enough, the figure came the third time, always dressed as he had been when he fell overboard. He didn't look to the right or left but proceeded directly to the cook's cabin. Nobody spoke, and nobody ever knew what brought him back. But they both saw him, and from that time he was never seen again."

Looking back to the days of sailing ships, names of

foreign ports like Buenos Aires and Hong Kong were often more familiar in our coastal towns than that of our own capital city of Halifax. This meant that there were long separations and, because life was dangerous, many sudden deaths. Bonds seemed to have been established between loved ones which were in no way dependent upon distance. An old man at Port Medway wished to drive this point home. As he prepared to tell his tale he straightened his rheumaticky back and sat up straight in his chair, his great hands clutching the arms as he spoke.

"My aunt was in a house and all at once an awful squash came against it as though a great wave had come across the window and against the pane. There's no sound in all the world that's like it. Her husband was away at sea at the time. When it stopped she lifted her apron to her eyes and the tears rolled down her cheeks.

" 'Judson's gone,' she moaned. 'My man has gone.' And she was right. He was lost at sea at that very time, and the sound of the wave had come to tell her so."

Going now to Cape Breton Island we come to Louisburg and Glace Bay. Many men went to sea from these ports and some brought home incredible stories. I am indebted to Mrs. Ruth Metcalfe, for this one which is her father's personal story. That being the case, it should be her privilege to tell it.

"This story goes back to 1862 when my father, Dan McPhee, was a prentice to John Hamilton, a shoemaker in North Sydney. He was only fourteen, but he was a big, sturdy lad. Sailing with him, but not so sturdy, was his cousin, Alex McKinnon. Together they shipped aboard a Norwegian. Some time later in Gloucester, Mass. they met a man prominent in shipping circles in Sydney, Sol Jacobs by name, and they were shipmates with him for many years.

"After a while my father had a chance to go with

the Black Ball Line and Alex stayed with the fishermen, sailing from the home port. Father was with the Black Ball Line seventeen years during which time he married and had two children. When they were aged five and three he was on a trip returning from South America when they were becalmed off Port of Spain, Trinidad. It was a very close and humid night, and father was lying in his hammock on deck. He said he saw Alex come up the deck. He was easily recognized, if for no other reason than by a characteristic pose, for he had a habit of holding the belaying pin on his shoulders with each hand, and moving it up and down. He came straight to father's hammock and said,

" 'Dan, I have Flora with me.' Flora was father's wife's name. Father claims he sat up on his elbow and Alex disappeared. He thought he must have dreamed it. But he appeared to him again the same night in the same attitude and said the same words. This time they were more forceful.

" 'Did you hear what I said Dan'l? I have Flora with me." With that father put his feet on deck, for he realized now that Alex could not possibly be on his ship. He was greatly disturbed and couldn't sleep all the way home.

"When they arrived in Boston he found news waiting for him at the shipping office, just as he feared. His wife had died at the Victoria General Hospital in Halifax on March twenty-eighth, and that was the night Alex had appeared to him. Father went down to Gloucester then to see if any of the Cape Breton boys were there who could give him a passage home. He met Sol Jacobs and, during their conversation, told him about his wife's death. Then he asked Sol if he knew where Alex was, and Sol said Alex had been lost off Sable Island that same spring. Father wondered what the date was, but Sol didn't remember. They looked it up in the shipping news and it was the same day that Flora had died, and could have been the same hour."

One such story was enough for one sitting. I found that it kept coming back to me long after she had told it. I was grateful therefore that she let me think about it for a few days before bringing up the subject of ghosts again. We had been recording songs she had heard in Cape Breton from her father and his friends, and one day as we put the microphone down she told the following story.

"On father's side they are highland folk, and one young man used to go fishing in the evening after working in the mine. He and another miner had an in-shore fishing boat and one night they went out in the boat and never came back. There were all kinds of stories made up about them. Some said they went on the Norwegian freighter that was in at the time, but none of the family believed that because there was no reason for their going. They were both happily married men. A few months after their disappearance my father and mother went to visit a sister of one of the men (father had married a second time, and I was of that family) and she told this story. On that night when they had disappeared, she had been lying on the bed with the baby. Her husband was on night shift at the mine, and she thought she heard someone call her name. Thinking it was her husband, she went downstairs, but there was no one there. It was some time later that she realized the noise had come from the skylight and not downstairs, and she always believed it was her brother who had called her. They were never heard of although the overturned boat came ashore. There was no storm, so something else must have upset them. They were wearing rubber boots which might have weighed them down, but we never really knew and it remains a mystery to this day."

Returning to the subject of knowledge being conveyed by strange means, we have a case from Shelburne.

Leander was a boy who wanted to go to sea, but his grandfather was opposed to it. The old man may have had a premonition of disaster, although it is more likely he wanted a better life for the lad than his had been. However Leander got his way but, before he sailed the grandfather said to the captain, "Now don't be too easy on him. I want him to get tired of it."

One morning the grandfather came downstairs and said, "Leander's gone."

"How do you know?"

"He came to me in the night and I saw the ship-wreck." It was quite right, for Leander's ship was lost that night, and he with it.

Such strange things happen sometimes. To the sceptical they are no more than coincidence. Perhaps that is the true explanation for the incident that follows. We will never know. A man from Victoria Beach was lost on a vessel and a pillow was washed ashore from the wreck. It had been made by his wife, and it was conveyed twenty miles against the tide to the shore beside his home and when it arrived she felt impelled to go down to the water. The pillow was the only thing washed ashore and it came all the way from Parker's Cove to Port Wade. How puzzled Mr. John Casey looked as he told me about it, and I could imagine people all along the shore trying to figure it out.

We have not had many stories from Liverpool. Here is one now about two brothers who were on the same ship. "A sailor named Big Henry made a great friend of the smaller boy. One day the bigger boy was swept overboard and drowned and that night Big Henry heard a voice saying, 'Take good care of my little brother.' He was sure it was the voice of the bigger brother and, to give substance to that belief, a midshipman had seen a form standing in a doorway and had asked who it was. Then the figure disappeared."

A story is told of a Tantallon family by the name of Silvers. "Mrs. Silvers was a widow with one son, Willie, who went away on a vessel to sea. One day his mother looked out the window and saw Willie coming up the driveway on a white horse. She said to herself, 'Willie must be in, but where did he get that white horse?' She went to open the door, but there was no one there. Fancy Willie's surprise if anyone had told him that when he died he would appear to his mother riding a white horse!"

At Port Medway the night was still and not a breath of wind was blowing, a fact that is noticed in a seaport where everybody is conscious of weather during every waking moment. Suddenly there was an awful banging as though every door had opened and slammed. The noise was so loud that it woke up the whole household, and the house itself shook. "Grandfather got up and examined the doors but they were closed and locked, then he went back to bed and thought nothing of it. But grandmother was worried. They found out later that on that same night their son had been washed overboard." In a story from French River where the son had suffered the same fate his father, at the time of his death struggle, paced the floor gasping for breath without being able to understand why he was being stricken this way.

A seafaring man has been seen at Myers' Point near Head Jeddore wearing a blue suit, bib cap, and having brass buttons on his coat. He was of medium height, and was reported by so many different people that some of the boys who took it all as a joke, decided to use him for their own purpose. They went skating on the pond, but it was too dark to see properly, so one of them called out, "Ghost, light up your light so we can put our skates on." Imagine their astonishment when the ghost obediently complied and lit up the whole pond.

Some Seabright men had much the same thing happen to them. "A man named Holigan had died. A few days· later some of the fishermen were out in a boat and they got to joking among themselves and, just for the fun of it, one of them started to call him. They all heard him answer, but it was from a distance. They hollered again and he came closer. They got frightened then and put for shore, and they'll never try that trick again."

Mr. Sandy Stoddard from Lower Ship Harbour had a strange thing happen to him. "I was out lobster fishing at Wolfe Island, and there was a crowd out gunning at the Crick. They went ahead of me to camp. There was a good trail, but you had to cross a sand beach. I seen this man coming from the camp on the clear open sand beach, and I thought it was someone I knew comin' for water. I thought he had landed and was going up the trail to the Crick. His face and hands were white and I realized then that I knew him all right, only he'd been dead for two years. I was too surprised to speak, but I intended to if I ever saw him again, but I never did, and neither did anyone else.

"You don't expect to see a man on a beach dressed in his best Sunday clothes, but this man was, and that took my attention first. He had on a white full-bosom tucked shirt, a cutaway coat, and cuffs showed below his pants. I stepped to one side, but he was so close to me that my shoulders should have struck him on the breast. As he touched me in passing I felt a hot breath all over me, and then he disappeared. I looked behind and there were no tracks like a human being would leave on the sand. The next day I went to the camp and talked to a fellow who lived there but he had never seen him. Perhaps it happened to me because I knew him so well. At the same camp there used to be a very pretty woman come and look in the window and, a few nights after, an

ugly one, who looked as though she had come up out of
the water. The man who lived in the camp and saw her
would never stay there again. Can't say I blame him."

Clarke's Harbour has given us many stories, and here
is one from a settlement near there called The Hawk.
"Years ago a man was drowned at The Hawk inlet. He
lived at the wireless station where there were five or six
men with a cook and a housekeeper. There was a little
hotel there at one time, and people used to come there
ducking (duck hunting) and fishing. One operator was
a South African, a veteran of the First World War, and
he used to have heart spells when he would pass out for
a while. He was a man who had travelled a lot and he
used to watch for letters from home. In order to come
to The Hawk for his mail he had to come by boat and,
before he came, he would 'phone to see if there was
anything there for him. Then if there was, he'd row
over.

"One night he came for his mail and when he left
it was after dark. He said he didn't mind, and he was
relieved now that he had his letter. The postmistress
had a habit of going to the door when you were going
off at night. This night she heard him haul his boat off,
so she came in thinking everything was all right. The
next day towards noon the officer in charge of the station
where he lived, and one of the others, came over for
their mail. We said he had taken it. They were surprised and called the station to see if he was in his bed,
but his bed hadn't been slept in. They thought perhaps
he had gone to see Lottie, the girl he was engaged to
marry, but he was a fussy man and wouldn't have gone
wearing an old sweater. And of course when Lottie
was asked, she hadn't seen him.

"Three weeks went by and somebody suggested he
might have run away rather than marry Lottie who was
older than he was. He was a Mason, so the Masons
offered a reward for him. In nine days his boat was

found partly full of water, but there was no sign of him. They were pretty sure by now that he'd been drowned so they searched and a fortnight or so later Marshall Smith stumbled over him face down on the beach.

"Well they brought him up and put him in the out-house (shed) floor. The Masons took the body and he was buried in The Hawk cemetery. They thought he must have had a spell just as he shoved his boat off, and that he'd fallen in the water. But here is what happened. The day after he died there was a steady shrill noise all the time in our pantry like a little screaming away off. We couldn't find what was causing it, and we couldn't stop it. It did that until after he was found, and then it stopped and we've never heard it again."

The eastern shore has a story in which one of their seamen played a leading role, at least according to Mr. Enos Roast of East Chezzetcook. "It must have happened sixty years ago that an iron vessel was found outside Halifax with nobody on board, but with the table set for breakfast. This looked as though it had been abandoned hastily. The vessel belonged to Liverpool, England, but people were suspicious of her and nobody wanted to take her back to her owners. Finally Captain Sprott Balcolm of Salmon River said he would. After they got out of the harbour one of the crew, Jack Donaldson, said to him, 'We've got a good thing here.' 'How's that?' and he told of finding a long chest. He said, 'There might be something in that chest.' The captain was curious then and went with Donaldson to see it. They stood talking about it and wondering what there might be inside and, after a while, they decided to open it. It wasn't locked, so all they had to do was to lift the cover. They did this and, right on top, was a lady's watch. The rest of the chest was filled with her beautiful clothes.

"The captain wrote it all down in his log and nineteen days later when they landed in Liverpool, an investigation was held. The watch and clothing were used as evidence, and it was supposed that the lady had been murdered." But why had the captain and the crew left the ship, and what had become of them? It must have been something extraordinary that would force them to abandon their ship, and so close to a large seaport. Mr. Roast could not answer that question, but in time the words of some of the old folk songs came to mind, and with them a possible solution. For in these songs it is not uncommon for a person who has been murdered to return and take revenge.

The story of Jerome has been written up so often that is it well known not only in Nova Scotia, but abroad. Yet the facts of the case as related to me at Sandy Cove are different in some respects from the usual tale and, for that reason, should be related. There is no suggestion of the supernatural here, but it is one of this Province's greatest mysteries of the sea. For this event we go to Digby Neck, a point of land that juts out from the mainland of Digby County like a long finger. It is one of our beauty spots, especially at the part called Sandy Cove. Here there are gentle hills on whose lush slopes white farmhouses give an atmosphere of peace, home, and plenty, and here too are sand beaches, one on either side of the narrow village.

Many years ago a man named Martin Albright lived close to the west sand beach. His house had only one window and it looked out over the beach. At that time otter were thick and he often used to watch them playing on the beach. One day he got up at daylight and, as usual, started the fire. Then he wandered over to the window and looked out, as he always did first thing in the morning. His eye was attracted at once by a moving object which he supposed at first to be a large otter. He went back to his fire then and cooked his breakfast and, when he was through, he looked out again. He was surprised to observe that the object had not moved, so he decided to go out and investigate. As he drew near it, he was amazed to see that this was a man. Upon closer examination he was horrified to find that he was helpless, for both legs had been amputated and he had been left upon the beach with a bottle of water and some bread within his reach. Mr. Albright spoke to him, but the stranger made no reply, nor did he ever speak in all the years he lived in Nova Scotia. All anybody could ever get out of him were the words that might have been "Colombo" and "Jerome" and he became known by the latter name. The amputation was half way between the knees and the thighs, and had been very well done for those days.

Mr. Albright hastened to his friend Mr. Eldridge and told of his incredible discovery. Together they mustered up some men and carried him to the Albright home where he lived for some years. Different people cared for him after that, but not always too happily. He is remembered as a man who could become very moody. When that happened he would refuse to eat or to do anything that was asked of him. The only person for whom he ever showed any sign of affection was Mr. Albright's ten-year-old daughter. It seemed to please him when she came near him. He never nodded his head or smiled when people went by, but he would show signs of gratitude for kindness. He could feed himself and, by his eating and other habits, showed signs of good breeding. He had a beautifully shaped head and an aristocratic appearance, and hands which the people of Sandy Cove believed showed him as a man of good birth. People came from far and near to converse with him in many languages, but he would never talk. The only clues they ever got to his past was in his reaction to the rattling of a chain. He could not endure the sound and it made him very angry. It was then he made the sound that might have been "Jerome."

To this day there are speculations about Jerome.

Where had he come from, and why was he left upon the beach? From the quality of his clothes and his general appearance the people of Sandy Cove thought he might be of royal blood, one whom it might be convenient for political reasons to put out of reach. He was a big man, and looked like a central European, either Spanish or Greek. Shortly after his arrival they recalled a strange full-rigged ship that had been seen the day before he was found. It sailed up and down and back and forth on the Bay of Fundy. It was a low-lying vessel, shaped differently from ours and of a superior quality, as far as they could tell from a distance and, from her lines, they knew her to be foreign. They also pondered upon another fact which may or may not have any bearing upon the case. This was that until then parties used to come to Ellsworth Island from Boston but, after Jerome was left on the beach, they stopped coming.

Jerome lived for many years, spending half of his life with the people of Sandy Cove and at the almshouse at Marshalltown. The last part was spent with the Roman Catholics of Clare who cared for him until he died. This account given here was taken down at Sandy Cove in 1947 from residents of that village and of Bear River who knew him well.

Mysteries are all very well to talk about, but captains do not like them on their ships. Granville Ferry told about a ship's steward who had a power that nobody could explain. He discovered it one evening when he was playing billiards and noticed when he set the cue in an upright position that it stayed that way with nothing to hold it. He began to experiment then and at one time had as many as five cues standing on the table doing gymnastics for him. His friends were so puzzled by this that they took him before a famous hypnotist who was unable to determine where his strange power came from. The ship's crew felt proud of him and thought the captain should be told what a prize he had on board. The captain listened with interest and said he would like very much to witness a demonstration. The steward therefore went through his performance and never with better results. The effect upon the captain, however, was not what they expected.

"I'm going to pay that man off," he said. "If he's got animal magnetism or anything like that over a billiard cue or a broom there's no telling what he might do to the ship's instruments." Then, even though he was the best steward they had ever had, he let him go.

With all the people I have talked to, I have only two reports of sea serpents. One, being in an inland lake, seems doubtful, so let us look at it first. Cranberry Lake lies roughly in the Sydney area. It is about a mile in length, and is always full of water. One evening about thirty years ago a man was standing by the lake, looking for cows that had strayed away, when he was astonished to see something move on the surface that looked like a horse's head. Then the neck appeared. In a moment the animal or sea serpent went under water, turning itself over so that the last he saw of it was its tail. He judged it to be twelve feet in length and it seemed to be looking for something on the shore. It all happened so quickly that he could not recall any other details. Others have also told of seeing it, and stories have been current for one hundred years.

As recently as six years ago a man went to the lake to wash his car and, as he was working, it appeared again. He was so frightened that he gathered his things together and fled. Shortly after this a company was formed to go to the lake and find and kill the animal. It was winter and they had to work through the ice, but they were unable to find it. Some say it is all a myth; others insist they too have seen it.

The other sea serpent was reported at Victoria Beach and was seen about forty years ago by a vessel sailing up the Bay of Fundy. The crew said it stood up forty or eighty feet in the air, that it had a head like a horse and eyes like saucers, and they described it as a wonderful (awesome) sight. They put on full sail and it followed them for sixty miles, all the way to Point Prim. Later, when it was blowing a gale of wind, it was seen by another vessel going to the West Indies. Then a third vessel sighted it. This all happened about the same time, but they have never heard of it being seen since.

In closing this chapter two ships should be mentioned, although I have little to add to what has already been written about them. One was the *Mary Celeste* which had been abandoned for no reason that has ever been determined. The other is the phantom ship that appears in the Northumberland Strait before a northeast wind. It starts as a ball of flame and develops before the onlookers' eyes into a three-masted ship. She has been seen as early as 1780 and is observed on the same night over a large area. Three years ago at the time of the harvest moon she was seen near Pictou Lodge.

CHAPTER SEVEN

Ghosts Helpful, Harmful, and Headless

HELPFUL GHOSTS

OF ALL the ghost stories I have heard, I know of none so comforting and touching as this from a man in Dartmouth. I had called him on the telephone to ask about a house he had once lived in and, when he had given that information, he rather shyly told me this story. He had cherished it quietly in his heart for many years, and it is with much pleasure that I share it now with you. He is one of our most successful business men, a pillar of his church, and is thoroughly liked and respected by all. I think of him as a matter-of-fact rather than an imaginative man, which characteristic gives added weight to his story.

"When I was a young man I was out courting and I had to come home over a lonely·road that had very few houses. It was a bright moonlight night. Before long I heard footsteps and noticed a shadow behind me. I walked a little faster, and so did the person following me. Then I slowed down, and so did he. When I got to within about two hundred yards from the house I turned around to see who it was and there, standing in the road was my father who had been dead for nearly three years. I saw him clearly, even to the gold watch chain that he always wore, and that I always connected with him in my thoughts. I was too frightened to speak, but ran in the house and got into bed and under the clothes where I lay shaking for the rest of the night.

"In the morning I got up and went to my work, and there I was told a very strange thing. There were three men who thought I had done something that I hadn't, and they had been hiding in the bushes as I walked home, planning to attack me. When they saw another man walking along behind me they didn't dare, and so I suppose my life was saved. It is many years since this happened, but it is as vivid today as it was the night it occurred."

I told this to an elderly clergyman who was much impressed and wondered if it offered an explanation to an incident of his younger days that he had never been able to understand. He was about to walk over a path across Citadel Hill in Halifax and was passing a place where there was a high board fence. It was a lonely spot, and the night was dark and gloomy. He began to feel frightened and, at the same moment, he heard footsteps behind him. He thought, "This man is walking faster than I am, I might as well let him pass me." So the man passed and he saw as well as heard him. That placed him between our young man and the high fence. By this time the road was better lighted and as he watched the man he was amazed to see him turn right instead of proceeding ahead towards the open path. But where had he gone? There was nothing on the right at that point but the fence, and this he could not have scaled without being seen. Nor was there a break in the fence through which he could have slipped from sight. He had just vanished. He went back the next day and examined the fence to see if there might be a hole or exit of any kind that he had missed, but there was nothing. He had puzzled about it ever since but now, in the light of the foregoing tale, he wondered if he too had been in danger· and had been given a protector. Why not?

A pleasant story comes from the headmaster's house at King's Collegiate School, Windsor, a place I mention because this incident will never happen again. It was told to me by Colonel Hebb who had the experience himself. When he was a young man he taught in the school. Another master there at the same time, a dominant but beloved character, was known by the nickname of "Pa Buckle." They often alternated their nights on duty, but Mr. Buckle always seemed to get the stormy nights, and it happened so often that he got into the way of calling fine nights "Hebb nights."

After the Second Great War Colonel Hebb was made headmaster and, when he arrived to take over his new duties he thought of his former days there and especially of his older friend who had since died. This was a stormy night; in fact a regular Buckle night. When he entered the house he was surprised to hear a step that sounded familiar. Surely that must be Pa Buckle; it could be no other. Then the lights switched on and off mysteriously as though someone were having a little joke with the new residents. At first he thought his daughter was doing it, but soon realized that she was as surprised as the rest of them. Nor was there anybody in the house to be walking around with Mr. Buckle's characteristic step. He thought about it for a moment and then felt very pleased, for he concluded his old friend had come back to see him take over, and was wishing him well.

Who of us has not wondered about the next life and wished some shred of light might be thrown upon the great mystery of our future? Two farmers in Newcastle, New Brunswick, were talking about it one day. They had been great chums all their lives and, at the age of seventy-five, they were cogitating over what might be awaiting them. Both were well versed in their Bibles and were faithful church attendants. Finally upon a summer day Rossier died while fishing, and his canoe was found by his old friend Briden on the river. Two years later Briden was fishing alone when his friend Rossier appeared before him.

"Don't be scared," he said. "You remember we said the first one that died, we'd come and tell the other one what it was like in the other world? You live the same as you ever lived and you'll go to heaven. I'm just going to heaven today, and the Lord said for me to come and tell you. I had to stay this time because I was not fit to go to heaven." Briden had no time to speak before his old friend vanished.

This reminds me of a lady from Newfoundland who went unwillingly with friends to a seance somewhere in the United States, and was amazed to be told that a child named Mary had a message for her. The message was, "It doesn't matter." She could think of no child by that name who had died, until some days later. Then she recalled a childhood friend by that name who was a Roman Catholic, while she was a Protestant. They had often wondered if it made any difference in going to heaven. She had little belief in spiritualism, but thought, could that be the meaning of that message?

HARMFUL GHOSTS

There are other ghosts that go out of their way to be a hindrance. For instance Captain David Hayden was going home from his ship one night and was climbing over a fence when some strong force that he could never understand pulled him back. It took all his strength to get away from it. There were no nails on the bars to account for it, or anything else that he could see. It was as baffling as the force that held a fishing vessel back as it was sailing up the La Have River. There was a good breeze, and these waters were familiar to all the crew. Suddenly the vessel was wheeled around in the opposite direction. The men were excellent sea-men but, no matter what they did, they could not get that vessel up the river until daylight.

There is a place between Rose Bay and Kingsburg that goes by the name of Goose Gutter where a phantom of a goose used to appear and bite people on the legs. It is supposed to be the ghost of Lucy Knock who perished there. Here too the traveller is held back by an invisible force. At Coot Cove in Halifax County a man said that whenever he passed a certain place his hat would fly right off his head.

Mr. Bobby Lowe of Moser's River said, "I was out late one evening playing cards and I hadn't been drinking. I was coming home and my coat was torn right off my back and I was knocked down on the road. It was pretty powerful to be a person, but it was too dark to see any-thing. It was raining, so there was not likely to be any-body hiding in the bushes. Just before I was hit I'd heard something right by me. That was fifty-five years ago, and I came home at a gallop and over the fence. After a little while I got curious and I went back with a lantern and a gun but there were no footsteps to be seen but my own. Then I could hear it coming again and I started to holler. It had four legs because it started to run, and I could hear the steps, but I ran faster. The next night it was heard again, and that was the end of it. The funny part about it was that it didn't leave any tracks though I looked for them that night and again the next day, and the ground was soft from the rain. I never knew what it was."

Our Indians experience these things too according to one named Glode at Hantsport. "I was living on a grant, a young man at the time, in Lunenburg County, and my uncle took sick. He knew he was going to die and wanted the priest. I had to walk eight miles to Bridgewater to get him but when I arrived at his place he wasn't there, so I left a message and didn't wait. That afternoon it rained, and it was winter. I travelled back in moonlight and at Northfield there was a church. As I got opposite it I could hear the church door open and a figure came out of it and was about a foot off the ground. He had a gown and a topknot and there wasn't much wind and still the gown was blowing and he came right out on the road. There was ice between me and this man. I wasn't scared then, just curious, and I waited to see what he looked like closer. I went forwards and looked up in his face and I said, 'You're trying to fool me.' I thought it was someone playing a trick, but with that he tripped me and my head struck the ice. I got up and he walked with me and if I walked fast he walked fast, and if I run he run, and at last he left me. Never a word, he just left, and that was the time I got scared, when it was all over. I don't know whether this had anything to do with it or not, but the second night after this my uncle died."

The next story comes from Mr. Reuben Smith of Blanche in Shelburne County in whose hospitable home I spent a pleasant afternoon. "There was an old black dog that used to jump out at people by the little bridge at Negro. One time grandfather Ross was going to Clyde on foot. It was late afternoon but not quite dark and he had his wedding suit on. He had to pass an old house with one or two tall trees beside it and, when he got abreast of the house, this thing came out and grabbed him. He could go back down the road, but it wouldn't let him go ahead, and it tore all his clothes off. The funny part about it was that it was light all around and still there was nothing to be seen. Whether it was the Negro ghost dog or something else he never knew. Another time he was going past Ely's woods and it was dark and dismal. He used to go by with his horse and wagon and this thing would come out and go round the wheel. It didn't stop him but it bothered him, and he never knew what to make of it either.

We come now to ghosts who were neither helpful nor troublesome but were content just to make an appearance. The first comes from Broad Cove, a delightful fishing village in Lunenburg County. "When we were sixteen four of us boys were walking towards Caleb Smith's house. On the way we met a man and, when I got home, I told father about it and described him. He wore a grey homespun suit, a cap without a peak, and he carried a club for a walking stick. Father recognized him at once and said that he had always carried that club and nobody ever thought of him without it. He had then been dead for forty years. We saw him just in front of his own place, and father said he had often been seen there resting on his club and looking out over the water. He had been regarded as a respectable old man so it was not thought that he came back to put anything in order. Could it be that this was his heaven, to be allowed to come back once in a while to behold this lovely cove again?

"A man named John lived across a bridge at Chester and he was a heavy drinker and quarrelsome. One night he was in town late and he and another man had a spot and he was pitched out of the house half drunk. He was gone two or three days and nobody knew what had become of him until one of the neighbour's boys was in swimming and tramped on something and it was his body. The place then became haunted and you couldn't get a youngster to go over the bridge at night because this man used to crawl up over the rail. He did that one evening when two ladies were going home, and he walked along the shore to the gate that took them home. He was easily recognized because everybody in the town knew him well, but only one of them could see him. I wonder if he had something on his mind and wanted her to speak to him?"

Mrs. Bishop has a nursing home a few miles from Dartmouth at a place called the Broom Road. It got its name from people who used to live there. "In 1910 my husband was out west and I was home with the children. I looked out the window about ten o'clock at night. The moon was full and the clouds were scuttling about in the sky. The lane to our house runs down about one hundred feet where it joins the Broom Road and, just as you turn up, I saw the figure of a man with a stovepipe hat. He was leaning on a stick and looking all around. I had a little cocker spaniel, and he ran to the house to get in and, when I let him in, he crouched down as though in fear. After I had let the dog in I looked out again and the figure was still there. He was dressed in grey home-spun pants, a dark coat of average length, not an over-coat, and he had a goatee and seemed to be looking around strangely. There was no one to ask what Mr. Broom had looked like, but I always supposed it was he. That is the only time I ever saw him."

Stories occasionally turn up in which a chair rocks with nobody in it. At Victoria Beach this happened with a cradle. It was told by Mr. Joe Casey and was added to by his mother. "My great grandfather had started out to be a priest but he changed and became a Baptist minister, and was married three times. He made a cradle that was as long as a cot and pretty soon they noticed that it rocked whether a baby was in it or not and they didn't see how it could rock by itself. Some people who used it said that hymn music would come from it." Mrs. Casey has seen the cradle rock but she has never heard the music, but she said that a friend who had borrowed the cradle was so frightened by the rocking that she returned it. The cradle now belongs to people who keep it in their attic. I called at the house hoping to see it, but circumstances made it impossible at the time. It has always been one of the mysteries of the village.

We do not expect to find balls of wool in our ghost stories, yet I have two. The first is brief and came from Mrs. Joudrey at Eagle's Head. "My mother told me once that a wool ball came in the front door and ran along the room." The other story came from Victoria Beach. The cook at the hotel that year had come from Litchfield and she knew that Mr. Casey and others were giving me stories and songs. One evening when she started to go upstairs she saw that I was sitting alone. She had been waiting for this opportunity and started to talk. The story that she had been saving, possibly hoping that I could throw some light upon it, was this. "My mother used to tell me that years ago a squaw had buried a baby near the cemetery and it was in a red handkerchief. After that this spot was known as the Ghost Place and people used to hear a noise like a squeak when they went by. Some people said it was the fence making the noise, and others said it was the ghost of the child.

"When I was a young girl the strangest thing happened. Another girl and I were taking cattle to the pound. In those days if people let their cattle wander they'd be put in the pound and they'd have to pay a dollar to get them out. We were walking along by the Ghost Place and it was broad daylight and I looked up and there was a little kitten with a ball of yarn coming down out of the sky, not straight, but sideways. I would have thought it was cute if I hadn't been so frightened, because the kitten was playing with the yarn. I called to the other girl to look but the cattle were making so much noise she couldn't hear me and by the time I got her attention it had vanished. I don't suppose it was a ghost, but it happened right there at the Ghost Place and, as far as I know, it never happened to anyone else. Now what do you make of that?" I am afraid I was as puzzled as she.

On the way to Sandy Cove a man is said to have come

down from the sky. He said, "I came down like thunder and I'm going back like thunder," and he did.

There is a Nova Scotia folk song that tells of the murder of a young girl. The story is that the murderer took her to a place between Loch Lomond and Gannet Settlement. Here he dismissed the driver and beat their baby's brains out against a tree. Then to rid himself of the mother rather than marry her, he murdered her and buried the two bodies beside the tree. But death is not always that simple, for the memory of his cruel act has been kept alive not only in song, but in rags that grow on the tree that was used for killing the baby. They may be taken down at night, and next morning they will be there. The tree is never without them, and in the snow of winter or the soft earth of spring there is never a footprint to be seen. I regret that when I was in this vicinity last year I did not have this story with me and could not recall the spot, and thus I could not see the tree for myself. However the story came from a native Cape Bretoner who is now a professor in one of our large universities and he assured me this is actually so.

A story quite different from any I have encountered came from Auburn and concerns what is called the Caney Call. At least I presume that is the spelling. The people concerned were Irish. They lived on Morden Mountain and, on a stormy night, one of the family died. The woman of the house ran out and gave a weird call with her hair down, and it is said that she wore mourning so the ghost of the person who had just died would not recognize her. The call is given whenever a relative of this particular family dies, and it is given with the hair down; that is, as women used to wear their hair before it was fashionable to cut it. My informant knew nothing more about the incident than this.

This story sounded to me as though it might have centuries of tradition behind it, so I wrote to the Irish

Folklore Commission and asked if they could throw any light upon it. The archivist Mr. Sean O'Sullivan, wrote in part, "The word Caney does not refer to an Irish clan. From the context, it is evident that it is a form of the Irish word *caoine,* which means a cry of grief or mourning. In Irish tradition the banshee (wailing fairy woman; synonymous with Death) was supposed to wail when a member of certain families (e.g. O'Keefes, O'Sullivans) died. Her wail was quite distinct from the mourning cries of the near relatives or of the "keeners," who were in olden days employed or called upon to mourn a dead person."

Our thanks to Mr. O'Sullivan for giving meaning to this strange custom.

The next story comes from Mill Cove. "I was coming down from Hubbards by the bridge and I saw a man. I was going to speak but I didn't know who he was. There weren't as many strangers around then as there are now. His face was like that of an ordinary man and he wore a suit of overalls and a dark hat. He just stood there and didn't move and there was something about him I didn't understand. I told another man about him and he knew. He was dead."

Mr. Bert Power of East Ship Harbour shook his head and said paradoxically, "I don't believe in ghosts; never did. But one time there was diphtheria at my sister's house and the doctor said it would be all right for me to go in if I had rum or brandy first, so I asked Will Chisholm to get me a gallon of brandy in Halifax. He went by boat and was due back on Friday before going to Spry Bay, so I went down to meet him. On the road there was a spotted dog in the wheel rut and I walked right up to it. The dog never moved, but looked right up at me. I walked all round him and then went on and when I got down about fifty yards there was this same dog in the centre of the road and a chill come over me and I walked around him again. Then something else caught my eye and I looked towards the lower gate and a barrel rolled up the hill right in front of me. I could of picked it up but I got that scared I went home and my father said, "What's wrong?" but I wouldn't tell him. I couldn't sleep all night and first thing in the morning we got word me chum Will was drowned. He was drowned right alongside his own door, and that barrel, it could have been the brandy. So I don't believe in ghosts, but there was something come—something to it."

A man at East River Point was so troubled by a "black thing" that blocked his passage on the road that he went back to his house for his gun, intending to shoot it and be done with it. His family would not let him have the gun, for they were afraid of what might happen. He may have been well advised because at the Allen Hartley's house I was told of a man who used to pass a graveyard at Eastern Passage on his way to work. He kept seeing a man there and decided to speak to him. There was no reply so he told his wife about it and said he was going to shoot the ghost. He would say, "If you're dead I can't hurt you, and if you're alive you should be out here on the road and not in the graveyard." He did this, and got the worst of it. The next morning it was not the ghost that was found, but the man who had shot him. He was lying dead in the road with three bullets in his heart.

In the same house they told of a man down the eastern shore who borrowed something from his neighbour which he had not returned when the neighbour died. Every night after that when he came home from work he would meet the dead man and he was greatly troubled. He said to his wife, "I've got to speak to him," and he did. Nobody ever knew what happened, but the consequences were plainly seen, for when he returned "his two eyes were twisted and his mouth was twisted, and he never spoke again."

Here too I learned of an old belief in the Hartlan family where I had gone for my first songs. It probably came from the German side of their family, and was said to have been practised by some of the older generation. They had claimed that if they put the lights out on Christmas Eve and sat in a room together, the dead of the family would come back and sit with them. Not, I should think, the most pleasant way to spend a Christmas Eve.

There is an old belief that grass will not grow on certain spots, and this is borne out by another story from this source. They said that there had been a mutiny at sea many years ago and several men were hanged for it on George's Island. One of these men said he had nothing to do with the killings on board; he had only taken some of the gold. His protests did no good, and he was hanged with the rest but, before the noose was drawn, he declared that the ground upon which the people stood to watch his hanging would never be able to grow grass.

Mr. Richard Hartlan, who gave me much of my first instruction in folklore, at one time owned a five dollar gold piece which he kept wrapped in a black handkerchief. There was a stone wall on their property where a ghost used to like to sit and it was near the Ghost House that they later abandoned. Mr. Hartlan enjoyed sitting there too and one day he took the gold piece along and sat with it in his hand. He may have been dreaming of the pirate ships that had left chests on Moser's Island and Back Cole Breaker on the Cow Bay shore. At any rate he absent-mindedly laid the coin and handkerchief down and forgot about them. When he remembered them a few hours later he hastened back, but handkerchief and coin had disappeared. The whole family came out to look. In those days there would have been neither visitors nor prowlers, so they assumed the ghost had taken it, particularly as it made only one more appearance and was never seen again.

A man at Upper Tantallon said, "My father had to cross a brook to see my mother when he was courting, and it's an old belief that a ghost can't cross water. Everybody knows that, and another thing everybody knows is that animals can see a ghost that humans can't see, and they see it sooner. This time he had a little black dog with him. They were coming along the bank and this little dog was fighting something all the way. It was behind my father but he couldn't see anything at all and when they came to the brook it stopped. Father always felt that he'd have got hurt that night if the dog hadn't been there, because he was sure it was a ghost and that it would have attacked him. That was the only time it ever happened to him."

Some years ago Dean Llwyd of All Saints Cathedral in Halifax passed away and he was mourned greatly by all who knew him. Two weeks after his death one of his fellow clergymen was attending the Sunday evening service when he saw the Dean go into the pulpit and look over the congregation as he always did. He thought his affection for his old friend and his sense of loss in the place where he had seen him so often had caused him to imagine this, so he made no mention of it. Some time later, however, one of the ladies of the congregation told him she had experienced a strange thing, and described exactly what he had seen. They checked the time and the service, and they were the same.

Seabright seems to go in for very tall ghosts. "A Seabright man used to go out every night. He was a bold old fellow and he'd never go home till twelve. He got to Prang's Lot by a brook one night and it was light enough for him to see an awful big man standing there. He was as tall as a tree and had arms like logs and he was all speckled. The Seabright man was very frightened but nothing happened to him and he was able to go on his way. There had been something happen there once like a death."

At Sambro the Gilkies told of a Scottish soldier who, hanged himself at Sambro Light and, after that, people saw his ghost for years, and they could hear him throwing casks around. Enos Hartlan may have been right when he said "a person that takes his own life isn't happy."

A mystery from Sheet Harbour goes this way. "As kids we used to go back to Heffler's gold mine and one day there was a chap from Halifax named Fraser with us. A storm was coming up that might have caused it, though I don't see how it could, but the most beautiful music I've ever heard came from the sky. The boys heard it and were petrified."

A Shelburne mystery did not take long to solve. "A number of us went out once with a buckboard and coming home we had to get out to fix the harness. While we were there a man with a long grey overcoat came out of the ground and stood with his arm on the wagon and looked at us. Then he went to the buckboard and did the same. There were prominent people among us and they were all mystified because he was so well dressed, and it would seem that some one would have known him. It was not until we left that one of them said, 'Do you realize that was Morvan's Hill we were on?' We remembered then that this hill had a ghost."

I have mentioned before that many pedlars seem to have been murdered in this Province. One was on the Hollow Mountain Road and passersby say they hear a singing and it says, "Don't kill me." The pedlar at Thorne's Cove is satisfied to jump out and frighten people, while another at Green Oak in Colchester County does no more than make an appearance. About a mile from the Causeway linking Cape Breton with the peninsula a dog that is not a dog is supposed to be the spirit of a murdered pedlar, while another pedlar whistles. They never seem to be vindictive, but just want to draw attention to their sorry plight.

Mrs. McGillicray of Marion Bridge said, "Cousin Catherine was dying and I was there. The pillows were behind her and we were supporting her, and as she was passing she said in a surprised voice as though she were greeting some one she hadn't expected to see, 'Papa!' Was she seeing her father through the veil that separates this world from the next?" This story makes me think of my own father's passing and how he suddenly sat up in bed, weak as he was, and looked far beyond me as at some distant goal. In that moment I became aware that I could be of no further use to him. He seemed to be struggling to keep his hold on the life he had loved, but a force far greater had taken possession of him. This must have lasted for several minutes during which time he breathed but was no longer a part of this mortal life. It is not at all uncommon for the aged to see their loved ones around them before they die. My mother saw various deceased members of her family. Whether they actually see them, or just go back to childhood memories, who of us can say?

HEADLESS GHOSTS

Spectacle Island lies about ten miles south of Yarmouth and ten miles west of Pubnico. Mr. Stanislas Pothier said, "The story was given by word of mouth from an old Frenchman who told some friends of mine to go to Spectacle Island and they would find a treasure. First thing they would find an oak tree and they would find a big flat rock with a row of beach rocks all around it. They were to go down further until they found another rock and, a little beyond that, they would come to Captain Kidd's gold. Seven or eight men went and it came out as he said, and they dug to the third rock. He had said if they found the rock there would be snakes and lizards come out, but they were not to mind them but to grab the gold. It was all going nicely when one man got out of the hole and he put a bucket over his head. They looked up and thought he was a head-less man and they were so scared they ran away. But many times since then they've seen men walking around on that island when there wasn't supposed to be anyone there. Two different men were on the island and they knew they were alone and they saw a third man. He was seen again only a couple of years ago by two men who were sleeping on the island, but there was nobody there. There used to be sounds of a ship's anchors, but that hasn't been heard for years. One Monday morning a bunch of fishermen and many women and children saw a man on the island and there was no dory and nobody there. They used to make a lot of it."

One evening I climbed up a very steep hill at Glen Margaret where a charming woman lived who told me a number of stories. Among other entries in my note book is the following. "Father said when he was a young man he used to go out in the evenings. At the first end of Hackett's Cove at Devany's Brook there was a story that people were always seeing a woman come up out of the water with something white over her, like a sheet and she had no head. One night he met two girls run-ning towards him and they said at the three brooks—Devany's Brook that is—they had seen this woman come up out of the water with no head. That's all I know about it. I guess nobody stayed long enough to find out anything more about her."

Another headless woman is one of my rare cases of suicide. This was a Mrs. McLaughlin of Victoria Beach who got up one morning many years ago and washed and dressed all the children, including the baby. It is so long since it happened that the motive for her suicide has been forgotten if, indeed, it was ever known. After finishing her chores she walked to the cliff and jumped over. Since then a headless woman wearing an apron has been seen there. Also, but probably having no connection with Mrs. McLaughlin, dogs without heads have appeared there.

At the foot of the long hill going to Seabright a headless woman has been reported, but nothing else is known about her.

Liverpool is the scene of our next story. "At Cape La Have a man had to go out at twelve o'clock at night on the first day of March to put a buoy down. From the same village another man went out at the same time to mow a swath, and what you mowed was your own piece. Well, this night as they were going to their different businesses they met, and it was at the spot where there is an old cannon. They both swore they saw an old-timer sitting on top of one of the old cannon in old-fashioned clothes and no head on. He was wearing a long split-tail coat."

Another headless man was reported from Victoria Beach. "He used to be seen up by Big Pond. They claim there is money there and the headless man is an indication."

The headless man who appeared at Upper Granville came mounted on horseback. He could be seen riding past a certain house with his head carried under his arm, and people often refused to pass over the bridge at night for fear of seeing him. You could hardly blame them. Twice I was told about this unwelcome visitor in Granville but he seems to have done nothing more than frighten the beholder. At Elgin, New Brunswick, I heard of a covered bridge at Bennett Lake where the ghost of a headless man used to come out.

An East Chester woman said, "My uncle was a contractor, and when I was fifteen he and I were going home to Mahone Bay from Western Shore. When we were in the woods I heard a horse and it seemed to be so close that I could almost feel its breath. I looked around and what I saw was a horse all right, but there was a man sitting on it with no head. My uncle didn't see it, and I was too scared to speak until we got home and then all he said was, 'That's nothing. Lots of people have seen that horse and rider.' Since then I have asked many people but nobody seems to know who the rider is supposed to be."

Captain Hatfield of Port Greville told of seeing a headless dog. He and one of his shipmates were on their way home from a sea trip. They were six or seven miles from Port Greville at a place known as the Ghost Hollow and they had been warned not to pass it after dark. They had an old team-horse and a lash and, when they were about two-thirds of the way up Mill Hill, a big white dog appeared at his side.

"The horse just stopped as if it had come to anchor but I wasn't frightened. I sang out 'Look at that dog,' and I jumped off the team and took the lash and struck the dog, and the lash went right through the dog as if it wasn't there at all and it didn't touch anything till it came to the rocks behind. Then the dog went under the wagon and disappeared. The man who was with me was scared to death. I was a lad of fifteen or sixteen then and I often went over that same place afterwards, but I never saw it again."

Our other stories of headless ghosts are mostly in the chapters on buried treasure and haunted houses. In some of these the ghost speaks, and in one case his breath is felt as he stands behind the person. You may wonder how that is possible, just as I have done. My conclusion is that the heads are there all right, but not visible to the human eye. My reason is this.

You will have noticed in all these stories that a ghost appears as it will be most easily recognized by the person it wants to impress, or in the manner in which it met a sudden death. Decapitation would be such a death. Or it may be identified by a characteristic gesture as Alex was when he moved the belaying pin up and down on his shoulder in the way his friend Dan always thought of him, as though just showing his face and form were not enough. Some people come back with deformities like the lame mother and the carpenter you have read about, not because their bodies have not been restored, but to leave no doubt of their identification. Thus a person who has lost his head wishes to bring out this important point and therefore the head becomes invisible. I have no authority for this belief, but to me it seems reasonable. If a ghost has the power or ability to reveal himself in garments of his own choosing and accessories, like the father whose son remarked that he appeared complete with watch chain without which he could not imagine him, then why could he not conceal his head if it suited his purpose?

CHAPTER EIGHT

So Many Wandering Women

EACH item of folklore that I collect is typed on an index card and filed away for future use. When I agreed to write this book I took out my file on ghosts and separated the stories under headings, and these headings became the chapters you have been reading. I had no idea until then that women are so restless after death and I was astonished at the thickness of the pile under this listing. Why are they so loath to settle down when life is over, and why do they wander about so much more than men? And almost always alone, poor things.

Of course many reported female ghosts are no more than mist rising wraith-like from road or marsh. This meets the cooler air and assumes a woman's form and her long flowing garments. It might float briefly above ground and then vanish as suddenly as it came. A timid person would take one look and run, not waiting to see the mist dissipate, nor to look for a physical cause. Old Enos Hartlan with all his belief in ghosts said, "They're nothin' but a puff of air." This may be true in many cases but there are others that cannot be dismissed so easily. Take the Grey Lady for example.

The scene for the Grey Lady was Stony Beach in Annapolis County just below the Habitation. She got her name from the colour of her clothing which never seemed to vary. Many years ago a vessel came to the Annapolis Basin and a boat was launched and went ashore. In the boat, according to Mrs. Burpee Bishop of Greenwich, there were two people, a man and a woman. When it returned, the woman was no longer there. A fisherman from Victoria Beach explained it this way.

"Up to Stony Beach there is a woman with no head. They claim there was once a deep-water fisherman who ran ships to foreign ports. He was married and had a family and one time he was going away on a long voyage when he got in with a nice young woman very handsome and he carried her on the ship for a long while. It was an Annapolis ship. At that time nice ships were built here.

"When he come back he had this woman and he didn't know what to do with her. They claim that he took her ashore and killed her, and she is the woman they see there. They claim that this woman wants to tell somebody about it, but nobody has ever had pluck enough to ask her. They say if you ask her in the name of the Lord that she will tell you. The reason she had no head is they claim he beheaded her, because she would appear sometimes with a head and sometimes without, but she was always dressed in grey."

If the Grey Lady really wanted to unburden her soul she should have realized that Rev. Mr. Gretorex would have been only too pleased to hear her story. He had always been interested in apparitions but, when he took his wife and a friend driving shortly after their arrival at Granville Ferry, he had no expectation of meeting one. Yet when they got to Stony Beach they saw a lady in grey gliding along beside them wearing a short skirt, a shawl, and a bonnet. Her feet did not seem to touch the ground, and she kept her place shortly ahead of them. They attempted to pass, as Mrs. Gretorex wished to see the face under the bonnet but, as they drew up beside her she disappeared. It was noted at the time that the third person in the carriage did not see her.

When they returned to Granville Ferry they told their experience and then learned the sad story of the captain's paramour. Mr. Gretorex felt sorry for her and wished to give her Christian burial. He looked in vain on subsequent trips but he never saw her again. It is an old belief that you will never see a ghost if you are looking for one. Be that as it may, the horse must have seen her because it sometimes shied and had to be led off the road when it got near this place. Yet even with this help it was never definite enough for him to say "this is the exact spot" and hope to unearth her bones. This happened about sixty years ago and he always regretted that he had not spoken to her on their only encounter and that he was never given a second opportunity.

Dr. Robinson of Annapolis Royal used to hear the story of the Grey Lady and, if my memory serves me faithfully, it was from his family that I learned of his meeting with her. It happened one night when he was driving home from a call. He came to an elbow in the road where there was a small bridge that crossed a brook, and there were alder thickets that grew close to the side of the road. As he drew near the bridge his horse stopped. The doctor urged it on but it snorted and jumped and stamped. He got out of his old-fashioned gig with its big spider wheels and went to the horse's head. There he saw the Grey Lady standing in front of the horse and trying to stop him. As he approached, she disappeared from sight. The horse was so agitated that he took it by the bridle and led it along. When they got to the bridge he discovered that it had been washed out by a spring freshet and, if he had not been stopped in this extraordinary way, he would probably have had a bad accident. He recalled then that other people had told of seeing her on this bridge, and that her appearance was usually a warning of one kind or another. This was a foggy night when he would not have been able to see the gap until too late.

Whether it was the same Grey Lady he saw upon another occasion or not, he was never able to determine. If so, she must occasionally have rambled. He was driving between the towns of Digby and Weymouth with the school principal of that time, Mr. Logan. They were both surprised to see a woman in a long grey cloak and bonnet upon the road who did not walk, but trotted. Several times they jogged the horse and passed her but in each case she quickly caught up again and took her place ahead of them as she had done to Mr. and Mrs. Gretorex. They noticed then that she wore hoops, and that her cloak was spread over them. She finally disappeared in the bushes that grew along the roadside. In this case they knew of no reason for her appearance, and it is possible she was an entirely different phantom.

A Mr. Mills of Upper Granville told quite a different story, and there was nothing pleasurable or helpful about the way he saw her. He said that he was on the marsh one morning when she appeared before him, but she was such a filmy wraith that he could see the fence right through her. She did not look to him like a person who had come to do a kindly service and he was so frightened that he took to his heels and fled. Another man who reacted this way was Mr. Roy Condon, according to my friends at Port Wade.

He was working on a wood boat and, in order to get back to it in time from the place he lived, he had to walk to the shore at two a.m. He noticed a lady coming towards him and he moved over close to her and said, "Good evening." She didn't speak. That surprised him and he wondered what woman would be travelling the road at that hour, so he turned to look at her again, but there was no one there. He recalled all the things he had heard about the Grey Lady then and when he did, he ran so fast he tumbled down into the bottom of the boat without even waiting to take the ladder.

Tales about the Grey Lady spread so widely that everybody in the district knew about her and she was often the subject of conversation throughout the whole countryside. But alas her story had a tragic end. You will have gathered long before this that Nova Scotians love to play tricks on one another and will do so at the slightest provocation. Those who feared the unknown were particularly vulnerable. In those days before the motor car brought new people and new thoughts to out-lying communities, and before radio and television invaded their homes, the staple form of entertainment was all too often the telling of ghost yarns. Children heard them almost from infancy and therefore grew up with an exaggerated fear of the dark. Well, the day came when the young people of Granville were to have an old-fashioned hay-ride and picnic and one young man thought it would be fun to impersonate the Grey Lady. He waited until the picnic party was returning home after dark. Then he jumped over a stone wall dressed in a sheet. Unfortunately one member of the party had a revolver, probably for target shooting at the picnic. Without waiting to investigate, he drew his revolver and fired, killing the impersonator. This seems like a strange way to lay a ghost but, from all I have been able to learn, the Grey Lady has not been seen since.

Clergymen are particularly given to seeing spirits which is not after all very surprising when you give the matter thought. Did not Jesus himself appear as a spirit? And others. We have had Rev. Mr. Gretorex in this chapter and we turn now to Venerable Archdeacon Wilcox who has been mentioned before. Although he was the rector of my church in Dartmouth I did not hear this story from him or even know about it until after his death. It came to me from Windsor, the town where he had spent his boyhood.

"Reverend Noel Wilcox was out shooting at Evangeline Beach one fall when he saw the figure of a woman walking well ahead of him. He had a companion with him, and the two had separated, the better to get their birds. Mr. Wilcox was afraid the woman would get hit by the other man's shots as he was unlikely to see her, so he hastened forward to warn her. At that time she was walking away from him. Imagine his astonishment when she disappeared. He couldn't believe it. He was, however, a man accustomed to the woods and an outdoor life, and it occurred to him to look for her tracks in the sand. There were no tracks to be seen. He hailed his companion then and told him what had happened and he was further surprised at the response his remark called forth. He said,

" 'Come on, we're getting out of here. There's going to be a gale of wind anyhow.' Then Mr. Wilcox recalled stories of a lady who walked before a storm. He couldn't credit the legend, but he had seen what he had seen."

Incidentally it is interesting, because of an old folk belief, to notice here that the apparition was walking away from the rector when he saw her. Whether a ghost is coming towards you or walking away is thought to determine the length of life for the person who sees the vision. If there is any meaning in this, it signified a short life in this case, for the archdeacon's career was cut off while he was still in his forties.

Another Anglican clergyman told me about a house he once lived in. I cannot mention his name because that would identify the house and it is not the purpose of this book to give a sinister name to any property. I shall only say that it is in one of the older residential

districts of Halifax. He said that he and his wife occupied the lower flat and that in the upper flat the occupants
found it very difficult to keep a maid. All who came
there to work were frightened, and all told of seeing a
woman in white behind the portière. They disliked being
in the house not only for what they saw, but for what
they felt, because it always seemed that there was someone standing behind their backs. He felt sure this was
not mere imagination because so many different maids
had told about it, and they all had the same story. It
would be quite natural for them to confide their fears
to the downstairs couple and, since these maids would
not have known one another or anything about the house
before working there, it would be more than coincidence
for them all to see and feel the same thing. Whether
the owners themselves have seen or felt anything I do
not know and I do not feel like asking them upon a
slender acquaintance. We can conclude however that
there is nothing really frightening about the house
because the same people have lived in it for many years.

In my book, *The Folklore of Lunenburg County,* I
have a story about Rev. Joseph Norwood of Hubbands
and an apparition that appeared to him. Some time
after its publication I took down a variant of this event
and still later heard that Professor Carmen Stone of
the University of King's College had the authentic version. Rev. Robert Norwood of whom he speaks was a
son of Rev. Joseph, and the Grey Lady in this story is
quite different from the one at Stony Beach. This is
Professor Stone's account of the event.

"We were at Seaforth in 1931 and my mother was
keeping house for me. Rev. Robert Norwood knew
my mother and he came to visit her. As she was coming
down the stairs and reached the first landing he looked
up from the hall below, raised his hand and said, "The
Grey Lady!" He was very dramatic, and told us the
story forthwith. I was there and heard it."

Dr. Norwood's story was that the apparition of a lady dressed in grey had appeared to his father when he was rector of the Anglican church at New Ross. Here he had to drive through thick woods, and the trip by horse and carriage would be lonely enough at the best of times without the unwelcome company of a figure from another world. Dr. Norwood did not say how often his father had seen the lady in grey but she must have come a number of times for him to grow so tired of her that he asked to be sent away. He was therefore transferred to Seaforth and occupied the Rectory later taken over by Professor Stone.

The lady, however, was not to be so easily dismissed and one evening shortly after he had taken up his residence in Seaforth, he looked up and saw her standing upon the landing in the very place where his son now saw Mrs. Stone. He decided then to face the situation so he signed himself with the cross and said, 'In the name of the Father and the Son and the Holy Ghost, speak.' She did, and her first remark was, 'Why haven't you spoken before?' thus confirming the belief that you must address a ghost before it can speak to you.

She told him then that a great wrong had been done in which she had a part and she related the circumstances which, however, his son did not mention. She then told him to go to a certain address on Morris Street in Halifax where he must deliver her message.

Although his father had seen the woman and had heard her speak he still could not believe that such things happened. Nevertheless he went to the address which was that of the apparition's sister. He asked the lady on Morris Street if she had a family album, and also if she had a sister who had died, and what her name was. The album was produced but he said, 'Let me pick her out.' He turned the pages until he came to a picture of the lady he had seen and then he said, 'This is the person you have here.' He then delivered the message and he was never troubled again.

The incident made a great impression upon Professor Stone who was a student at the time. For one thing Rev. Robert Norwood, a native son of the Province, was then rector of St. Bartholomew's Church in New York and was famed for his powers of oratory. Always dramatic, he told this story in a way that would never be forgotten by a young man, so that every detail was burned upon his memory. Besides, think of the implications in such a story and what they would mean to a young man about to embark upon the ministry as his life's vocation. Was this not proof that life continues after death?

In another variant of this story the reason for the visit was to tell the sister how to find a certain document whose whereabouts only the apparition knew. In still another, it was to ask forgiveness for a quarrel. In this case the sister remembered the disagreement, but said it had been forgiven long ago. Still another says that the person he was asked to visit was the widow of a fellow clergyman who was in great difficulty, and that he was able to help her. The details may vary, as the story has been passed around by word of mouth, but the theme is substantially the same wherever it is told.

Most of the incidents in this book have taken place in Nova Scotia, but we need an occasional one from outside to confirm experiences here. I have a story from England which parallels the last one in some of its salient points. It is both strange and beautiful and came to me in a surprising way. I had spoken to the School of Community Arts at Tatamagouche one evening and dropped in to see some friends there the next day. In the hall I met Rev. Mr. Minton from Lockeport. Yes, you have guessed rightly, for he too is an Anglican rector, and so is the man of whom he spoke. Knowing of my interest in ghosts, he asked if I would like to hear a story from England. He had heard it from the sister of the man to whom it happened, and she has been a friend of many years' standing. The Norwood story will not seem so inexplicable after this.

"Rev. Mr. Gray belonged to a large family and had been recently ordained. This was in the early Edwardian period. He had taken a parish in the East End of London. His housekeeper had gone to bed and he was sitting in his study smoking his pipe and thinking out his sermon for Sunday. Presently the door bell rang—a spring bell—and he went to answer it. Standing under the gas light in the fog stood a little old lady in poke bonnet and shawl and a once black skirt now green with age. She pleaded with him to go to an address in the West End of London. She said he must go because he was urgently needed. The young clergyman tried to put her off as it was very late, but she pleaded so earnestly that he finally promised to go that same night.

"He took a cab and at length arrived at the address. It turned out to be one of the large mansions in the West End and it was lit up and obviously there was a party going on. After he had rung the bell and waited, the butler came and the clergyman said, 'I believe I'm wanted here. My name is Gray.'

"The butler said, 'Have you an invitation?'

" 'No, but I've been asked to come. Some one needs me.'

"The butler asked him to wait in the little anteroom and presently brought back the master of the house. He was a well-known titled gentleman. Mr. Gray then told him what had happened and the man looked very odd and asked if he could describe his visitor. As he did so, the man looked terrified. He then confessed to having led a wicked life of crime which included white slavery, whereupon the clergyman tried to help him. He urged him to stop this life and make his peace with God, and the man finally made what appeared to be a serious

confession. The clergyman then gave him absolution and
said in leaving,

" 'Just to show that you're in earnest, I'll be celebrat-
ing holy communion at eight-thirty in the morning and I
want you to be there.' Then he went away.

"The next morning as the priest turned to administer
the sacrament it was obvious that the man was not there
and he wondered what he should do about it. After
breakfast he decided he should see him again. He
arrived at the mansion house, now still and quiet, and at
his ring, the butler came. When he asked to see his
master the butler told him he was dead. Mr. Gray said,

" 'It can't be true. I was talking to him last night.'

" 'Yes, I know. I recognize you,' the butler said. 'He
died shortly after you left.'

"Mr. Gray asked if he could see the body which he
knew must still be in the house, and the butler took him
up to a very spacious room. There, lying on the bed,
was the dead body of the man he'd been talking to the
night before. He stood for a moment thinking, trying to
puzzle it out and, as he did so, he glanced around the
room. His eye caught an oil painting above the bed. It
was of a little old lady in a poke bonnet and shawl—
the same little old lady who had come to him and had
sent him to this house. He said to the butler,

" 'Who is the little old lady?'

" 'That is the master's mother. She died many years
ago.' "

I listened to the story which was told with great
earnestness, and then we sat quietly for a moment on
the spacious lawn in front of the Tatamagouche school.
There was so much to think about but, by this time, the
students and staff were coming back from the beaches
and there was no opportunity to meditate. I went back
the next day, however, to ask about two points which
had occurred to me later. Had Mr. Gray realized that
the little old lady was not of this world, and was that

why he had carried out her mission so faithfully? No,
it was not until the butler told him whose picture hung
above the bed that this realization came to him. The
other question was not so easily answered, but it is one
we may all consider well. Obviously the mother knew
that her son was about to die, and she must have wished
for his repentance since she sent a clergyman to see him.
Was she then, in this last-minute confession and the
giving of absolution, able to redeem his soul? Who can
give the answer, but it is a beautiful and breath-taking
thought.

Now let us come back to our own Province and also
back to laymen and their experiences. Pugwash will be
our next port of call and we will sit on old Mr. Teed's
doorstep. On the day when I first met him he happened
to mention that he used to sit up with old people who
were dying, so with such an opening I asked of course
if he had ever seen or heard anything. The result was
seven good stories to add to my collection. In the midst
of them he stopped and said, "Well now, this is kind
of funny, me telling you things like this." I assured him
that lots of people did, and he picked up the thread
again.

He said there was a house where a boy and girl had
been taken to live and they were supposed to work in
return for the care they were given and the home in
which they lived. One day their foster parents went
away and, when they returned, they found that the girl
had disappeared. He did not know how much they had
tried to find her, but she was never heard of again.
After a while the family moved away. Years passed and
then one day when the father was working in his
garden, he was greatly startled to see this girl on the
edge of the road, and he could see at once that she
was an apparition. She said, "Don't be scared and I'll
tell you what happened to me." The man listened in
astonishment as she told him that the boy had killed

her with an axe and had buried her under a tree stump. Her foster-father supposed she had returned for revenge and said, "What do you want me to do? Go and find him?" But she said no, he was dead too. In time he had left his foster home and then had killed another girl. His second murder had been detected and he had been hanged. Then, having told her story, she disappeared.

The poor man was greatly upset and talked the matter over with his friends. They concluded no benefit would come to anybody by verifying the story which would be difficult as he no longer owned the property or even lived in the same town. The conversation however had been real enough and was held in the full light of day. But why had she waited so long after her death to make the facts known, and why did she wish them to be known anyhow? If she had wanted a proper burial she would have asked for it. Or would she?

Mr. Teed then told this story. "When I was fifteen I was out one night and I went to a house where there was a large family. The father had been married twice but I didn't know it. I saw a woman come towards me and she walked up to the ditch by the fence, and then along by the fence towards an old barn. I heard a dog bark and looked behind and, when I turned my head again, she was gone. I went home and after I got in the house I began to laugh.

" 'What are you laughing at?' Mother said.

" 'I'm laughing at the funny old woman I saw in a coat and hood.'

" 'Where did you see her?' I told her and she said I'd better stay home at night. I begged her to tell me who it was because I could see she knew, but she wouldn't tell me for a long time. Then she said it was the man's first wife and my mother knew her well. Her cattle used to stray. Many a time my mother went with her to call them in and she always wore that coat and hood."

Another first wife was seen after her husband's second marriage, but under quite different circumstances. This was at Port Medway. There were several children by the first wife and their stepmother was always kind to them. But one of the children became ill and was not expected to recover. The stepmother was getting tired, so two friends of the family came to watch over the child at night while she got some rest. As they were sitting quietly in the sick room, they saw a woman come in and bend over the child and go out again. They said in astonishment, "That's Annie Wharton!" (the child's mother.) She did not look at them, but both recognized her. Telling of it afterwards they insisted they were not afraid.

In this case there were the two mothers both caring for the child, a love which they shared. They were both good women. Not so a stepmother reported from Sambro. She had beaten her stepchildren and then had thrown them in the same crib. They cried but she paid no attention. When midnight came she heard a little sound and looked up. To her horror the children's own mother was standing looking down at them. She was so terrified that she persuaded her husband to leave with her the next day and the children were left to the care of neighbours. Perhaps that was what their mother wished for them when she allowed herself to be seen bending over their crib.

Spry Bay also has a story of two mothers. Here a mother had died and the father was being married again. The child was to be sent away to be brought up by another woman. One day the stepmother-to-be went to the well and the child's mother appeared to her. She advised her not to send her to the place they had planned, and said what they should do for her.

That was done, and the story has been told in Spry Bay for years.

My singer, Mr. Nathan Hatt of Middle River in Lunenburg County, was getting close to his proud record of recording eighty-six songs. He had just sung one called "The Dreadful Ghost" which turned his thoughts to something he had once seen. His face could change suddenly from the merriest laughter to the most solemn expression and it now became sober. His aged, blue eyes looked into mine intently.

"I saw a woman one time dressed in white in the noonday. She had a white nightcap on her head and two long white ribbons hanging down over her bosom. I didn't say anything about having seen her at the time but later I got talking to a friend and I told him. He said, 'I believe I know who that was. I believe it was my sister. She married and she had a foolish girl (mentally deficient) and, just before she died, she called this girl to her side and said, "What'll become of poor Ruth when I'm gone?" So you see she had trouble on her mind and that's why she came back.' The place I saw her was at Beech Hill, just a little piece from where she lived. Ruth was there at the time and the young fellows were tantalizing her. The woman was pale and deathly and I could see she was no living person. She watched those fellows with her eyes and she whipped away so quick I didn't see where she went to. Her eyes looked natural. The man I spoke to was sure she was Ruth's mother, and well she might have been but, as far as I know, I'm the only person who ever saw her."

Was the mother able to protect her defenceless child? Could we but know the answer to that question!

Marion Bridge has a story of a mother who died many years ago at Trout Brook. "She had been a good-living person and would not allow any card playing in her house. After her death her son and daughter did all the things their mother had objected to and the house became known not only for its card playing, but for its general depravity. One night John, the son, was coming home from Mira Ferry when he saw his mother coming towards him. He took to his heels and ran, terrified, and he kept on running the whole way home. It happened a second time and a third. By the third time he felt he must speak to her and end this business of being followed, so he said, 'Hello mother, what do you want?'

" 'I wondered how many times you'd have to see me before you'd speak. If you and Cassie do what I tell you, you'll never see me again.'

" 'Well tell me what it is, but hurry up.'

" 'You must give up your card playing and live decent lives. If you do that and live right, I'll never trouble you.' He went home and told his sister what had happened. He also told his friends and for years they would tease him and say, 'John, have you seen your mother lately?' Needless to say they obeyed her wishes and she was never seen again."

How much do the dead see of what their loved ones do on earth, and to what extent do our misdemeanours keep them from their well earned rest? Such isolated instances as I have been able to give you may well make us stop and think.

In both song and story the idea is put forth that the dead cannot rest if the living grieve too much for them. In the First Great War my brother Terry and his dearest friend Jack Carson enlisted and served overseas. Jack was killed and his mother in some way knew this immediately. I did not hear of this until after her death, so I do not know how the information came to her. But a few weeks later she was walking alone through the grounds of Dalhousie University, dressed in deep mourning, when Jack appeared to her. He assured her that all was well with him and that her grief was holding him back from his new life. His mother immediately changed her way of thinking and no doubt was comforted in the knowledge that she could still serve her son. I have placed this story here because it follows our train of thought.

Most women who return seem to do so with a desire to be helpful as we have seen. Another pleasant story of a helpful ghost comes from St. Isidore, New Brunswick.

"I was fishing with me father way back of Shippigan and that night a big storm come and we had a very small vessel, about thirty feet long and three sail on it. We were not coming very fast but we got lost and we couldn't see the Tracadie light. We looked and there was a woman dressed in white and a torch in her hand and her two feet dragging, and she was canted this way /" (Here he held his hand up to show that she was not standing upright, but at a slant.) "Me father took the wheel then and he followed her for twenty minutes and then she disappeared and, as she went out of sight, the Tracadie lights came into view. I was about fifteen years old then. I'm eighty-eight now, but I never forgot that. I don't know who she was, but I guess she saved our lives all right."

An odd thing happened to a cousin of mine about fifteen years ago. She was doing clerical work in one of the big Bermuda hotels and she worked every second night. Her afternoons were spent playing golf, and then she slept. At exactly three minutes to six each evening, at the time she was due to arise, the figure of a woman with her hand upraised would come to her in her sleep, and waken her. She was never able to distinguish her features because all she ever saw was a shadowy form. This went on for the whole six months she was there, and it always happened at three minutes to six and never at any other time. There was never any sensation of fear about it; on the contrary, Marjorie was grateful. When she returned to Nova Scotia she wondered if the woman would follow her, but she has never seen her since.

A family named McDonald lived at Trout Brook many years ago and, after Mrs. McDonald died, they began to have unusual disturbances in the house. Then she was seen walking near the house and finally appeared sitting on the railing of a little bridge nearby. A man who knew her well confronted her.

"What do you mean," he said, "coming around here frightening people?" She gave him a message to give to a certain person at Donkin (then Dominion 6.) The next morning he harnessed his horse and went to Donkin and delivered the message. That much he told, but what the message was or to whom it was sent, he kept to himself. After that she was never seen again.

This reminds me of a strange thing that happened to Mr. Alex Morrison's brother. It frightened him nearly out of his wits.

"At that time John was courting a girl named Belle who lived at Hillsdale. Country roads can be awful dark at night, you know. They used to be pretty rough and, with a horse and buggy, the going would be slow. It was pretty late, and John was driving home alone when he saw a woman walking ahead of him dressed in black, and the next thing she was sitting alongside of him in the buggy. It was light enough for him to see her, and who should she be but someone he knew who had died a few years before. She told him she wanted him to go to see her daughters, and to tell them to take care of themselves and be good, but he must never reveal to anybody else who she was. He never did. He came home and unhitched the horse and was too scared to take the harness off, and he got into bed with all his clothes on. He went to see the family and told them what had happened, but nobody ever knew who they were.

"Any time after that when he wanted to go that way somebody had to go with him. I know that well enough because I came home about that time and it was usually me. He would never go that way alone again, and perhaps that is why he stopped courting in that direction. If he hadn't delivered the message she would have come back but, after that night, he never saw her again."

Most people think of ghosts as apparitions that float through the air and appear at unexpected times and places but do nothing that a human would do. At East Petpeswick a fisherman told of seeing a ghost in an unusual position. He was rowing by when he saw her walking along the shore with a pair of stockings in her hand. He kept his eye upon her and said he distinctly saw her stop and sit down on a rock and put her stockings on. As so often happens in these stories, his attention was diverted for a moment and, when he looked back, she had disappeared. Others had seen her with her stockings in her hand and it was always supposed she had something to do with buried treasure.

Anne Boleyn may be the most famous woman in history to be seen without her head, but she is far from being the only one. "There was an old gentleman who lived at Wild Cat, Head Jeddore, and he was walking along a road where people used to see a woman with her head off. He'd heard the stories and thought they were pretty crazy, so he thought this would be a chance for him to see for himself. The faster he went the faster she went, but in time he caught up with her and put his hand on her shoulder. Then he got the surprise of his life because there was nothing there, so he said, 'That's the ghost all right.' "

Perhaps this is the same woman who was seen at nearby Oyster Pond. "One evening a young couple were sitting on the bridge below my house when a woman came down from the field and seemed to step right over my fence. She was in white without a head and it looked as though she was coming right for them. They'd often heard of her because she'd been seen before and was supposed to be concerned with buried treasure. The girl was so frightened that she fainted."

Also connected in the minds of local folk with buried treasure, and thought perhaps to be its guardian ghost, is another woman who appeared at Oyster Pond. "One time Mrs. Sydney Myers and I were coming by the United Church wall and a woman was there in light grey. Her dress was long, and her head looked draped in the same colour as her dress. We both saw her and thought it was somebody from around (from that vicinity). Just before we got to her she started to walk ahead of us, and her dress shimmered like silk in the bright moonlight. All of a sudden she disappeared. Do you suppose she was trying to get rid of a treasure?"

Duck Island in Jeddore Bay has been mentioned before, as being on the way to Goose Island. "A man went there once and a woman appeared to him. I don't remember how she was dressed but I think it was in white. She had buckle shoes on I know, and she told him to get off the island or he would starve the same as she done, and he had to leave." In all these accounts of female revenants their dress seems to be remembered in detail. It seems odd in this case that buckle shoes were such a noticeable feature of her apparel.

Many years ago a girl from Granville Ferry used to drive a double-seated wagon and a span of horses. One of the horses was known to be frisky and her parents had warned her not to drive it. With the high spirits of youth she felt herself equal to deal with any horse and drove off quite happily to a picnic at Victoria Beach. It was a good picnic and she left to go home with a feeling that all was well in this best of all possible worlds. But on the return trip the frisky horse got out of control and, before she could get command of the situation she was thrown out of the wagon, dashed against a tree, and killed. It happened by what is known now as Johnny McGrath's house. Since then every seven years a horse and team are heard going down the hill clatter clatter. People step off the road to let it go by although they never see anything. The ground shakes and they feel a wind like that of a passing vehicle. According to some, you must be close to hear it.

Women ghosts in the old days liked to run along beside moving vehicles. About fifty years ago a woman in black used to be seen at Port Wade near the scene of our last story. She would appear about nine o'clock in the evening. One man tried driving so quickly that she couldn't keep up with him, but she was able to match his pace. He decided then to go to a friend's house for a while. He stayed until he felt he had shaken her but, when he started away, she was at the horse's head again. If he had any idea who she was or why she was there, he did not reveal it.

Modern transport in its swift movement is no deterrent to restless spirits. This has been demonstrated in the United States by the frequent appearance of what has come to be known as The Vanishing Hitchhiker. I have often inquired for such a story here and finally got one from Mr. Earl Morash of East Chester. The hitchhiker, of whom he had never heard before, appeared to a Toronto man about ten years ago in Winnipeg. He told Mr. Morash who passed it along to me. That is its only relation to our Province.

"This friend of mine had seen a girl at a railroad crossing and he stopped to pick her up because he could see that it would be a long walk for her to go from there to anywhere. He asked her where she lived and, as it was not far out of his way, he decided to drive her home. They talked all the way in the ordinary conversation of strangers but, after they'd arrived at her home and he had opened the door to let her out, she wasn't there. He couldn't remember afterwards whether his arm had touched her as he reached across to open the door or not. He couldn't understand it, so he got out of the car and searched everywhere. She couldn't possibly have left the car without his knowledge, but she had disappeared completely. He was so mystified that he decided to inquire for her at the house. A woman of about fifty answered the door and he told her what had happened. She said to come in, and then he saw her husband sitting in a chair. He started to cross the room to shake hands with him when he saw the girl's picture in a frame. "There she is," he said. "That's the girl I drove home."

"That's our daughter," they said. "She was killed two years ago at the railroad crossing." This tale follows the usual pattern reported as having occurred in cities from New York to San Francisco except that it is usually a car that has killed her. Neither Mr. Morash nor his friend had ever heard of it happening before.

It may have been a would-be hitchhiker who stopped a team with a man driving and two women in the carriage at Salmon River. They were too frightened to take her in, so they failed to learn her story.

A woman at Clarke's Harbour told a strange story. It is one of many in which the man was more frightened than the woman. I have ceased to be surprised at this, for I have found in so many cases that women will face a supernatural ordeal that men find completely devastating.

"There is a big rock at Centreville Woods called the Ghost Rock. When my mother was a girl about fifteen she was at Centreville visiting her sister. When she decided one night to go home, my uncle said he would go with her rather than have her go through the woods alone. They were walking along without saying very much when all of a sudden they saw something white crossing the road ahead of them, over and back.

"Did you see what I saw?" my uncle said.

"Well, I saw something white crossing the road," she said. They walked on a little further and it came again in front of them across the road, and it looked like a woman dressed in a white gown and the tail of it was long and sweeping and trailed along behind her.

"You can keep on going to Stony Island or come back with me, but I'm not going any further," my uncle said. My mother decided to keep going and, just as he was turning back, she saw it in front of her again and from then on she knew nothing until she lifted the latch of her own front door. When she told what had taken place her mother asked her why she hadn't stopped at her brother's store, but she had no recollection of having passed any store. It was as though she had been picked up and carried home. It was not until the parcel she was carrying fell to the ground and startled her as she touched the latch that she was conscious of her surroundings."

We hear occasionally of people wanting to come back after death to warn their friends or to convey some message about the future life. "Al Pearl, Al Langille, and Bella Young all lived on Tancook Island and they made a bargain whatever one died first would come back and let the others know if you could come back. Bella was the first to go. She was a little crooked woman and couldn't be mistaken for anybody else. One time a few years after she died the two Als met on top of a hill. They looked down by a brook and they said, 'There's Bella.' It was just getting dusk. She was dressed like when she was alive. She had said she'd come back if she went to heaven. There was no conversation; just seeing her told them what they wanted to know."

Similarly at Jordan Falls two young women were talking and one said if she died before the other she would come back to apprise her of the event. It so happened that this young person died at some distance from the other. That night, just after retiring, the friend felt a hand slapping her gently on the side of her head. For some reason she could not understand it made her think of the other young woman. It transpired later that she had died at just that time.

The Acadians left treasure buried in Nova Scotia, not all of which has been recovered. At Pubnico, Cyriac d'Entremont's wife said before she died that the first thing she would do in the next world would be to find out where this treasure was buried. A couple of weeks after her death some of the men of the village were at St. Anne's Point digging for kelp when she appeared before them. They were so frightened that they dropped everything and fled. When they told about her visitation people recalled what she had said, and they supposed she had come to take them to the spot. But alas, this explanation was not thought of for some time and, by then, the men had forgotten the exact place where they had seen her.

Bridges are favourite haunts for spirits, largely because they have so often been the scene of tragedies. Lank's Bridge at Parrsboro is supposed to be haunted following a murder many years ago. A horse is supposed to come by with a headless driver. And at Frog Hollow Bridge a girl has been seen and heard screaming. She had fallen off the bridge one Hallowe'en and had been screaming when she touched the water before being drowned. At Sambro I heard of a man named Bill Gray who used to see his mother at the bridge. He talked it over with a friend and they concluded she must have something on her mind she wished to tell him. He therefore said in the approved words for addressing a ghost, "In the name of God what do you want?" No message was forthcoming but she was evidently satisfied, for she disappeared and was never seen again.

The bridge at Blockhouse Creek also had its ghost, such a sad, unhappy wraith. "Long ago the road went up around, not where it is now. This woman was murdered and they used to see her ghost down by the bridge. She was dressed in white, and you would see her running up the creek, always going away from people." Still afraid, or shy of humankind?

I often wonder what happens to ghosts when the place they frequent is taken away or changed completely. Until very recently there was a covered bridge at Avonport. Here, according to a man from East Walton, a woman in white used to appear not only at night, but also in the daytime. He said she walked along the bridge and disappeared. The bridge near his own town also had its woman in white as well as other disturbing phenomena. A team of horses would come down the hill and disappear, car lights would come and vanish, and a man has been seen dancing and on fire on the hillside. Add to this the sound of chains rattling as you come up the brook and you have a lively setting. A girl told me that when she was in her late teens she saw the woman in white standing on the bridge at night and she was so frightened that she ran. When she went back later, the figure was gone. At Amherst I was told, "a girl at Rockport drowned herself and they always used to say they'd meet her on that bridge but nobody would speak to her for fear. She just walked by, dressed in white. As my friend Enos Hartlan said, "People who take their own lives can't rest."

You will have noticed that women appear in a variety of wearing apparel, usually the clothes associated with them when on earth. At Martock in Hants County a man named Wilkins was said to have had a house where officers from Halifax used to visit many years ago. One time two of these officers were sitting having tea when two nicely dressed ladies walked into the hotel and just vanished. "I've heeared that since I was small," said my informant. "I don't know whether anybody else was ever known to see them. Nicely dressed they were."

White and grey are popular for colour, but there is no set rule about it as this Seabright story testifies. "About fifty-five years ago when I was seven or eight I was walking with my mother and sister along the road. It was twelve or one o'clock at night. We met two women in long black dresses that glistened, and black hats. They were very tall. They passed us but there wasn't any sound from their feet on the ground or from their dresses. We all three of us saw them." .There are two interesting features about this story. One, that the women were seen by three people, which some say never happens, and the fact that two women were seen together. Only one other story tells of women in company. It came from Mahone Bay where a man saw two women in white walking around a vacant house. Men are not so lonely, and a whole ship's crew may be seen at one time; women always seem to be solitary in their peregrinations.

When Mr. Caspar Henneberry of Devil's Island was going past Fort Clarence on foot at a very late hour many years ago he saw a girl who, he learned later, was supposed to have been killed at that place. She had a round face, long black hair, black eyes, and she was dressed in black. She faced him on Battery Hill first and then walked along beside him. He was so frightened that he took to his heels and returned to the house he had been visiting, and all the way she ran along beside him. He then did a most unmanly thing—he fainted.

In the summer of 1939 Mrs. Reva Marshall was working at the Ashburn Golf Club in Halifax and, at half-past six, she and a friend named Joan left to go out for the evening. As they were walking down the woodland lane Joan saw a woman coming towards them and said in a startled voice, "Look, she's not touching the ground."

In the light of the summer evening every detail of her dress was plainly seen. She looked wrinkled and very old and she wore a black skirt, a white blouse, and a black shawl over her blouse. The blouse had a little piece of lace at the top of the high neck. On her head she wore a bonnet with a hood and the bonnet had ribbons under her chin. It had a wide brim at the front and tapered down at the sides.

As she came towards them she looked neither to right nor left and her feet, which did not touch the ground, made no sound. In her excitement Joan pushed her companion so that she almost touched her and, in her embarrassment Mrs. Marshall said, "Good evening madame." The old lady paid no attention to this greeting but went on her way to the end of the lane and then up a driveway and finally disappeared in the woods. As far as Mrs. Marshall knew, this was her only appearance.

Victoria Beach reported a tall woman in dark clothes, a former resident, and Mill Cove told of a woman dressed in brown. Our next was dressed in a sugar bag. An organist told the grandmother of my informant that she was going through the lower hall of a house in Annapolis Royal when she met a coloured child dressed in a sugar bag. The child not only walked towards her, but right through her. When the grandmother heard the story she did not seem greatly surprised. She explained that a former occupant had kept slaves and one day she had tied this child up by the thumbs and locked her in a closet. She went out then and forgot all about her. When she returned and went to release her, the child was dead. Others had reported seeing her, and that is why the grandmother was not surprised. Miss Charlotte Perkins, Annapolis Royal historian, carries the story a little further and adds that after the mistress found the slave dead, she sealed her body in the fireplace.

In this same house, the oldest in the town, an old woman often used to be seen sitting in a rocking-chair wearing a plaid or grey shawl. According to the writer, Beatrice Hay Shaw, this was not the owner of the slave, but a sister of one Andrew MacDonald who always appeared in the dress she had died in, and in the rocking-chair where her death had taken place. Women who saw her used to be filled with fear, but she did not have this effect upon men who always spoke of the kindly smile upon her face. She was first seen before 1821 and she was known as the Chequered Lady on account of the pattern of the dress she wore. The story, in the *Sunday Leader,* May 8, 1921, goes on to state that in all her appearances the chair continued to rock for some time after she left it.

It seems possible to me that the chequered dress would have a shawl-like collar which, from the street, would give the impression of a woman wearing a shawl. All stories agree upon one point; that is, that it embraced several of the quieter colours.

A story in which the reason for the appearance is far more important than the description of the dress, comes from Pugwash. "One time a man came here who had been in Rockhead Penitentiary and I asked him what he was there for. He said it was for stowing away on a ship from Newfoundland. I said if he'd been a stow-away they'd send him back; it must have been more than that.

"Well, one night we were both out seeing girls home down the same road. I waited for him and it was very late when he came. We were walking along and I saw a woman coming towards us and I thought she was one of the MacLeod girls and I thought I'd see if it was and why she was out so late. I went up close beside her and looked right in her face. It was as white as these gladiolas there. If she'd been real she'd have stepped to one side, but she kept right on. Her hair was coal black. You remember those basques women used to wear? Well, she was wearing one of these and a black skirt. She was neat and well dressed. The other fellow was with me when she came along but he had taken to his heels and run. When I got up to him he was standing at the corner shaking.

" 'Who was that?' I said.

" 'I don't know,' he said, but I think he did know, and that it was because of her that he'd been in Rockhead Penitentiary. I didn't go out with him any more after that."

We have several cases where the gift of seeing has been given to children. This is from Tangier. "When Uncle Bill was a small boy he was one of a large family and was put to bed with the hired help. At dawn he woke up and looked towards the door and saw a woman looking in. Then she left. In the morning he told the girl and described the woman whom she recognized as her mother. They learned later that she had died at that time."

At East Chester a story is told of a Mahone Bay woman who had always wanted a new house. She dreamed of it, and planned how she would fix it up, and the thought was so dear to her that she could think of little else. In fact it was almost an obsession. Finally the dream came true and the house she had longed for became hers. She moved in and was happier than she had ever been in her life. It lived well up to her fondest dreams and she loved the new house with all her heart. But alas, she had been living there only for a short while when she fell ill with tuberculosis. In those days little was known about this disease and it caused many deaths in the Province. She realized that her days were soon to end and her one sorrow was that she would have to leave her house. After she died, the woman who had nursed her stayed on and she told that every once in a while the face of her former patient would appear against the wall. No more of her was seen, and nothing happened, just the face.

Sometimes a sound is heard, and that is all. Pity the poor soul told about at Tatamagouche who drowned over a hundred years ago at Blockhouse Creek. She has never been seen, but she is still heard to this day wailing as she must have done at the hour of her untimely demise.

One evening a group of girls decided to regale one another with the sort of ghost stories they had heard so often in their homes in various parts of the Province. They got a delicious thrill from most of them, but that ended with the tale of a spectre from Springhill.

"My father went out one evening and he had to cross a meadow. On the way he met an old friend who had been dead for some time. He said she was dressed in the old-fashioned clothes he had last seen her wearing, and that she carried an umbrella in her hand. When they were through talking they shook hands and went their different ways." It was the thought of a hand-clasp that frightened the girls and, to this day, it sends shivers up the back of the one who told it to me. The father however suffered no ill effects.

Finally we have a story from Prince Edward Island, given me by Mr. Neil Matheson, M.P. It happened in a Scottish settlement called Strathhalbyn. Duncan and Flora had been sweethearts in their earlier youth, but in time Duncan's affections changed and he married else-where. Flora sickened and died, and many said it was from a broken heart. One day Duncan was driving between Hartsville and Rose Valley when he noticed a good-sized pig following him. Although he had a speedy trotting horse the pig kept up with them, with its snout just under the rear axle of the wagon. It finally got on his nerves and he stopped the horse, took the whip from its socket, jumped down, and struck the pig several solid blows. Then to his astonishment a woman's voice came from the pig. Flora's voice. She said, "Why did you strike me, Duncan?" Now why would a woman slighted return to her former lover in this ungainly form?

CHAPTER NINE

There and Not There

In Nova Scotia there are many instances of things having been seen which, upon investigation, were not there at all. Take for instance the strange occurrence on L'île à Frisée as reported by Mr. Stanislas Pothier of Pubnico. This is a small island which may once have harboured buried treasure. A hole lined with beach rocks indicates that a chest once rested there. It is also thought that a Frenchman had been murdered on that island, although that probably has nothing to do with our story. What is important is the erection of a lobster factory which took people to the island and resulted in one man seeing something that has puzzled him ever since. Mr. Pothier's story follows. "This man had come on a vessel and on landing decided to go for a stroll. He was walking along by himself when he came to a place with no trees or grass, but with a beautiful flower garden in the middle of a clearing. He couldn't understand how such a garden could be in such a place, particularly at that time of year when it was too cold for flowers like that to be growing along our coast. He didn't touch the garden, but went back to the vessel and told the other men about it. They thought it very strange too, and a few of the crew went back with him to see it for themselves, but he couldn't find the garden then or at any other time. As far as we know, nobody else has ever seen it either. It's a belief here that flowers represent buried treasure, or the ghost that guards it. That's the only explanation any of the fishermen have ever been able to give for it." (You will observe how often ghosts and buried treasure tie up together in the thinking of our people.)

Mr. Pothier also told of Spectacle Island in the same vicinity. "A few years ago a man from Clarke's Harbour was going along the shore of Spectacle Island in a skiff with his boy and they saw the prettiest flower in a pot on the bank. He said, 'Look a here, we'll get our firewood and when we come back we'll find our flower pot and take it back with us,' but when they went back, there was nothing there. He told it to a lot of people, and nobody else could find it either."

Men who live in the country know their way around and are not likely to get lost any more than a city dweller would in his own metropolitan area. This Annapolis Royal man knew his territory, and that is why his experience seemed so puzzling to him. "Some years ago I found myself in a place where a ring of spruce trees had been set out close together in a circle about the size of an ordinary room. I thought the spot was about where the Catholic church bell had been buried by the Acadians. I knew the spot well. A few years after I'd seen it, I took two other men with me to see it but it wasn't there. I looked and looked and I've gone back since and there's not a trace of it. I never could find those trees again."

Duck Island has been mentioned in connection with buried treasure, a tiny place off the eastern shore. "Uncle Joe and Uncle Arthur were out there one day and they saw a human bone, a leg bone. They overhauled it and Uncle Joe said, 'We'll take that up and we'll bury it when we've had something to eat. We'll, lay it down here until we're ready. It looks as though it's been washed ashore.' Uncle Joe thought the owner would probably like to have it put under the ground. After they finished their meal they came back to get the bone but it wasn't there. There wasn't a dog or a crow on the island to have carried it away, nor any other human being. Where had it come from, and where did it go?"

Mr. Sydney Boutilier of French Village also knew of a mystery. "Two young fellows, brothers of mine named Sandy and Will, were digging around for a cabbage bed. We always sowed cabbage seed on Good Friday. They cut up some seaweed for fertilizer and carried it up to mother but she wasn't ready just then to help them. There were two big willow trees near the house and, while they were waiting they sat down, and there was a hole underneath one of those trees, and in the hole there was an egg. They both saw it, but Sandy said, 'It's my egg. I saw it first.' They both ran their hands in the hole then, but they couldn't find the egg. Sandy thought Will had taken it, but he hadn't. They went in the house at last and told mother and she came out and looked too. One other time three of the most terrifying howls were heard beside those willow trees, and we never knew what they meant either. All the rest of their lives they wondered about that egg, but it was never seen again." It was like the gold pieces that surrounded a man named Misener at Lower East Chezzetcook "one handsome moonlight night. He shouted in his excitement and bent over to pick them up and they disappeared." Could it be that the egg and the gold pieces indicated treasure, and that speaking had caused them to be removed?

Far more extraordinary however is the appearance of a person in one place who is known to have been somewhere else. Anybody in a small town is bound to be well known by all the other residents. It is not only the face that is familiar but also the manner of walking and even the clothes that are worn. I was greatly surprised therefore, when I went to Digby in the year 1947 and talked to Rev. Mr. Gaskell. He told me of an incident that had happened there. One of the townswomen had been on her deathbed and, the day before she died, she was seen walking up the main street of the town. He said there was no mistaking her, but of course, she wasn't there.

The mother of Mrs. Fred Redden of Middle Musquo-doboit had an experience along these same lines, but with a more definite purpose.

"One day a man came to our house and asked for eggs. My mother went to get the eggs but when she came back he wasn't there. She looked everywhere and couldn't find him and she was afraid he was hidden somewhere in the house. She kept the children in two rooms until my father came home and she made him go through every room but he couldn't find him either. She knew who he was; he lived alone but at a little distance. Everything was too open around the house for him to have got out of sight in the short time she was away from him.

"My father couldn't understand it any more than she could, so the next day he got his nearest neighbour and they went to see this man. When they got there they found that he was dying. In his weak condition he couldn't possibly have come to our house, yet my mother had answered his knock on the door and had gone for the eggs after he had asked for them. He must have been thinking of her, and wanting someone to come and help him."

Then we have this from Ingramport. "Not long after I was married we lived in a little cottage that had four rooms and, from the kitchen, we could look into all the other rooms. One afternoon I was ironing when I saw a strange man walking from one room to the other. He was wearing dark trousers and a white shirt and he had his braces down over his hips as though ready to shave. Then I didn't see him any more and I began looking and I couldn't find him, and there was no way he could have left the house without me seeing him. I got scared then, so I called the men from the mill and they came up and searched. There was no trace of him anywhere. That night there was a man hanged himself in the mill. He was a stranger and when I went to see him, who should he be but this same man."

Mrs. Sydney Boutilier of French Village had this experience. "One day I took the milk pail and went for strawberries. When I started home I had the pail in my hand and, at the gate of Will's house, I saw a woman coming towards me. I recognized her right away as Mrs. Keddy who had lived there, but she was at that time in Halifax, and dying. She wore a long dress and a coat to her knees. Her hat hid her face, but I could see that she had a long chin. Her shoulders were rounded as she was going through the gate. I looked at her, but I didn't realize she couldn't be there until she went through the gate. I didn't exactly see her disappear, but all of a sudden she wasn't there. A couple of days later she died in Halifax where she had been all the time."

Mr. Earl Morash of East Chester said, "The night before Mrs. Charlie Bond died I was driving home from Mahone Bay. Near the church a woman appeared at the side of the road and suddenly she glided out in the road right in front of the car. I jammed on the brakes but there was no one there. She was the same size and built as Mrs. Bond, but she wouldn't show her face, but kept it away from me. I heard next morning that she had died, but it was after I had seen her."

Another living woman was seen at Big Pond and was

reported from Victoria Beach. She came up out of a corner of the pond wearing a cotton dress, and the man who saw her recognized her immediately. He was very startled, for he knew it was a forerunner of her death, which soon followed.

No one could look more jovial one moment and so serious the next as Mr. Richard Hartlan, brother of Mr. Enos. Even his moustache caught the feeling of solemnity and bristled against his ruddy face as he prepared to talk of the unexplainable things in his life. He said, "Before me brother died they seen him in the evening. He walked past the house with his hands in his pockets, and him too sick in his bed to move out of it. They said, 'It's a forerunner; he's going to die,' and the next day he was dead."

Going now to Tiverton, we find there is a story of a haunted house at East Ferry where people, or a person, are heard walking upstairs. "A bus driver was staying there once and one morning he came downstairs and he saw walking past the door an Englishman who was a boarder but, at that time wasn't there. The sounds are always heard in the morning."

Most of my Shelburne stories came from the Allen family, who had more than the usual gift for seeing things. They said there was always one member of the family who had second sight, and that their grandfather would sit at the table and talk to what would seem to be only a chair. But to him there was someone in that chair, unseen by the others. Their stories go like this:

"We used to get milk at the south end of the town on winter nights. The girls in our family wore tobogganing suits such as nobody else wore. One time I was coming home with the milk when I saw my sister approaching from the opposite direction, so I waved to her and shouted, 'I'll race you to the house.' But when I got to the house and put my hand on the knob, she wasn't there. She hadn't been there at all, yet I saw her until the moment when her foot was lifted towards the step. Then she disappeared. I wouldn't tell about it for ten years because it was considered such bad luck to see a person who wasn't there."

And again: "One day when we were youngsters I was steering the toboggan but after a while I suggested somebody else do it, and I passed it over to my cousin. She said, 'No, I don't want to take it.' I was surprised because she never refused anything if there was fun in it, so I said to her later, 'Jessie, why wouldn't you take the toboggan down?' She said, 'Because there was a man standing there.' So I said, 'That's why I wouldn't go.' There was no human there of course but, for our eyes only, there was a strange man. Nobody saw him but Jessie and me."

A strange thing happened to a man from Peggy's Cove. "A friend of mine was a great hunter, especially on a Sunday. One Sunday he and two other men were off hunting and they got separated. Soon afterwards my friend saw one of the other men coming towards him, and suddenly he disappeared. Later, when they were together again, my friend asked him why he hadn't come all the way. He said he hadn't come at all; he'd been off in another direction. Well, they talked it over and it puzzled them, so they all went to the place where he'd been seen. It was winter and there wasn't a track in the snow, yet my friend had seen him as plainly as could be. It scared the other man so much that he took it for a warning and, since then, he has never hunted on a Sunday."

Another warning, which unfortunately was not recognized as such, came to Earl Henneberry of Devil's Island. Or was it a forerunner? To put it down as a warning would be less frightening. "Earl was eating his supper one day when he looked out and saw his brother Ben coming up the road, but Ben didn't come. Earl was frightened and said, 'Mum, something's going to happen to Ben. I'm going after him!' Ben had rowed some friends to the South-East Passage shore. Earl borrowed a boat and two of his sisters asked to go with him, but he said, 'No, one of the family's enough to go at one time.' " (By this you will see that he anticipated a calamity as the result of having seen his brother when he was not there.)

"After Earl left, Ben came home and was surprised to hear what had happened because he hadn't come before. They waited for Earl to come back but he didn't come. The men went out then to look. You know how high the waves can get off that South-East Passage shore?"

Indeed I did know, only too well, for two friends and I had been all but swamped there ourselves. Apparently Earl had not been so fortunate, for they found his over-turned boat. The following day they dragged for him, and Edmund Henneberry and Ken Faulkner brought his body to the surface. I do not know how the brothers missed each other on such a short run. It was probably fog, but that is a minor point. Why had Ben appeared?

At French River in Colchester County Mrs. Tony Tattrie said, "Tony's mother was reel-footed (club footed). I seen her coming towards me and I went to meet her, and my sister and I both saw her plain. Then she disappeared. That was before she died and we knew she was somewhere else. After she died I saw her only once. She was coming across the field after sundown. One time three of us started down the road and we saw George Tattrie crossing the field and he kept on going, and all the time he was home in his bed. That was after twelve at night."

A fisherman at Paddy's Head had an experience with a boat. "I came in one time after fishing and there was a boat hanging to her club (mooring). I steered straight up towards her and I could see her all the way, but when I got up to it there was nothing there at all. That boat didn't come in till later.".

And from Glen Haven, "Before my brother died a woman in white came to my doorway, and suddenly disappeared and, before my sister-in-law died a woman with a shawl over her head went down the hill ahead of me. I wasn't exactly frightened in either case although I was pretty sure something was about to happen."

One bright moonlight night at Victoria Beach Buzz Ring said he had gone down the steep hillside to the wharves, and he walked along by one of the sheds. He was only a boy at the time, but it was not unusual for a lad to go fishing with the men. He saw a man in yellow oilskins walking ahead of him so he called out, but the man did not speak. He thought it was one of the Everett men and, since they are all friends in this small community, he wondered why he didn't answer him. He kept his eye on him, however, and distinctly saw him go through an open door. This too seemed odd, but Buzz supposed he intended to jump out and scare him. He therefore lit a match which he fully expected to have blown out by the other man, and peeked cautiously around the door. Nothing happened, so he drew the door back carefully and there was nobody there; neither was there a place to hide nor any other way to get out. He was dumbfounded. Shortly after that, and at about the same time of night, an older fisherman saw a man walking at the same place. He called, "Clifford," thinking it was a friend of that name, but he, too, received no answer. He was angry at being ignored and said, "Can't you speak to a fellow?" at the same time catching him by the arm to stop him. But there was no arm to catch. Nothing was there.

A man from Wallace having put his hand on the shoulder of a man who wouldn't speak to him and finding nothing to grasp, said in describing his experience,

"Do you known what it was? It was a nawthin'."

In his book, *Exploring the Supernatural,* R. S. Lambert tells about an event which took place in Sydney in 1785. After I had read it, Miss Eva Worgan of Sydney told a story so similar that I thought it must be a variant of the Lambert tale. It seems now to have been an entirely different incident, for Miss Worgan said it happened in 1873 or thereabouts. She had often heard it told by her father, Capt. Worgan, R.N., and her mother, both of whom knew many of the officers stationed there, and had heard it first hand. I later called her sisters in Halifax, and found that one of them knew the story well as it had been told in their home. None, however, could recall the name of the officer whose appearance caused such consternation.

"The Military Barracks used to be at the old Victoria Park. One of the officers stationed there at the time of our story was called to England to see somebody who was very ill and, while there, he took sick himself and died. On the night that he died, his brother officers were sitting having dinner when this man walked down the stairs, passed the table, and went into an adjoining room. They looked at one another spellbound and finally one of them said, 'That's So and So. Did you notice the look on his face?' Everybody in the officers' mess saw him, and they all agreed it was this man.

"In those days news was slow in arriving but they learned in time of his death which, upon further inquiry, had taken place at the exact time when he had been seen passing through the mess."

Another story, also from Cape Breton was given to me by Mrs. Ruth Metcalfe. "A young couple in their thirties lived at Reserve Mines. She was a tall and lovely lady of highland Scottish birth. He was a miner named John McNeil. In those days it was the custom for cows to be pastured on common land and one summer afternoon Mrs. McNeil started out to bring their cow home. She was dressed in a beautiful black silk dress with a white apron which was the usual costume for that class of highland woman. She had not gone far when she met a neighbour and they walked together, enjoying the early afternoon sun as old friends do who have met unexpectedly. Their conversation was interrupted by Mrs. McNeil who said with surprise, 'There's John. I'll go for the cow later,' and she left to go to her home and husband.

"I'm going for my cow, so I'll bring yours home too, Lizzie,' her neighbour said, and she did.

"When the neighbour came back with the two cows she stopped first at her own home, and was surprised to see her husband there, for he was not expected for some time.

" 'Why are you home so early?' she said.

" 'John McNeil was killed in the mine this afternoon,' he replied. When she recovered from the shock she asked the time of the accident, remembering how his wife had looked towards her house and how surprised she had been to see her husband there. She realized then of course that he had appeared at the moment of his death."

An Ellershouse man had to stop his car one day when a friend appeared on the road either before or at the time of his death at distant Springhill, and Mr. Jim Apt of Victoria Beach saw a man and learned later that he had been murdered in another place and at about the same time.

Now let us run up to New Brunswick and see what a man from Newcastle has to say. "When I came here in 1916 there was a man had lived here I never saw in my life, Tommy Taylor. I was sitting down in John's father's kitchen, where he often used to visit, and I riz my eyes up and this man was looking in the window. I sez to John's father, 'Look at the man looking in the window.' He looked up then and said, 'That's Tommy Taylor. When did he come home?' He went out the door and he sez, 'Come in Tommy.' There wasn't a soul around. He sez to me, 'There's something happened Tommy Taylor.' I sez, 'Where is Tommy?' He sez, 'He's in the asylum.' Well, Tommy had died all right and they brought his body home next day. I went to see him and I sez, 'Yes, that's the man I seen looking in the window!'"

Also from Newcastle: "My wife seen me coming in the main road. She seen me coming with a parcel on my back and a little stick. The house was on the top of a hill. She seen me coming to the door and she run to open it and there was nothing there. An hour after, she seen me coming again, and this time it was me. I wasn't there at all the first time. We could never understand it." Then he added an observation about ghosts in general.

"A ghost don't appeal to anybody if he don't need anything, but if you can help him, you can see him."

I picked the next story up at the Pictou County Exhibition. At Taylor's Stone House I had met Mr. and Mrs. Ernest Ferguson of Baie Comeau. When they saw me later at the Exhibition and also a Pictonian, Mr. Scott, they thought there might be an interesting exchange of stories. We were therefore introduced and stood in a little group talking. The following went down in my notebook: It was experienced by Mr. James Simon Fraser, a hardware merchant of New Glasgow, who had a summer place at Melmerby Beach. His wife was staying there at the time, and he joined her for weekends. A man named Kelly, whose first name Mr. Scott had forgotten, lived at King's Head, a mile from the beach, and Mr. Fraser knew him well.

In the late summer we often have what we call an August gale. Mr. Fraser was preparing for his weekly trip when the wind came up and the rain fell in torrents. He did not let this deter him, but hitched his horse to his light buggy and, beneath the waterproof top that covered it. got what shelter he could. It was dark as he drove along and his one lantern glimmered faintly. There were frequent lightning flashes and in this sudden light he saw Kelly walking up the road towards him, dressed in his fisherman's clothes. Mr. Fraser stopped his horse and leaned out to speak to him but, although Mr. Kelly walked close to the carriage and looked Mr. Fraser in the eye, he said nothing, but continued on his way. This was so unexpected, and so unlike Kelly, that Mr. Fraser remarked upon the event to his wife soon after he got in. It was then eleven-thirty.

The following morning the Frasers were late in rising, but they had no sooner made their appearance than they were told that Kelly had disappeared. No one had seen him since the previous day, Saturday, when he went out fishing.

"I've seen him since then," Mr. Fraser said. "I saw him last night walking up the road." However that night, the one after Mr. Fraser had seen him, they found his body. By its condition they knew he had been drowned from his boat early Saturday afternoon. The Frasers were so taken aback by the strange occurrence that they said nothing more about it for many years. They finally told it to Mr. Scott's mother, and he kindly passed it on to me.

On the southwestern shore at Boutilier's Point a woman said, "I was at a party when I was in my late teens and I had to walk most of the way from Oakland to Mahone Bay alone. A friend walked with me until I saw a girl ahead in a fresh white dress and I recognized her at once. I told my friend I would be all right now and I would keep close behind her, so he left me and I kept the girl in sight, but suddenly she disappeared. I wasn't frightened because I was sure she was somebody I knew going home just as I was doing. I even stopped and looked under boards on the shore to make sure she wasn't hiding. There was no sign of her anywhere and I was puzzled. When I checked up, I found she hadn't been on that road at all. I told my father and he shook his head. He said my description reminded him of a young girl who had been drowned just across the road from the Church of England and had been seen several times at that place. So which girl it was, a living or a dead one, I don't know, but I certainly saw someone."

Now from Victoria Beach: "One bright moonlight night when there was snow on the ground four of us were walking towards the Moose Hollow Bridge when I saw a woman in white coming towards me with a white sheet over her head. She was only about twelve feet away when I turned to speak to the men behind me and, when I looked ahead of me again, she was no longer there, and there were no tracks in the snow. If it had just been me who'd seen her I might have thought I'd imagined it, but two of us saw her and two didn't. She had been walking easy."

We go now from the bright light of the moon to the broad light of day. "It happened about forty-five years ago that a man was walking from Herring Cove to Pennant. It was about five o'clock on a Sunday in May. The day was fine and the atmosphere was clear. Half a mile from Portuguese Cove a woman stood in front of him and walked a quarter of a mile side by side with him. He spoke to her and got no answer and she disappeared as suddenly as she had come. He never knew who she was or why she had come there at that time."

On another fine Sunday a few years ago Mr. and Mrs. Bagnall and their son set out from Glace Bay for Gabarus. It was a beautiful day, free of fog, and so clear that every leaf on every tree stood out distinctly. As they drew near their destination they saw a familiar figure coming towards them, dressed in his customary clothes which included a green pea jacket, peaked cap, and rubber boots turned down. His wife said, "Who is that?" and her husband told her. There was no hesitation because Mr. Bagnall had grown up on a part of this man's land. The driver's arm was resting on the top of the turned-down window and they were so close that they could easily have touched him. When Mr. Bagnall told his wife who it was she said, "Yes, I thought so, but that man is dead."

"I know it," he replied, and reflected that if he had been alive he would have stopped and spoken to them. Instead he seemed quite unaware of them, never raising his eyes nor looking at them. After they got by they talked it over and recalled that this man had a nephew who might look enough like him for a mistake to be made, and possibly he might be wearing his uncle's clothes. To settle the matter they called the nephew's sister but she quickly dispelled any such idea. "Would he have any resemblance to your uncle?" they asked.

"That's foolish," she said. "He's only thirty-five and our uncle was seventy-five." They realized that she was right, but why he had appeared to them in broad daylight they could not imagine. And for those who say that one or two people, but never three, may see a ghost, this theory is again refuted.

About four years ago the family in our previous story lost a son, a doctor, by death. It was, of course a grievous blow. His mother said, "One day Mr. Bagnall and I were sitting reading when I felt somebody close beside me. I put my book down and looked up, and my son was standing by the oil stove, the one who had died. I looked behind me and Mr. Bagnall was still reading, not realizing what was happening, and I made no sound. When I looked back my son ran his hand through his hair as he often did, and smiled at me. He did this twice, smiling each time. I was a different woman after that." I have often noticed in our stories how the dead make themselves known beyond any doubt by some article of wearing apparel or a characteristic gesture. The running of his hand through his hair was evidently something that she always connected with him. Unlike Jack Carson's appearance to his mother, this son did not speak. His happy face was sufficient to assure her that grief was superfluous.

Clothes seem so important in our Nova Scotia stories that this description from Richard Hartlan of South-East Passage cannot be ignored. He had no idea who the man was or why he appeared to him one "starlit night about ten o'clock. I could put me hand onto him when he got up close. He had a pair of white duck pants on, a black waistcoat, and a pair of fishin' boots. I just cast me eyes down, and when I looked up he was gone."

What a useful thing snow is to prove that one has seen a ghost. Mr. Edward Gallagher, retired light-keeper at Chebucto Head, said, "We were fishing at Sambro and we went to a pie social. It was a moonlight night and there was snow on the ground. Two hundred yards from Sandy Cove road there is a clear bit and, as we were walking home from the pie social, we saw a fellow ahead of us all dressed in black. I said, 'There's one of the Finks or Nickersons, we'll catch him up.' There is a place called Clay Hill where chains have been heard rattling, boats have rowed up by the Head, and lights have been seen. It was always thought these things meant pirate money was buried there.

"When this man got to the top of Clay Hill he went off into the bushes. We could hear him but we couldn't see him. I said, 'Let's go and find him,' but the other fellows wouldn't go. Next day it blew a gale so we didn't go fishing, and I was curious about what we'd seen. No new snow had fallen and, although I knew exactly where he had turned in from the road, there wasn't a footmark. Another time I saw a light on the top of Clay Hill like a candle, but when I went up to investigate there was nothing there."

The Hartlan estate, you will remember, was at the

eastern approach of Halifax Harbour and, in the old days, it had a steep bank close by the sea. Mr. Richard Hartlan said, "My father was settin' by the windy a-lookin' along the public road and he sees a man comin' towards the house and he watched him a-comin'. He didn't come to the door. He just went around the house and when he did that my father went out and watched him goin'. There's a big bank where we live and he went over to the edge of the bank and just kept on goin'. My father said, 'That man's killed himself,' but when he looked over the top of the bank there was nothing there at all. If he'd been real, his body would have been lyin' on the rocks below."

The next apparition was seen by four people, and I heard about it at Tantallon. "There were four men in a boat, Lester my son, Doc Fader, James Boutilier, and one other. They had been on a trouting trip and they were coming down Big Indian Lake in a boat. One of them faced ahead and he said, 'Look, what's that on the dam?' They put down their oars and looked, and they all saw a man in a rubber coat and a sou'wester walking along the dam and, when they got almost to where he was standing, he was gone. They landed and could find no sign of him although the four men had all seen him plainly. They found out later that the same thing had happened to one of the operators there and, when he saw the man, he was just as puzzled and investigated and couldn't find a thing. The dam goes right out to nothing, so there is nowhere for a man to go. They kept it quiet for a long time till somebody else reported it, and then they told what they had seen. It came out then that two women and three men had been drowned at that place quite a while before, so they always thought that might be one of them. They could never forget it."

"There was a man at Glen Haven named Josey Joe, and a crowd would collect at his house and tell ghost yarns until everybody was scared to go home. One night my mother was being taken home from one of these evenings and, going through the woods, a terrible row come up. They thought it was a bear, but nobody had seen a bear around there for a long time. She said it made a roaring sound. The next day they went into the woods at the same place and they couldn't see a thing out of place. The bushes weren't broken down and there weren't any tracks." A man named Williams was going from Jeddore to Ostrea Lake when "something came in front of him like a great big horse. He was terrified, but kept on going and there was nothing there at all." A Seabright man heard footsteps by a bridge but could find no person.

Then, "I was coming from Tantallon one winter's night. I was by the hemlock tree when something started right at the top of that hemlock tree and it was the most hideous sound I ever heard in my life and it sounded as though it broke every branch. It commenced at the top as if it was up there with a three ton truck and it was loaded and dropped down that tree. I never slackened my pace. I had to pass it, and when I got close beside it, it happened again and, as I got a little further away, it happened the third time. The next day I went back and there wasn't a broken branch, nothing to account for it. It was close to the Bel Snickle Road where people used to see a man with no head, just half a mile before Glen Haven."

The next two stories are enough alike to be considered together. "I was going to Albert (New Brunswick) about eleven o'clock. I was walking and alone and I had to go down a little hill. I heard a horse and carriage behind me and I looked and could see a man driving it. I said to myself, 'That man will give me a drive when he goes by,' but he came up abreast of me and disappeared. They came down to me and never passed me."

The twin to this happened at Blue Rocks and was told by Rev. Mr. Gretorex. He used to go out there at times and, if he were very late, he would stay until morning. This night he decided to walk into Lunenburg and sleep there. As he was walking along the country road that skirted the sea he saw a team ahead with a couple in it. He supposed they were lovers and thought if he could catch up with them that they would take him in. He therefore called out to them, hoping they would hear his voice above the sound of the wheels but instead, the whole thing disappeared. (No interrupting of love's sweet young dream for them!) The next morning he told of his amazing experience and was informed that he had seen the Blue Rocks ghost. The team with the couple driving to Lunenburg had been seen by other people. The incident happened many years ago, and it is quite likely this would be an ox team since it was moving slowly enough for him to catch up with it afoot, and the ox was used by so many people in that community.

Another "nawthin'" story comes from Seabright. "One time I had to go to Hackett's Cove and the fog shut in and they told me I'd have to stay all night. About ten o'clock we started to bed and I stepped outside and the stars were a-shining and I said, 'I'm going home. If I wait till morning I'll meet all the boats coming out from Glen Margaret.' So I sailed home and I put my boat up, and then I had quite a little walk to my house. As I started up the hill I saw a man ahead of me. I hastened my steps and caught up with him but he didn't stop. When I got abreast of him I put my hand out to touch him and there was nothing to touch." His mild blue eyes looked into mine and he said, "Now what was the meaning of that?" ·

Another Seabright man said, "When I was sixteen my father went to Hubbards in the boat. After he'd gone I came down the hill and although he was in Hubbards by that time I saw him and then the barn hid him and, when I came in sight of the wharf, he wasn't there. I said to my mother, 'Is father home?' and she said no. What made me see him when he wasn't there? I even saw the smock he used to wear when he went fishing. It wasn't a forerunner because there wasn't any death after it. I could never understand it." This man was well up in his eighties. Perhaps then there is some truth in the statement that "if you see a person who isn't there it means you'll be a long liver."

Mrs. Sadie Clergy of East Petpeswick has never been able to understand a strange thing that happened once to her. She said she had gone to a dance one evening and had talked to an old friend who was stout and was wearing a black dress. When Mrs. Clergy left, her friend said she thought she would stay at the dance a while longer but, when the Clergys came to a bend of the road, they heard her voice behind them saying "Sadie, why don't you wait for me?" She said to her husband, 'Here comes Mrs. Young.' Mr. Clergy turned around and couldn't see anybody, but Mrs. Clergy saw her plainly. She said it was her friend Mrs. Young all right but, instead of being dressed in black as she had seen her, she now had a white silver shawl over her shoulders, and her hair was snow white. Then she disappeared. Mrs. Clergy asked her the next morning if she had been on the road that night behind her, but she had not left the dance hall for a long time. The incident which happened many years ago, has mystified her to this day.

Although Mr. Clergy's eyes were closed to the apparition seen by his wife, he saw a vision of his own. About a mile below his own house at ten-thirty one night as he was returning home, he saw a boat in the air above him coming from the west and going in an easterly direction, although there was nothing east but woods. He said it was a low, flat power boat that went racing through the air without making any sound. As far as he knows nobody else ever saw it.

Sandy Cove had perhaps the strangest story of all. "One time a man named Hiram was coming home from hunting and it was hazy and at night. There were trees all along the road and, as he came towards a little hill, he saw a white form that seemed human, yet reminded him of pictures of angels. It was going back and forth on the road. He was puzzled and stopped to watch it and after a while he began to think he would speak to it and he did and it made no sound. Then he said, 'I'm going to bring you down. I've got a gun loaded with big shot, and I'm going to shoot you.' He fired and whatever it was vanished. A short while after that his wife, Pheban, died and he grieved from that day. Although he hadn't recognized her, he felt that was who he saw on the road and that he had killed her."

In every one of these stories, the person telling it had a furrowed brow. The event had puzzled them at the time, and had disturbed them ever since. While some ghost stories came easily at a first meeting, these personal mysteries were saved until a firm friendship had been established and they could be related as a confidence. The tales all had one thing in common, a shaking of the head at the conclusion and words to this effect, "I could never understand it."

CHAPTER TEN

Ghosts as Animals and Lights

ANIMALS

IN MANY of our stories ghosts appear as animals, with the dog the most common. The Hartlan men used to tell about dogs six feet high, but they are not always large. They may be very little dogs, and they may be black, white, or spotted. Horses come next in favour, and we also have three pigs. You will recall the rejected lass in Prince Edward Island who followed her lover's carriage in the ungainly form of a pig. Port Wade had a place called Pig Bridge, so called because on a very dark night a phantom pig used to be seen there. Our third pig came into a house now demolished, but once owned by the Allan Hartlings at South-East Passage. It ran through the rooms to the terror of one of the children, and his mother had to take him from room to room to prove that there was no pig there. He is a grown man today and still insists that he saw it. Incidentally that same house had doors that opened mysteriously when nobody was near the old-fashioned wooden latches to lift them. It also had a number of bottles of preserves stored upstairs. One night Mr. Hartling had just got into bed when there was a terrific noise as though all the bottles were upset but, upon examination, nothing was out of its place. It was a house his wife had never liked because of the unexplainable things that happened there.

We have stories of kittens and cats, and we also have a gopher. I heard of it from Mr. George Perry of Ingomar when he was working at Ragged Islands Inn. He was a great talker, and had often regaled Miss Arnold's guests with his stories. "The gopher was something that appeared at Ingomar and people wouldn't go near the place where it was seen. Nothing had ever happened there to account for it as far as anybody knew, but they dassn't pass it. It died away after a while, but not before frightening a lot of people.

"One night a woman was going down past this place and she wasn't scared of anything. It was a pretty moonlight night and, when she got that far, she looked across and there stood a big yellowish coloured dog with handsome dark on it. She went over and put her hand on it and it disappeared. She thought, 'that's funny,' and she went on a little way and then come back and the dog was still there, but headed in the opposite direction. So she went up again and patted him and said, 'There, there, little dog,' and it wasn't there. She said, 'I was just as sure it was a dog as I am a woman.' Whether it was this gopher or a dog or what it was I'm blest if I know."

Whether their gopher light had anything to do with this animal I could not determine, nor could I understand why it was given this name.

"There were two boys out gunning (shooting birds)" Mr. Perry said, "at Cape Negro once and they both got shot by accident. Ever since that time up to forty or fifty years ago, and never before, a gopher light has been seen. It would come over the water before a storm in the place where the boys shot themselves and would go back at the same place. It would start small and would get big as a washtub, and there was a man in the light swinging a lantern. One time three men went out in a dory to see if they could find out what it was. They took a gun and started to row and they got just so nigh and the light would diddle up and down and it took down the harbour and they couldn't catch it, so they shot at it and gave it up. People got scared of it because after a while it began to move around the shore. It would go down and come up and you could see this man swinging his lantern. When you saw it you always knew there would be a storm. One woman told her man that if you watched it, the light would come right across the harbour for ten minutes, but he wouldn't believe it. So she said, 'Will you get up if I call you when I see it?' He said 'Yes,' so the next time she see it she called him. The gopher light was coming right towards them and it dilly dallied up and down and then went back.

"One night my brother and I were out and I said, 'That's the gopher light right in the middle of the medder' (meadow). By and by it blazed up and we could see the man swinging the lantern. We rushed home and told mother and she ran out and saw it too. It was coming down the harbour and it diddled up and down and then went back."

We will have more stories of lights later on. Let us look again at our dogs. A Seabright fisherman said, "Father was in a house once where in the first part of the night there was a big dog in the kitchen under the stove and he couldn't get it out. He said, 'I'll get it out!' and he took the horsewhip. He lifted it up and was going to strike and it disappeared in a little flash of fire. That house was haunted."

Do you remember the dog in an earlier chapter that

used to put its paw in a doorway and was supposed to be the devil? And the forerunner that came in the form of a halibut?

"I was coming home one calm moonlight night at twelve o'clock. Just below the church I seen a white dog with its tongue hanging out, and a black ring round its head and tail and I had to step out of the road. If I'd looked over my left shoulder I wouldn't have been frightened (this evidently would have dissipated the power of the ghost). Then I saw a man with a split-tail coat peeking round the building. It was a man I knew when he was alive, and now he was dead. It was funny that he'd come as a dog first and then as a man." So said a Negro at Sackville. I have often wondered why so many of our phantom men appear wearing split-tail coats. It must have been the garment they were buried in.

At Scotsburn it is said that dogs hear a phantom called a Black Dog. Other dogs get very excited, but nothing can be seen by humans. It is also believed there, as elsewhere, that horses see things before people. It is a Victoria Beach legend that a big dog used to appear at the top of Parr's Hill. Then if you went to Andrew's Hill at the right time every seven years you would not only see a dog but you would hear him rattling his chains. Nobody knows why he came or what the story is behind his appearance. His time has been up for some years, for he is not seen any more.

Many stories of dogs appearing in the dark may seem far-fetched, and the reader thinks of all kinds of physical explanations. At Port Wade one day I was talking to a kindly old man and his wife and they told that they were coming home once when they saw a strange dog. It followed them so closely and so persistently that the man got cross and kicked it. Imagine the surprise they got when his foot went right through it. They both assured me this was so, for both had seen it. Much the same thing happened at Glen Haven to one of my elderly singers, Mr. John Obe Smith.

"I seen something over here one night coming home. I seen a big black dog coming towards me and his eyes as big as two fists. I went to fire at him and the rock went right through him. I threw another one then and it disappeared altogether. By this time I was pretty scared and I was only young anyhow so I took to me heels and ran. There was supposed to be somebody killed by an Indian years before and this was its ghost. Lots of people saw it about seventy-five or eighty years ago."

Mr. Angelo Dornan of Elgin, New Brunswick, said there used to be a big black dog in one of the houses when he was a young man. It would go up the stairs every night and go through the rooms but, the moment the lamp was lit, it would disappear.

The next story comes from Mrs. Tony Tattrie of French River who lived before her marriage at McPhee's Corner. Her ghost was a horse. "There were eight or ten men going to work on the Midland (railway) and they went to a house to sleep, but the house was full. It was too late to go anywhere else and there weren't many places that could take them anyhow, so they said they'd sleep in the barn. There were no animals in the barn, so they knew it would be quiet there. It was a nice summer evening and none of them minded sleeping there. They closed the barn door and they all chose to sleep on the barn floor except Joe Weatherbe and he slept up in the mow. That is why he is the only one who didn't see it.

"The people in the house didn't say anything to the men about the barn being haunted, but they said to themselves, 'They'll not get any rest tonight.' A pedlar had been killed in that barn and they knew something would probably happen, because things had happened before. The men in the barn had all gone to sleep when George

Tattrie felt a horse's breath blowing on him. He woke the others up and they all saw the horse. George put his hand up and felt the horse and he thought they were all going to be trampled on. It didn't take them long to skedaddle out of there and, after that, the people who owned the barn told them it was a ghost."

We have seen before that horses can be heard in a mysterious fashion when there are no horses there. For some reason which nobody knows, a sound of horse's hoofs has been heard for years coming up the driveway of a place at Upper Falmouth. They would be so distinct that the hired man would go out to greet the guests and attend to the horse for them, only to find no one there. It always happened at night and is heard every once in a while. A few years ago it was still happening, but now with an automobile taking the place of horses.

"Mr. Bond at East Chester is supposed to have seen a big horse come out and put his forefeet on the fence. One time at that same place three young people were stealing apples when they heard an awful noise and snorting like a horse would do. Then it appeared. It stood on its hind legs and snorted and ripped the boards off the fence and they all ran away, frightened to death. The next day they went back to see how much damage the horse had done and the boards weren't ripped at all. In another place here at the turn, people would hear a horse galloping along and it would be behind you and by you and then it would pass you and fade away. Real horses are supposed to see things that can't be seen by humans. There is an old saying that if a horse rears, you should get down and look between his ears, and you'll see what the horse saw."

They used to hear a horse and wagon at Thorne's Cove. It would start at one of the beaches and go a mile towards Victoria Beach and then go off the side of the road and disappear. One man tried to race it, but he couldn't catch up with it. Different people reported having seen it.

Riverport had the most common type of story about a horse, but the scene was laid at Port Hawkesbury. "There was an old man who lived twelve miles east of the Strait of Canso and kept a respectable place. One night he was driving a horse team from Port Hawkesbury and he hadn't gone far when a lady came running along and put her hand on the arm rest of the carriage, and kept it there until they came to a church. He had no whip but an Indian withe, an alder branch, and he used it to hit her left arm where she was holding on. He urged the horse to go faster, but she went faster too. This kept up until they reached the church and then she disappeared. This happened when he was coming from Port Hawkesbury on the road to West Bay. She was on the driver's side which was then on the right. He almost broke his withe trying to hold her back."

LIGHTS

When ghostly lights are seen it is usually supposed that treasure is buried nearby and that the light is showing the way to it, as you read in a previous chapter. Not all lights have this meaning. The Keyes' place had a frightening name to people in Queen's County as recently as ten years ago, according to a man from North Port Mouton. "I was coming from Fairy Lake to West Caledonia one night after playing the fiddle, and it was about one o'clock. The man in the horse behind me said there was a light following right along to the old Keyes' place. I had a nice up-to-date horse and team and didn't see anything myself. Older people used to see something at that farm, and there was no one living there.

"Tom Perns was an old Cornish shoemaker and he used to see something half a mile this way from the farm. A lot of people were scared of the place, and the reason was that Keyes was killed in a pit while getting gravel for the road. It was low and swampy where he lived. The Indians and lots of others thought he used to come back, and they wouldn't travel there after dark. People driving near Fairy Lake would report lights that would appear under the wagon and follow right along and then disappear."

Mr. John Dan Ferguson of Bay Head, Colchester County, had a strange tale to tell. "At the top of Spiddle Hill there is a place where a ball of fire used to be seen. It was a common occurrence and people used to talk about it, but they didn't think too much about it. It was called Ross's torch and it floated over the Ross farm for years. It was a round bright light and lighted the whole place but, when they left, it left.

"One time about sixty years ago a farmer named Murray was visiting his neighbour on the next farm and it was crusty weather. He saw the light and was watching it so closely that he went off his course and up there on the hill beside the light he saw something, but he would never tell what it was. After he saw it he went home and collapsed and, although he lived for a while, he never got out of his bed again. The Rosses themselves didn't appear to think anything about the light, but in time they moved away. The light didn't follow them, but it was never seen after they left."

At the time of the expulsion of the Acadians there was a settlement between Diligent River and West Bay called Gascoigne. The French were being sent away, and one old chap refused to go, so they cut off his head. Since then, said my informant from Moose River, he has been seen ever since going from place to place carrying his lantern.

Hall's Harbour has a very modern ghost. "In the fall of 1946 a car with lights on was seen to come down the road by the Schofield's and to disappear as quickly as you could have snapped your fingers. It was seen again at the same place by two girls who were going to a meeting. A person is supposed to have been killed and buried in a pasture at this particular place, and they wonder if this might be his ghost."

Another ghost that deviated from the usual pattern appeared at Shag Harbour. It came at various times, but mostly before a storm and in the form of lights. These lights danced before the astonished onlooker and formed the figure eight.

Although many of our people are Irish, it is a rare thing to hear of a banshee. I was therefore surprised when one turned up at Annapolis Royal which I look upon as one of the least Irish sections of the Province. The banshee was described as a ball of fire that bobbed over the marshes. People often used to see it, and they called it by that name, but my realistic informant added his impression which was that this was probably phosphorus rising from the swampy ground.

Spirit Hill, appropriately named, goes through the Centreville woods of Cape Sable Island, and people going that way pass what they call Ghost Rock. "Lights are seen there. There may be more than that, but the old people who told about them didn't wait to look."

If you should go down to what they call South Side on this same island at two o'clock in the morning and at the proper season of the year, you might see a light on the beach. Those who have witnessed this light say that it is like a ball of fire that floats through the air and, they say, one man tried to shoot it and it burst his gun. Another man on the island had a light follow close beside his horse and team, but the faster he drove, the faster the light went beside him. He thought he was a man without fear until this happened but, when the light left without any harm befalling, he realized that his spine had stiffened and his teeth were chattering.

The house at Seabright where the apron was pleated on the clothesline in a mysterious way and there were sounds of lumber falling, has another tale to tell. A young man went to the door for wood. As he reached the woodpile he saw a big ball of light coming up the fence. "It came up behind the buildings and took to moaning like a person in pain, and it followed him to the platform (stoop). It kept the form of a ball of light until it reached the woodpile, and then the light disappeared but not the sound that went with it. That followed him as far as the door, but not into the house."

At Scotsburn, which is a farming community in Pictou County, they said, "Angus McKay drove one of Murdock Anderson's boys home and on his way back he saw a light following him along the other side of the dam. It went on until it reached a gate on the mountain road, and then it went out. Then McKay saw what looked like a stump burning so he went back and got Murdock up and they went to the spot but there was no stump burning or anything, and they could never account for it."

Dead stumps have often been taken for phantom lights. At Port LaTour boys used to take the phosphorus off the stumps and write names across the road to frighten people who would think their time had come. It was quite a trick they said, and they could only do it on certain nights. Phosphorus on a stump might be the answer to the stationary light seen by Mr. McKay, even though he could find no stump in that particular place, but it doesn't explain the light that followed him to the gate on the mountain road.

Here is an odd story from Glen Margaret. "There was a man by the name of McDonald from French Village who was visiting Moser's Island. Up by Wodin's River there was an old road and the story was that it was haunted. McDonald told them that he was going to take a short cut that way and he said, 'If the spirit is supposed to be seen, I want to see it tonight.' He said before he left the island that when he got to

the graveyard he was going to say out loud that he hoped
to see the spirit, and then he would see what happened.

"Well, when he got up to the old cemetery there
were two bright lights come up out of the burying ground
and they were so bright that he couldn't see. They
blinded him and he couldn't get clear of them till morning. No matter how he tried, all he could see was those
lights. He went back to Moser's Island then and was
sick for a week, but he didn't mind because he claimed
he had seen the spirit." This story belies an old belief
I have heard expressed many times that if you are
looking for a ghost you will never see one. He was
apparently satisfied that the light he had seen was the
spirit he had heard about, and sought.

FAIRIES

When I was having my car serviced in Sydney in 1956,
I mentioned to the mechanic, Mr. Charles Turner, that
I had heard a great many ghost stories in Cape Breton.
He asked a few questions and then turned out to have
a fund of stories himself. It was on the last of several
visits to the garage that he told of having seen the little
people. I had often inquired for fairies but, until then,
it seemed that they had not crossed water from the old
land. This was the exception.

"When we were children we lived in a house at Point
Edward. There were six of us sleeping upstairs. The
upper part of the house wasn't finished off and there
were rafters above that could be seen from both of the
bedrooms where we were sleeping. This morning we
were lying in bed and we looked up and we could see a
dozen little people like pixies or elves with brownish
bodies jumping back and forth on the beams, carrying
on and having a time of it. I can't remember their
clothes, but they were about a foot high and wore high
pointed caps and shoes. I called my sisters and they

were watching the same thing. It happened only once, and it lasted for about ten minutes. Then they vanished and were never seen again. With all their jumping round they didn't make a sound."

I visited one of Mr. Turner's sisters later. She could not remember the incident herself, but said her brother had all his life insisted it had happened.

CHAPTER ELEVEN

Haunted Houses and Poltergeists

HAVE you ever thought what it would be like to buy a house and then discover that it was haunted? Such a possibility would never enter your head nor mine. And if by any chance we hear of a house being haunted our eyes sparkle expectantly. We feel a delicious shiver running up our spine and we probably make some flippant and thoughtless remark and then forget all about it.

When I was collecting folklore in the summer of 1956 and also working upon this book, I mentioned what I was doing everywhere I went. In this way word got around and people were ready with their stories when I called. Others sent messages by friends and one of these concerned a house where hauntings were taking place at that very moment. I listened to all that was known about it but the stories did not always agree. Finally I realized that if I wanted to include the story in this book I must stop listening to rumours and visit the place myself.

It was a lovely day in August when we set out, and we had thirty miles to drive through a wooded back country road. My companion, at whose house I was staying, knew the people in the few scattered farms we passed, and I was glad of her companionship. By myself it would have been a lonely drive, and I would have bounced over the unpopulated sections at breakneck speed. No one had described the house we were looking for but, as we entered the village and saw a large frame house set well back in its own grounds I said without any hesitation, "That's it." I still have no idea why I was so sure.

The house stands back about one hundred feet from the road with an open field in front of it, a few apple trees beside it, and thick woods behind it composed mostly of coniferous trees. Although the house is large it would pass unnoticed were it not for a decorative piece attached to the centre front. This has three long windows with rounded tops both upstairs and down which, with its pitched roof, give an air of distinction to an otherwise plain frame dwelling. There are verandahs on either side at the front of the house, but the railings are broken and look as though the owner has lost heart in his place. Most of the small posts that would have given a finished touch in the old days have broken away and the result is depressing. The house is also in need of paint but could, without too great an expense, be made into quite a handsome dwelling. Why it has been allowed to get in its present state you will understand very soon.

When we began this trip we did not expect to find the owners at home, for we had been told they had left it. Possibly I would not have been so lighthearted if I had known I would have to view it both inside and out. A truck in the driveway gave evidence that it was occupied, and it was with quite a pleasant feeling of expectancy and adventure that we turned in at their driveway. We were in the midst of something now that was far removed from the usual daily round and our pulses raced quite happily.

There is a built-on porch at the side of the house next

the driveway and here I stopped my car, carefully turning it in case I might wish to leave suddenly. It usually happens in country places that someone comes to greet a stranger but here, the only person who seemed interested, was a lad about five years old. He was a quiet, nice-looking boy, and his appearance gave a sense of normality to the house. My companion remained in the car, not because she feared going in, but because she felt I might make better progress alone. In answer to my knock a woman's voice invited me to "come in."

The young wife was tall with auburn hair, blue eyes, and a restrained but not unfriendly manner. I realized she would want to know my business and lost no time in setting her mind at rest. Nevertheless I felt embarrassed. I had been told that she and her husband would talk freely and willingly, but I hadn't thought how difficult it would be calling on a perfect stranger to say, "I hear your house is haunted." I sensed at once that they did not treat their peculiar situation lightly and that they were in need of all the sympathy and warmth I could give them. I soon convinced her that we had not come from idle curiosity, and then she told me everything that had happened so far.

She pointed out that the house is not old, for it had been built in 1910. They had bought it in 1949 and had moved in then immediately after their marriage. They looked forward to working a good farm while, in the off season, there would be employment for her husband in the woods nearby. It was a bright outlook, but it did not last long. They had been in the house only a short time when they heard a person walk downstairs in the dead of night. Then they heard horses galloping up the driveway. It was April and there was snow on the ground, but no tracks. This continued for other nights so that they were losing their sleep. At first they kept their trouble to themselves and then decided to invite a few friends in to listen with them. Some heard the sounds of galloping horses, while others heard nothing unusual. By this time their nerves were frayed but they thought they should wait and see if the footsteps came again. When that happened, they moved to the wife's former home and stayed there until that September. They returned then to their own house where they lived undisturbed until April of 1956 when it began all over again.

This time the disturbances took the form of footsteps walking upstairs and the sound of heavy objects being dropped. When asked what sound these objects made she said it was a dead sound. That would mean without any echo or reverberation. There did not seem to be any pattern in these noises except that they always came at night. They might come before or after midnight and last only for a couple of minutes and stop, or they might go on for irregular intervals over a three- or four-hour period. One night when the footsteps were heard the wife's brother was sleeping there. He heard the steps come into his bedroom and he was struck on the face with a soft object which he has never identified.

One day the young couple were sitting in the kitchen when they saw an aspirin bottle quietly leave the pantry shelf. They watched in fascinated amazement as it slowly made its way to a shelf in the porch, with no human agency to transport it. The husband and wife were always together when strange things happened, so it was a shared experience. The footsteps have been heard mostly in the upstairs hall and bedroom, and never in the attic. Upon one occasion, when sitting together in the kitchen, they were frozen to their chairs as they heard slow, careful steps on the stairs as though an elderly person were making his way down. They had never seen their unwelcome visitor, and wondered if the mystery would be solved now. Instead, the steps turned in the opposite direction at the foot of the stairs and went into the parlour.

It was just before we arrived that the most shattering thing of all had happened and it was so alarming that they were once more frightened out of the house. (They were now occupying their own place during the daylight hours only, and were driving three miles every night to sleep in peace at the wife's former home as they had done before.) It had been a bright moonlight night and the wife was sleeping. Her husband was lying awake when the bedclothes were suddenly lifted off the bed to the height of about a foot above them where they were shaken violently, turned upside down, and dropped back crosswise upon the bed. As they dropped, the wife awakened. At the moment of their levitation her husband did not disturb her, probably because he was too terrified even to breathe. Not then, nor at any other time, did they see their tormentor.

All this was told by the young wife with a quiet dignity and a complete absence of anything dramatic or hysterical. I was thankful that we had come to the end of her recital before her husband decided to join us. I have seldom felt so sorry for any human being as I did for him, for he looked utterly crushed. He walked over to the couch which is part of the furniture of all our country kitchens, and huddled down in the farthest corner. I expressed my sympathy for all they had been through and said, "Do you mind talking about it?"

He replied truthfully, "It doesn't help any," and little wonder. His friends, no doubt with the best intentions in the world, kept telling him he only imagined these things and he was thoroughly sick of their remarks. When I asked if any of these doubting youths would sleep in the house alone he gave the nearest approach to a laugh I'd heard, and said very definitely, "No." The only real interest he showed was during the time I suggested things that might help them, for I wanted desperately to ease their burden. For instance I told them that I had been hearing of houses like this ever since I first went out looking for folk songs in 1928, and that my very first visit had been to the Hartlans of South-East Passage. There, I said, the family had built small houses around a dwelling which still stood in the centre and which they called their Ghost House. And, I said, they were very proud of it.

Proud of it? The young husband looked at me with an expression of complete incredulity. Proud of owning a ghost house? How could they be? If there had been any doubts in my mind about the sincerity of their belief in what they had told, they would have been dissipated now. It was beyond his comprehension that anybody could take pride in a situation as desperate as his. This then was no act they were putting on for the sake of notoriety; it was sheer misfortune.

We talked a little longer and then I left, but I asked if I might take photographs of the house. They showed no objection and, I think, were rather pleased although they were careful not to be taken themselves. I took pictures from all angles and, in some of these, included the little boy. I hoped they might show a shadowy figure in one of the windows perhaps. (Actually when they were developed I could see a form there, but it was caused by the draping of the curtains.) However these pictures did serve one useful purpose for, as we drove away, my companion remarked that she supposed they had shown me over the house. I said I had not gone beyond the kitchen. She was surprised because she had distinctly heard a window being raised upstairs while I was inside. On checking up later with the owners no window had been raised by them that day, nor was there anybody else in the house when I was there. Yet the picture shows a raised window.

After that it was impossible to forget the haunted house and its unfortunate occupants. The wife was serious, but it had not upset her as it had her husband. I learned later that he had been a robust young man before this happened, but that now he was wasting away. The continuous strain of fear engendered by the un-known, coupled with the realization that he had invested in a property that might be worthless, weighed heavily upon him. He had what can best be described as a beaten look. I therefore wondered if my going there was mere chance, or was it all part of a pattern? Could I perhaps help in some way, and what would that way be?

Not long before this I had met Mr. R. S. Lambert, and had been given a copy of his book, *Exploring the Supernatural*. We had also met briefly in Toronto. Since his book deals mainly with haunted houses I wrote and outlined the case, and asked what he thought about it. He replied promptly and at length. Then with his suggestions which included the assurance that nothing could happen to them beyond a very bad fright, and my own all too limited knowledge, I wrote them as reas-suringly as I could. I also tried to infuse a feeling of interest in their house by asking them to write down any-thing that happened so it could be used in scientific research. I thought this might give them something new to think about as well as a fresh feeling of self respect which was greatly needed at that time. I also sent them a copy of a book I had written, *The Folklore of Lunen-burg County*, thinking that perhaps some of its ghost stories might help them, and told how they could get the Lambert book at the nearest library.

From then on whenever I settled down to my night's sleep my thoughts would turn to the young couple and the atmosphere in which they lived, and this was also the experience of my companion of that day. I decided then to talk to everybody I could find who might have information about the place in the hope that some help-ful light might be thrown upon this case. I learned first that they had both grown up in the same village, but that ghost stories were not much of a subject of conversation in the wife's home. In the husband's home, however, they were often talked about and believed, and many of their beliefs had been brought from Scotland by their ancestors.

First I visited a man of middle age who had once spent a night in the house, with the intention of speaking to the ghost if it appeared. It had been a quiet night with the intense quiet you get nowhere but in the country. There was not a sound, not even a mouse, for the house is free of rodents or any other animals; he was disappointed. He told me of a friend, however, who had spent a night there when he heard steps but, upon looking back, he could not remember whether they had been going up the stairs or down. But they were indoors; of that he was sure.

From various sources I learned about the former occupants and also that the present owner attributed the visitations to drownings in a nearby lake. In both cases these had taken place in April just before the noises were heard. I soon discounted this theory because the people who were drowned had no connection either with the house or any of the people who had lived there. The occupant immediately preceding the family I had gone to see had lived alone. He was described as a quiet, respectable bachelor, and one not likely to have left any unsolved problems behind when he died. There had been other houses on the property, but not on this particular location.

Only one unexplainable event seems to have taken place in a former occupancy. It happened one evening when a few young men were in the house playing cards and the lamp shade suddenly lifted itself up from the lamp, rose a few feet in the air, and then returned to its place on the lamp again. This sort of thing occurs occasionally before a death in a family, but that was not the reason in this case. If this was caused by any supernatural force it would show that strange things happen whether the present owners are there or not. Rumour has it that a group of boys drove up to the house one evening this year when it was empty and heard strains of beautiful music flowing out, but I had no opportunity to check on this. What I did hear from an eye-witness came from a man of middle age, rather serious and quiet, who is deeply concerned for the misfortunes of his young friends. He said that he was driving home from work at five o'clock one evening when he and his friends noticed a door on the side porch of the house slightly ajar. There are two doors here, but the one facing the road is securely bolted and is never used. They drove up to investigate and, as they expected, there was no one home. They found a storm door outside somewhere and nailed it over the open door so that no one could make an entrance. Then they reported it all to the owner who said he had left twenty minutes before, and everything had been intact.

There is now no way of discovering whether the first occupants ever heard anything because they have all passed away. If anything had happened during their lifetime they kept it to themselves. A former school teacher who spent two winters there is sure nothing happened while he was in the house. He knew its history and said that only one other family had ever lived there. They were old when they died and one, who was blind, had suffered a long illness. Another was an unmarried woman and a tyrant who made it her business to see that everybody worked hard. She not only organized the home but the people of the village as well, presiding over various organizations where she was feared by all, for her word was law. If any departed spirit had come back he felt she was the logical one. The farm had been prosperous in her day. Now it has only one man to work it, and he spends much of his time in the woods cutting timber. Could it be that she resents this fact and hopes to frighten them away, thus making it available to another family who might keep the place up according to her standards? I passed this thought on to the young couple because a crabbed old woman being a nuisance would not be as formidable as some of the horrors they had envisaged. My only other suggestion is that the house may have been built upon an unknown grave.

In the midst of this investigation I was invited to appear on television. I told a ghost story, but not this one in case the place would be besieged with curious visitors. Later I told the interviewer without, however, mentioning the location. The following day he called on me, for he too could not get the family off his mind. Feeling sure that he would not exploit them I finally gave him the address and he wrote some months later to say he had been there and had cleared up some of the doubtful points for me. It seems they had read in my *Folklore of Lunenburg County* that a ghost comes only every seven years, although I am at a loss to know where they got that information. Nothing however had been heard since my visit, so they were planning to remain there as long as the place keeps quiet. Nevertheless they no longer take any pleasure in this house so they are preparing lumber for a new one and, as soon as the sawing is completed, they will start to build.

For the present that is where the matter rests. They have promised to let us know if the sounds return when we will go there for a night or more if necessary. This ghost is unpredictable and never comes at specified times. I cannot say that I look forward to it with any great joy, but I would like to get to the bottom of it. I shall probably face it with chattering teeth and knocking knees, but not alone. Oh no! I'm not that brave. And who knows? With a prayer of exorcism in hand we may be able to release some poor earthbound soul to an eternal rest and, at the same time, make life a joyous thing again for the present owners. Confidentially however I will admit that if this can be done by other means than mine I will not cry with frustration. Would you?

This is not the only case we have of houses in which blankets have been removed at night. They are usually pulled off rudely and without warning. A Clarke's Harbour ghost seems to have been given to tidy habits. Here Miss Beth McNintch was sleeping in a room where an older woman had died two years before. Up to that time all had been quiet here. This night however she had her cat at the foot of the bed. "It was daylight, about eight o'clock in the morning, and suddenly the clothes were pulled off and folded over evenly as though in pleats. They went all the way to the foot of the bed and at this moment the cat jumped and fled from the room." This was not repeated because she made no attempt to sleep again, unlike the father of my New Brunswick singer Mr. Dornan, who was sleeping many years ago in a New York house. He was wakened with a heavy weight on his chest; then the bedclothes were pulled down. He pulled them up and went back to sleep only to have them pulled down again, this time to his feet. Now fully awake, once more he pulled them up, and had a good grip on them. He held them as tightly as he could, but they were jerked away and he was left completely uncovered. He asked who was there but received no answer so he swore at the unseen intruder, also without any response. He never slept there again, and he said it was his one encounter with the supernatural.

The story is told of a man who taught school in Antigonish and who roomed a short distance from the town. In this house the lights would flicker and go out, the bedclothes were lifted above the bed, and the bed would shake. He said nothing to the people who owned the house, but he found a room elsewhere and left. Eventually he told some of his friends about it and they thought it very funny. They dared him to go back, so he did. The owners were delighted and probably wondered why he had left and then returned. By this time the ghostly visitant had retired and nothing more occurred.

Another house with a history of bedclothes being removed was at South Uniacke. This was a big two-and-a-half-storied flat roofed house that used to be a tavern, and a woman is said to have been killed there after a fight. "At night we would hear a rumbling. There was a winding stairs in that house that went all the way to the roof and there was a nice place up there to sit. When we first moved there we would hear a noise on the roof and go up to investigate but, by the time we got there, the noise would be downstairs. It sounded like a barrel going bumpety bump when it was downstairs, but like cats when it was on the roof. The light in our room would go out and there'd be nothing wrong with it, and once, when I was there alone, the door opened and shut.

"My husband knew something about the house he wouldn't tell me, any more than that I was not to go to the back end of it. Any time we went up to the roof we always took the baby with us because we didn't like leaving it alone. The people who had lived there before us couldn't stay, and we heard later that children who slept there after we left, had the clothes ripped right off their beds. When we were there I provided meals for lumbermen and sometimes the men slept there. It was a big house and in good repair. One night there were so many of these men that the place was full and some of them had to sleep on the floor. They were still awake when a sound disturbed them and, from the one dim light that was kept burning, they saw six men in old-fashioned clothes walking through the house. They used to say too that at milking time people would hear the tinkling sound of cow bells, and several nights when the men were playing cards the door would open and shut with no wind, a stout latch, and no person to touch it."

There are people who get used to sounds made in their homes by phantom visitors and look upon their arrival as a sign of good fortune. At East Ferry near Tiverton one house had an occasional welcome ghost of this kind and another, where a man lived alone, had one that was there most of the time. It was company for him and, although they never talked together, he was glad to have him around.

Such cases are the exception and certainly did not apply to a house in a residential section of Halifax. About seventy years ago a well-known family named Tuttle lived there. Miss Tuttle, who was elderly at the time she talked to me, remembered as a child being in a room and something white going through it which left a cold breath of air in its wake. She was old enough at the time to notice when this happened that the older women in the house were very frightened. When she grew older, her mother told her that the fire tongs were often moved about in that house and that in one room they were particularly active. Also that often she had no sooner put the children to bed than the clothes would be off them, but not cast aside as a child would do. This was a frequent occurrence. (I often pass this house today and wonder if these things still happen. I doubt it, for it has been occupied continuously and has a prosperous look.)

The cold breath of air left behind by the figure in white reminds me of an Oyster Pond house and an icy hand felt there. "My daughter and her husband had a rented house. They had a little boy and they wanted me to stay with him one evening while they went to a big supper and dance at Head Jeddore. It was a rainy night and I didn't like being there alone so I told them to be sure to shut all the doors and windows and, when they left, I tried them to see that this had been done.

"It was some time before the baby went to sleep but, after I'd got him settled, I thought I'd lay down on the couch in the kitchen beside him. After I'd been there just a little while, and before I'd had time to fall asleep, there was a hand like ice came over my face. I opened my eyes and it went swish into the next room and over the piano. I got up and thought, 'What can that be?' I didn't think of a ghost, but I was very frightened and I got the baby ready to leave in case we had to get out for any reason. When the young people came home at twelve o'clock and I went to let them in, my teeth were chattering. Jack said, 'You're cold. Why didn't you keep the fire going?' I didn't tell them what happened but I had to sleep there because it was pouring rain, and the room I slept in was just above the dining-room where the icy hand had seemed to come from.

"Soon after that I was at Aunt Lide's house. She was going there to stay and I said, 'Aunt Lide, I wouldn't be you and stay in that house tonight,' and her daughter said, 'Aunt Jessie, what did you see?' I told them and then Aunt Lide told what had happened to her one time when she was there. She said she was sitting by the window and the window pane took to shaking. Her hand was steady, so she tried holding it against the window but the pane still shook. She said the same thing had happened one night when Elsie and Jack were there alone, while, at the same time, the pump kept running and nothing they could do would stop it. The house had a name of people moving out almost as fast as they moved in and somebody asked the owner one time why that was.

" 'There's nobody lives in that house can live there in peace,' he said, 'because there was a family there once who had turned their own father out and had treated him cruelly. While he was still alive things began to happen. First a son had gone to sleep when he heard a racket like someone at the window, so he got his gun and went out on the road. It was a beautiful moonlight

night and he couldn't see anyone about, so he went back
to the house but he didn't even try to sleep. Nothing
happened until another night when he was reading the
paper. After a while he got sleepy and laid down on the
couch. The paper was still in his hand when it was
whipped off on the floor. There was no wind to have
blown it there. He picked it up and put it on the table
and whip, off it went again. This happened three times,'
he said. 'When this same son was buried and they were
ready to take the coffin out, there was the awfullest racket
under the house like a beam falling. Everybody heard
it, and three men went down to investigate, but nothing
was out of place. It happened just under his body. They
allowed that whatever it was, went out of the house
with him. It had been a very unhappy house and something of that must have remained when Jack and Elsie
were there, but it must be all over now because the
people in the house today have never heard anything.' "

Cornwall tells of a fine old couple who had been
treated badly by their sons. After they died, voices were
heard at night, and the sons were forced to build a new
house. They moved out, but the house continued to show
signs of occupation by showing lights at night as though
they were still living there. In Charlottetown Mr.
Dougald McKinnon said that it was a belief that the
spirit of a person who oppressed the poor might be
around for generations. It would be heard going through
the house slamming doors and moaning, but it would not
be seen, and it could not rest.

There is a house at Thorne's Cove where slaves used
to be kept and were said to have been treated cruelly.
Also at this same spot a pedlar lost his life. Pedlars
seem to have been fair game, judging by the number
reported to have been murdered. It must have been a
temptation, for they carried what money they made with
them, and they would be defenceless on a lonely road.
One man who passed this particular house would do so

only in daylight because he said when he went there at night a pedlar always came out and chased him. Whether it was the pedlar or the slaves who caused the hauntings inside the house has not been determined, but the doors rattled there, their latches lifted, and there were strange noises that had no meaning. Mr. Abram Thorne came home one night and had just got into bed when he heard a sound in the hall "like the jumping and shuffling of two men. I thought it was my father playing a trick but when I got up to see, father and mother were both asleep in their bed and there was no one to be seen. I often seen doors open and close in that house and no explanation for it. Only certain ones would hear and see them. Others would live in the house for years and never hear a thing."

A curious legend has grown up about a stick that murdered a pedlar at a place in Cape Breton called Slios a Bhrochan. Here, according to my informant, a professor, the stick can be chopped up at night but, in the morning, it is always back in its place intact.

An interesting haunting took place in a house about a mile and a half from St. Croix towards Ellershouse, where Mr. Freeman Harvey is supposed to have been murdered by an Englishman named Stanley. "This Stanley used to do a lot of buying and selling. He was a small man, very polished and polite, but he must have been strong because Mr. Harvey was strong too, although at that time he was deaf. We think they must have had quite a tussle. This would be about seventy years ago.

"The reason Stanley murdered Harvey was because he wanted to buy his place. Mr. Harvey was a tax collector and Stanley got in with him and then wanted to buy him out. Harvey got talked round to selling, but he wasn't in any hurry about it and thought he'd like to go away first on a trip. Stanley didn't like that idea and he got impatient. Maybe he didn't intend to go that far but he killed him, and cut his head off as well, so he must have been carrying a knife.

"When Harvey was dead, Stanley had nothing to take the body away in so he pushed it into the cellar under some potato bags and he put the head in a bag under a bucket—a wooden measure. Then he moved a family in with him named Fisher and told them Harvey had gone away. They had a friend named McCarthy who lived with them and they all drank a lot. They were there for a whole week and ate potatoes from the bag without knowing what was under it.

"After the murder, noises began in the kitchen at night that sounded like wrestling. The Fishers would investigate and the noises would move to another room. They allowed the fight had begun in the front hall because there were splashes of blood there and there was a bloody imprint on the wall that nobody was ever able to cover over. It would come through paint or whitewash or whatever they put on. It was the same in the cellar later on, for no matter how much they dug, the blood could not be dug out of the spot where Stanley had put the body.

"After a while the Fishers got suspicious and McCarthy informed on Stanley and suggested that Harvey had been murdered. Nobody paid attention until one day when Fisher went down the cellar. Until then Stanley had always got the potatoes himself and wouldn't let anybody else go down, but they decided it was time they looked around themselves. The first thing they found was a boot under the potatoes, and then they gave the alarm. Stanley had bought a wagon intending to take the body away, but it was discovered before he could get it off his hands. He confessed then, and it all came out. Other people lived in the house later but, until the time that it burned down, the blood stains remained to remind them of the murder."

In another old house in the same village the owners

used to hear knockings on the floor and table, and the local people thought there had been sudden death here following a fight between the French and English. The sounds went on for quite a while and then stopped.

Nova Scotia fishing craft have always sailed beyond our own waters and on one of these cruises Mr. Doyle of West Jeddore was in the crew. "I saw a man. We were in the Labrador. We started down there in a barque and she went ashore. There was a little island with a factory on it so we went in there to spend the night and we left our provisions in the dory.

"In this factory the place was full of cages with just enough alleyway to go through. We went upstairs to the boss's room. There were some big boilers abreast of that room and the window was clear so there was plenty of light while it lasted. We went in and sat down and sang songs. I'd sing and then my brother'd sing. There were three of us. After a while we decided to lay down and go to sleep and we each found a bag to use for a pillow. By and by we heard a boat rowing. It was moonlight then and calm and my brother went to the window but he couldn't see any boat. We got laying still and we heard it again and it was getting closer and we still couldn't see any boat. Then we heard it next to the window. It was light as day, but no boat to be seen. Then we heard it again and this time he was up to our dory.

"By now we didn't like it much but we laid down and tried to get some sleep. Then punkedy punk we heard the man from the boat in the factory below. He carried on for an hour and I couldn't get any sleep. I was lying there looking towards the door and first thing I see a tall man with a slouch hat and two tossels hung down from the hat and his face was white. He stood and looked down at me brother Joe quite a spell. Then he came to me and I looked right up at him. Then he looked at Cedlock and he went to the window and done the same thing coming back. You couldn't hear a sound from his feet as you would of if he'd been human. When he left us and went downstairs again I took the gun and woke the other men. By this time he had stopped his noise so we decided to sit up and make a fire in the stove.

"At last I got so hungry and thirsty that I couldn't stand it any longer and I went out those long steps and through that alleyway and when I opened the door it shut behind me though I had purposely left it open. I got to the dory and I got a big drink of water. Then I got the grub and got the door open again; I kept going and it was just like he was grabbing me from behind. All the time I felt something trying to pull me back, but I kept going and finally reached the other men. For the rest of the night we took watch about and kept the fire on but towards daylight Joe said, 'It's all right now,' and he went sound asleep and he knew nothing more till he found himself standing up on the floor. He never knew how he got there, nor did we. My brother Joe died quite a spell after that and he was the first to go. Whether this had anything to do with it or not I don't know, but I have often wondered if that was why Joe was the first one he looked at."

In the days when Devil's Island had some fifty inhabitants there was one house that was noted for the extraordinary things that happened in it. This treeless little island at the mouth of Halifax Harbour, one mile in circumference, was then a thriving fishing community. Small boats were used, and men would fish singly or with a companion. The Atlantic Ocean was at their door, so they did not have far to go.

One day when Henry Henneberry was out, his wife heard him return and walk into the kitchen. The flopping of his rubber boots was a familiar sound. At that particular moment, as she heard him moving noisily about, he was drowned. In his absence she had been painting the floor, and his footsteps appeared in the fresh paint. She had also washed a mat that morning and had left it lying on another floor and his footprint was plainly outlined here as well.

Fires used to occur in this house in a mysterious manner. You could put your hand on the shingles and they would not be hot even though you could see the fire burning. All of the people who have lived in the house have been Roman Catholics, and they always put palm in the rafters for protection. This palm, blessed in the church and given out on Palm Sunday, would never be touched although the fire would burn all around it. Different families lived in the house, and they all had the same experience. One man described the fires as five or six blue blazes that were not "natural" fires. One family insisted that the house collapsed on them one night and that they got out of bed and said their rosaries after which the house went back to its proper shape again. They even tried putting the house on a different foundation but it still caught fire, this time under the roof. Here, with no water supply except from wells, it would be a major calamity to have a house catch fire because it would be almost impossible to put it out, so this is further proof that the fires had some strange unexplainable quality.

One day another Mrs. Henneberry was sitting beside the kitchen window with her baby daughter Henrietta beside her when she saw her husband fall out of his boat. He must have been knocked over by the boom because the boat kept coming towards the island as though he were still in it. She was very ill after he was drowned and lived only a few years but, during that time, she often heard her husband and mother calling her. Friends staying with her would hear the voices too, while others would hear nothing. She could not be left alone, so one evening two of the men went over to sit with her. "I was sitting by the window on the south side when all of a sudden there was one of the awfullest odours that ever could be smelt by anybody came in through the window. It came and went, almost like a flash of lightning, and we both smelt it. When her mother died Henrietta was hale and hearty but when we came back from the funeral she was sitting up in her high chair dead and nobody knew why. After that they locked the house up for nine months and then Dave Henneberry moved in. One night his friend Alf Welch was visiting him when they jumped almost to the roof from the sound of lumber moving. There was lumber in the house at the time, but it lay neatly in its place. Mr. Welch was so frightened that he had to be taken home."

Dave stayed in that house three years and then his brother John moved in. During John's occupancy there were three fires and the family heard unaccountable noises. Then Mr. Edwards took it and tried shifting furniture around upstairs and all manner of things to make it habitable, but the ghost would not be quieted. One midnight as they were leaving after a party one of the men had his hand on the door latch when he heard three knocks. They were heard only by the owner and the man who told about it. They came a second time, but there was no one asking for admittance and anyhow, on this island where the people were all related, nobody waited to knock but just walked in. The third time the knocks came they were heard from inside the house and by all the assembled company.

These, however, were mild compared with what the children told. Some were frightened because they saw a man in oilskins walking through the rooms, but the worst experience came to a young son of one of the occupants. He would come to his father in the night and say there was a baby in bed with him all dressed in white and that he couldn't pacify it. This baby was supposed to be Henrietta.

The house was finally demolished, but some of the

neighbours decided to make use of the wood from which
it had been built. Almost immediately they had bad luck.
Nobody ever liked the house. One couple who lived
there always had something happen on the twentieth of
the month. The Islanders say that one of the early
owners of the house was drowned while he still owed a
small debt upon it and they think if someone had settled
the debt the disturbances would have stopped. As far
as I am concerned personally, I regret that I was not
more interested in the house when I was staying on the
island. Every waking moment was devoted to collecting
songs. Fortunately I jotted down most of the things
they told me, and I can recall the fear in the voices of
both men and women as we walked by and they talked
about it. I am sure there were many more experiences
that I might have had first hand if I had realized then
the importance of every slightest detail connected with
the haunting of a house. In those days it looked to me
like a bleak, unpainted, and unfriendly frame dwelling,
and I was glad to leave it to the wind and the weather
and any family unfortunate enough to have to live there.
The house is gone now and so are the people; there is
no one left but the lightkeeper and his family.

People brought up on stories of the spirit world do
not necessarily look for them at every corner. Nevertheless when things take place that follow certain familiar
patterns they are not slow in coming to a conclusion.
Men who hunt and fish and spend most of their lives
in the woods or on the water are not as a rule afraid
of the dark. They are accustomed to bunking down in
all kinds of places and give it little thought. I have
been amazed however in talking to retired sea captains
to have them occasionally admit that there are certain
houses they would never sleep in again, due to visitations
they have experienced there. Guides too have their
stories like this one from Moser's River.

"I was up early in the fall one year on the trapping

ground and I got acquainted with a fellow and he let me have his camp. It was brand new and beside a big lake; Liscomb Lake it was and I went up early in the afternoon. There was an old dam there, and by the outlet there was a boat turned over and no oars in it. I needed the boat because the camp, was on an island. I hunted up a pole to use for oars and tipped the boat over. Then I let the water out and rowed the best I could with the pole to the island. When I got there the door of the camp was open and I thought that very strange. I cut myself some wood for the night and then I went inside. There I saw a bench upset on the floor and a cup and saucer and a piece of bread with one bite taken out of it. A bucket of water stood on the floor and there was a bag with bread in it that must have been a month old. I began to think about the boat having drifted down to the dam and the door being open and things so upset and I thought it must have been left in a hurry. I remembered too that the owner hadn't been out for a long time, so whatever it was, he wouldn't know about it.

"The door was big and heavy and I thought I'd feel better if I closed it and I even put a bar against it. There were strawberries there in a bottle and I ate these with some bread I'd brought with me and I put a fire on and made a cup of tea. There were no blankets, but I'm used to sleeping in the open, so I had a smoke and then laid down on the bed and went to sleep. It didn't seem that I'd been asleep long before I woke up and felt cold. I got up and found that the door I'd closed and barred so carefully was wide open. I had set the table on its legs and put the mouldy bread back on it, but now the table was upset, the bread was back on the floor just as I'd found it, and the wood that I'd moved was back where it had been when I arrived.

"I shut the door again and put another big bar against it and I piled all the wood I could get and put it on the table and shoved that against the door too. I had another smoke and went to sleep a second time and again I woke to find the door open and and all the things put back as I'd found them. No animal could have done it, and certainly no human being, and anyhow a guide like me wakes up at the slightest sound and it wasn't noise that woke me but the cold air from the open door. I got up and closed the door again and made up another fire, but this time I decided I'd had enough sleep for one night. After that nothing else happened and I left after daylight.

"The next year I went back, but this time I had a friend with me. When we got up to the camp we saw a sign on the door and the sign said, 'This place is haunted.' Somebody else must have slept there and had the same experience. I never was able to get to the bottom of it." (If this had happened to those of us who live in the city we would at once have written to the owner and started an investigation. Many of our country people are not like that but will await a hoped-for meeting. If this fails to take place nothing more is done about it, even though the desire to talk it over is very great. Our guide and the owner had never crossed paths again, and so the mystery remained unsolved.)

We go now to what was known as the old Robinson cottage on the New Ross road. Mr. Croft said, "We'd been told that it was haunted but we were young and not afraid. One night we were sitting in a large room on the ground floor when we heard what was like a man with heavy boots on going upstairs. There were people living on the other side of the house and I wouldn't have thought anything about it if I hadn't heard stories about the house, so I thought I'd see if one of them had gone up. They hadn't, so we got axes and knives and clubs and went upstairs but we couldn't find our man. Some weeks after, we heard him coming down the stairs again.

"One night I'd been shopping at Chester Basin and

had just come back when I heard some womankind run through the hall and brush against the wall. Women wore long skirts then, and hers made a swishing sound as she ran. I thought it was a friend of my wife's playing a joke, so I went through to the kitchen. I said to myself, 'I'll put my parcels down and light a lamp and find her.' I hunted through every part of the house and, all the while, our little dog was barking so hard I thought it was going crazy. I couldn't find anybody. Then I thought it must have been my wife, but she'd been in the next house all the time.

"That was bad, but the worst of all happened to a man from a vessel who stayed here before we took the house, and he used to sleep upstairs. There had been a child born in that house and it was known to have done a lot of screaming. This man heard the child in the night and in the morning he asked the woman of the house what was the matter with her child that it screamed and cried all night. At that time there were a lot of ships' knees here and they were stored in the house. When the last ones were finally moved away they found what they thought must be the body of this child. It must have been murdered and hidden away. My wife heard of these stories and they got on her nerves so much at night that she would dream of a child with nothing but bones coming down the chimney hole asking for food. We decided before long that we'd had enough of that house and we moved away. In time it was burned down because no one could live there for long."

The next house is still standing so I cannot reveal its location. "I was born in Amherst and, when I was a few months old, we moved to a great shell of a house. It had been partly built by a man whose son went overseas in the First World War. It wasn't finished when he left, and his father kept working on it until the son was killed. He abandoned it then and eventually sold it to my father in 1919. Daddy was a carpenter, so he made a very nice looking dwelling of it.

"From the time I was old enough to notice things I didn't like that house. I was afraid of the living-room although it was light and airy and had a southeast exposure and six windows. I felt quite safe in the kitchen and dining-room, but I had literally to be paid to go upstairs on errands for one of the family. Mama always kept the light burning at bedtime because I was afraid of the dark. When I was nine my sister became engaged. One evening she and her future husband were keeping house and they were expecting mama to come in at any moment. When they heard the front door open they rose to greet her but the steps continued up the great stairs and they didn't sound like her steps which were light. The stairs are three times wider than you find in houses built today. The person wandered into all the rooms but, when Vic and Freda called out, the steps ceased. They were young and afraid, but they knew I was sleeping alone up there so they took the lamp and searched in all the rooms, even going to the attic. They could find no one, so they went back to the dining-room. They had just got seated when the footsteps started again. They came down the stairs, through the dark kitchen, and then the door of the dining-room where they were sitting began to push open. They were terrified. Vic called, 'Get out!' The steps retreated to the front door. It opened and closed, and silence reigned. They made a dash then to see who was walking away from the house but there was nobody in sight and not a footmark in the fresh snow. Until then they had supposed it was a human who had walked in, but now they were really afraid and they were huddled together on the couch when mama finally came home. They told her about it and she only laughed at them but, from that time, Vic has never spent a night in that house. I often wondered after they were married why he always left the house at bedtime, and it wasn't until I was twenty that I found out. Nobody had told me what had happened that night, so this had nothing to do with my fear of the house.

"One Christmas there were six of us at home when a great crash sounded through the house. We pushed our chairs back and all rushed to the living-room crying, 'The Christmas tree!' for we were sure it had fallen over. There stood the tree in its finery intact, and not so much as a needle was out of place.

"One fine summer day Freda, Hazel, and I were listening to the radio in the living-room when we heard groans as if someone were in agony. My dad had nightmares sometimes and that was what it sounded like, but he wasn't home. The groans were terrible and Peggy, the spaniel, howled and the hair stood up on the back of her neck. She would always go anywhere with me for she was my beloved companion. I tried to coax her down the cellar with me but she wouldn't go. This cellar was well lighted, so we three girls went down, following the groans until we came to an alcove and there they ceased. I was all for digging right there on the spot, and I've always felt if I had that I'd have found the cause of all our trouble. Perhaps someone's bones were there, or the son who had been killed might have put something in the ground and wanted to tell us about it. We moved away soon after that, and mama would never let me ask the people living there today if they have heard anything. We were all glad to get out of that house."

Our next haunting took place in Tantallon. "My uncle married a crippled woman who walked with a cane. When her fifth child was born she and the baby died and, after that, my uncle tried to get a housekeeper but, no matter who he got, none of them would stay. One was a fine educated woman and the children liked her so much they wouldn't sleep anywhere but in the room with her, and the little ones had to be right in the bed with her. She said that at night she could feel a hand reach across and cover the children in her bed.

"When she left, he got a married woman who said she wasn't scared. She said she'd take two children with her for the day, and the other two would go to school. They did that but, when they'd come back to the house at night, there would always be something in a different position from the way they left it. One night everything was upset, including the pantry door that wouldn't stay shut any more. One evening my brother came home and said, 'I saw a woman standing in Uncle Jack's window with long black hair and a baby in her arms.' She was the children's mother. I was in the house a lot after that and I often thought I could hear her coming up the steps, and I could hear her cane.

"For years the pantry door refused to close, so in time they tore the pantry out altogether and practically the whole of the downstairs was changed. To this day the oldest girl who lives in the States won't go in that house by herself. It seemed as though their mother just wouldn't leave them alone, but had to be around covering the children up at night and doing things in the house to make sure they would remember her."

Another Tantallon story is about a man named John Hershman who was supposed to have had money. When he was dying he said, "I'll be there to watch it; I'll be there to watch it." "Years ago the old Halifax road used to come up around the shore and over the hill, and old Hershman used to take a short cut along this way. When my father's house was built it went right over his footfalls, and father and mother would hear his footsteps coming in the front door and out the back, but he was never seen. Father had heard that if you moved the doors around a ghost couldn't find its way out, so he moved the back door and a window. That didn't stop it and the sounds went on until they felt they couldn't stand it any longer and the house was torn down. He had a certain way of walking and, after they heard the sounds first and realized they were Hershman's, they remembered those last words and that he had so often walked this road, so they felt that must be the reason for it."

In a Port Medway house where the family cherished its small holdings lights would be seen in the kitchen after they died. The saying in the village was, "Three lights in John McVicar's kitchen. Where's all his gold and silver now?"

A Shelburne house was supposed to be haunted. "I can assure you it was, for when we were children our house was burned and we slept there. All the first night there were sounds of men running up and down the stairs and I said to my mother, 'Why don't those people keep quiet?' I was only eight years old and my mother didn't say anything. She couldn't understand them herself, and she didn't want to frighten me.

"Another night a truck kept running up and down the steps, or at least that is what it sounded like. It was very noisy as you can imagine. Another time five of us were there when someone came to the door and asked for my father. We said he was out, and then the windows opened by themselves and shook, and this kept up for two hours. At the same time the heavy batten doors opened too. We thought there must be a lot of fishermen outside who were trying to get in. Then in the midst of all this confusion there came a little ring on the door as gentle as it could be. A woman was there and she was surprised when we told her what had happened because she had not seen a sign of anybody around the house as she had come up to it, and that was when the noises were at their worst. In the same house musical instruments played without anybody touching them, for they stood in the corner all the time. We couldn't understand what it was all about until after we left, and then we heard that the place was haunted. We'd have been a good deal more frightened if we'd known that."

A house that used to stand on Henshaw's Point had a reputation for being haunted, but the only thing anyone is known to have heard there was a man saying the Lord's Prayer. In a Seabright house near there we find another tidy ghost like the one at Clarke's Harbour who folded bedclothes in pleats. "A lame carpenter used to own this house and he had a lot of lumber. One night when I was fourteen I had just gone to bed when this awful racket started like a crippled fellow moving around upstairs. He'd hobble to one end of the room and back, and he'd drop the lumber bang on the floor, and he kept this up for a quite a while. Others in the house downstairs didn't hear it. I was too frightened to get up and look, so I didn't say anything. The man had been dead ten years. I wasn't the only one who knew he came back because a woman who lived there before us said she saw him one night." The mother then took up the story.

"For two years whenever I put the clothes on the line I'd find them all knotted. There's plenty of wind blows around here, but wind couldn't do it like that, and there was no accounting for it and, when I'd go to put on my apron, it would be pleated as lovely as could be. Next thing the head of the lobster pot would be shoved out of place. There were nights when I couldn't go to sleep for the noises. I often heard a fellow walking upstairs when there was no living person up there at all." The sceptical reader may say the noises were caused by rats, but this is a house where I spent many hours and I am sure nothing of that kind would have been tolerated. In fact to me the house had a pleasant atmosphere, unlike some that I have been in. This of course may have been caused by the present owners who are kindly, giving people.

Murder can be followed by something worse than hanging as one man could testify. He lived with a farmer in the Annapolis Valley, and there was a settlement of negroes nearby. One day a negro came close to the property and the farmer told his helper to fire at the coloured man. He only meant to frighten him, but the farmhand was a better shot than he realized and he killed the man. He was considerably shaken by his act and left the farm and went to Sherbrooke where he rafted logs. But there was no peace here because whenever he rafted them a black figure would climb up on his raft. He moved his house three or four times, thinking this might help, but he still came. Whether he changed his occupation or the ghost got tired my informant did not know, but he said it was a very frightening experience while it lasted.

From Liverpool there is a story of a house at Brooklyn near Taylor's Mill. A sea captain used to live there. "Two men were there when they both heard casks rolling upstairs and, when they went up, the casks were heard down below. This is quite a trick of a ghost and they decided to beat it at its own game, if this is what it was, so one went up and the other down. That only made it worse, for the sounds were heard everywhere. A while later a carpenter took the house and he had a man come to work for him and he gave him a room at the head of the stairs. In the night he woke up and heard someone come up the stairs and walk along the hall and get a piece of lumber and take it down again. He wondered about it because it was such a strange thing for a person to be doing in the dead of night. He supposed it was the carpenter and, in the morning, he asked him why he was up getting lumber in the night. The carpenter had to say something so he dismissed it lightly.

" 'That's nothing,' he said, 'I've often heard things like that.' Then the workman asked if the house was haunted and the carpenter had to admit it was and after a while he too moved away."

A house reported from East Chester had the same kind of aggravating steps that moved to another part of the house as soon as the first place was investigated. They could never find out what caused the steps, and they concluded someone must be buried there, perhaps beneath the house. No one could live there in peace.

In some places where a ghost is too active the family will build a new house on the same property hoping to live there without being disturbed, but this does not always happen. There was a house on the Georgefield Road between Kennetcook and Shubenacadie whose former owner was buried nearby. It was a big house and was occupied by a coloured family but, among other things, the doors slammed and things were thrown around to such an extent that they found the place uninhabitable. It finally got so bad that they built shacks all around the property. The former owner, whom they felt was responsible for the trouble in the big house, was not satisfied with this either, and followed them to their little homes. At last they decided they might as well give up the struggle and they abandoned the property. It is the only place in the Kennetcook area with a story of being haunted. This sounds like a poltergeist case, but I did not have an opportunity to meet any of the family, and so could not learn any further details.

Victoria Beach reports a gun being haunted. The reason is that it has been in four different houses and they have all burned down. This seems more than coincidence, so the gun is held responsible.

There are stories about the Sam Slick House in Windsor and the Uniacke House at Mount Uniacke, houses that were occupied by prominent families in earlier days, and have been restored by the provincial government and opened for public inspection. I have little information about the Uniacke house except that a former member of the family is supposed to have been seen on numerous occasions sitting in a chair in the beautiful garden that overlooks a lake.

The Sam Slick House has Miss Flo Anslow, a lifelong resident of Windsor, as its curator. She loves every inch of the grounds and every tiniest splinter in the house. She told me that many years ago a number of the Black Watch regiment were marching through Windsor to Annapolis and they went through this property. As they were passing the pond one of the men dropped his watch. He reached over to get it, lost his balance and fell in. He was never seen again. The man was a piper, so the place became known as Piper's Pond. "As children we were told that if we ran around the pond twenty times a soldier would come up on a horse's back. People often ran nineteen times, but they always lost their courage on the twentieth. The old pond was reputed to be bottomless but it was cleared in 1939. It was fifteen feet deep. Wagon wheels were found in it and lots of other things, but no bones. They lined it with stones and put a mud turtle in, but the turtle wouldn't stay."

From other Windsor sources I was told that Judge Haliburton was supposed to come out through a secret door in the panelled wall of the reception hall where he would wander around and then disappear through the panel again. Two former residents said they got quite accustomed to having him around. The house was in great disrepair before being restored, and children in Windsor used to hear the old people telling that it was haunted. They used to go up to the house and peek through the windows and they claim to have seen ladies and gentlemen of an earlier day dancing. Miss Anslow says she has stayed in the house many evenings and has never seen anything, but that does not prove anything because she may not have what we might call the seeing eye. However she did have a story of the panel. One former resident had a cutting made so that part of the wall was movable, and a chair placed behind a panel so that when he saw a visitor coming he disliked, he would go in there and sit down. That may explain some of the reports of a man being seen coming and going there, but it would not apply to the two families who grew accustomed to having Judge Haliburton around. Another thing that a former occupant could never understand was that every evening at nine o'clock her dog would bristle up, for dogs are supposed to be aware of spirits that are not seen by humans.

My own town of Dartmouth is not immune to ghostly visitations, but again I must be careful not to give the location away. Mrs. Hirtle said, "I lived in a house in Dartmouth when I was fifteen or sixteen. It was built on a hillside and had a basement kitchen and dining-room, both above ground. One day we were in the dining-room, father, mother, a visitor, and I, and I heard what sounded like a breathing just beside me. It frightened me so that I ran to my father and he thought I was crazy, but my mother stood holding the teapot in her hand and said, 'Did you see that?' She and the young man who was visiting had both seen it. This was a man without a head standing right behind me. We learned later that a pedlar was supposed to have been murdered in that house." I was fortunate in knowing a man in the town who had lived there until his marriage, the same man who saw his father, as described under Helpful Ghosts. He had never heard of a headless man being seen, but he said there was one room where it was impossible to sleep. Sounds were heard and he has slept there himself when not only the bedclothes were taken off, but the bedspring itself would be lifted up off the bed. The family closed it off and it was never used again for any purpose while he was there.

There was a barn behind this house. He said he would often be out there rubbing the horse down when he would hear a noise like a hand pushing along the wall. It would make its way slowly until it came to the barn door, and then the horse would jump. He said you would not only hear it, but feel it as it approached, and often when he was in the house he would hear the horse jump as if frightened, and nothing there. The noise was always on the outside of the barn.

There is another house in the same vicinity where a sailor got into trouble one night and had his eyes gouged out. He left in the utmost agony and fell over a bank and was killed. For years, according to our Dartmouth historian Dr. John Martin, his agonizing cries could be heard and from that time on, there were strange and unaccountable noises in the house.

On the other side of Halifax Harbour at Birch Cove they used to say many years ago that you must not pass by a certain place at night or you would see a black dog crossing the road. There used to be a big rambling house there with a room that was uninhabitable and had to be sealed off. In the Duke of Kent's time, said a Halifax lady, a woman was supposed to have been imprisoned there.

The Hartlan's ghost house at South-East Passage has been mentioned in the Prologue and referred to several times since then. This house, made of wood washed ashore from wrecks, finally got the better of its inhabitants and sent them off to build small dwellings around it. Mr. Richard Hartlan lived there once and he said, "When I was young at home every night after I'd go to bed my room door would open and I used to get up and close it not once a night, but three or four times. That went on four or five years. We couldn't see nothin' but there would be knockings and where it started from, it ended. It went all the way around that house. When Ferdinand was there he used to hear three knocks that would come every night between seven and eight. First they come to his porch door and the next night to his bedroom windy and the third night to the back door. He said, 'The next night they'll be in the house,' so

we were all there and it was like three or four heavy
boards falling down and nothin' fell at all, only the
noise. Another night we were settin' there and something fell from the loft on to the table and behind it
and we couldn't find a thing. Another time Ferdinand
was on his knees saying his prayers and something got
him by the toe and hauled him round and something
struck the bedroom door three times and it swung open
and struck the bedpost.

"I used to hear footsteps outside my room at night
and I'd think my brothers were up, but there wouldn't
be anyone there, and night after night I used to have
the bedclothes pulled right off me and in time I couldn't
sleep in a bed; I had to sleep on the floor. Sometimes
before the door would open you'd hear creak, creak,
but you'd never see nothin'. One night my father and
mother were in town and they were to be home at eight.
We heard them comin' and the horse pullin' the wagon
over the road and we lit the lantern and went out to help
them in and there was no sign of them. They didn't
come for an hour. Another time I heard me wife talkin'
and I opened the door and she wasn't there.

"The only time I ever saw anything was one Sunday
afternoon. After I ate my dinner I went and had a lay
down and I fell into a doze of sleep as I thought. After
I got to sleep there was somethin' pressing me and I
couldn't wake or couldn't turn over for about half
an hour and, when I woke, I seen this person go from
me to the windy and she was a woman with a black and
white spotted dress on and I was in a lather of sweat
with the water pouring off me as big as marbles. Whatever it was, a witch or not, God knows." Well, they
concluded this was a witch and they stopped her from
coming back by putting nine letters from the German
Bible reversed on a board and nailing it over the door.
The ghost, however, was thought to be a former owner
who was said to be a wicked man. He had a spinning

wheel and would sit at it from morning till night. When the threads broke, as they did with great frequency, he would curse and swear. He also drank a lot and must have done other things to give him such a bad reputation.

I had never heard of knock-a-balls until I visited the Smith family at Blanche, and I have never heard of them since. They are knockings which have no natural explanation. "If we took the Bible and opened it we wouldn't hear a sound but, if we closed it we would hear knockings. The reason we heard these sounds was on account of a girl named Cordelia. One time a fellow had been cast away from a ship on the shore near here and he stayed around these parts for a while. He took a shine to Cordelia and went around with her but, when he wanted to marry her, she wouldn't have him. He got mad then and said he would send something to annoy her. It was then we began to hear the knock-a-balls.

"When they first started, the rest of us were afraid, but the girl wasn't. She would ask questions and it would knock out the answers. We supposed he did it through a medium. One night a friend of hers slept with her and she got frightened because it knocked beside the bed. Other things happened too like my gun being thrown rattle thrash bang across the room and all the wood falling out of the woodpile. Mainly though it followed Cordelia. It would follow her down the stairs and even to the barn. People came from all around to hear it and they stayed in the room with her, so she couldn't have done it herself.

"My father wasn't frightened of anything, and he asked it a question once. He said, 'Are you from the devil?' It said, 'Yes.' (Three knocks meant yes.) Then he said, 'Are you from the Lord?' and it didn't answer anything. Only the Bible opened would make the sound stop." Like other such cases it was of short but noisy duration.

That no doubt was a poltergeist, with a young girl emotionally upset the centre of activities which no human being could accomplish alone. This Province has had three more poltergeist cases and they have aroused international interest. They took place at Amherst, Caledonia, and Eastern Passage, and have been written up in detail in R. S. Lambert's book, *Exploring the Supernatural*. I am not sure that the Caledonia case was that of a poltergeist; it has been suggested that it might have been something much more frightening. I remember passing the house one dark night with people who lived nearby and being thankful when we finally got away from that unhealthy atmosphere.

There are other houses in the Province that are supposed to be haunted now. In one, a man comes out of the side of the wall and consumes food. Perhaps in my next field season I may learn more about this strange case.

Epilogue

IF YOU think back to the chapter on Hindsight, you will recall a story in which a young woman spent a night in a house in Halifax and had the terrifying experience of looking back upon an incident of the past. You will remember, too, that she had never mentioned this to the friends living there at the time, mainly because she wished to forget it. At my request, however, she finally wrote them. They were horrified, but not greatly surprised, for they could believe anything about this hateful place. They had disliked it for its location which was particularly objectionable in wartime. Among other distressing events, they once witnessed a murder outside a dance hall nearby that had seen so many skirmishes it was nicknamed "The Bucket of Blood." Their memories were of actual events; they had seen nothing supernatural.

You will also recall when I visited the haunted house that I was told of manifestations which had twice begun in April. I mentioned this to the McMasters at Port Hastings when telling about the house, and Mr. McMaster murmured, "Yes of course, it would be April." Later, in thinking about our conversation, I wondered if there could be any significance in his remark and, upon inquiry, learned that the older people believe ghosts to be more active in that month. I had never encountered this before, so I do not know whether the belief is widespread, or is confined to Cape Breton.

After this book was finished I appeared on the television show "Graphic" and, in the course of the interview, told one of our stories. It was no sooner concluded than my telephone rang and a voice, shaken with emotion, told me that he had experienced the very thing that I had related. His name was Donovan.

"I was steam engineer at the Light and Power in Halifax," he said. "One morning at four o'clock I was sitting on a bench in the boiler room and my helper was taking out the ashes. Something seemed to tell me I should turn my head, so I did, and I noticed my father standing by my left shoulder. Not the whole of him as it was in your story; just the head and shoulders. He had an angry look on his face. I turned away because I couldn't understand why he should be angry. Then I looked back and this time he started towards the boiler. I thought then he must have come to warn me, so I got up and examined the boiler, but I couldn't see anything wrong with it, but I had just sat down again when the most awful explosion came and I was covered with soot and ashes. I can't say that he saved my life as the father did in your story, but he must have come to warn me about that boiler."

I have now come to the end of my story which covers every phase of supernatural belief I have been able to discover. It is quite possible that I have missed incidents that would come under other headings but, if so, they would be isolated cases. As I said at the beginning, some stories in the book are the result of imagination and superstition. Others, like our first Helpful Ghost, and the appearance of Alex to his friend Dan at sea, leave no doubt with me. I could mention many more, but that is unnecessary.

I have attempted to show you how extensive our belief is and how often it is wrapped up with the sea that

surrounds us. You have seen how we think upon these
subjects, and how we express our thoughts. You will
have discovered too that the supernatural in Nova
Scotia is not a subject talked about for the sole purpose
of entertainment but that, for many of us, it is a part of
our way of life.

Internationally known collector of Maritime Folklore, Dr. Helen Creighton was born in Dartmouth, Nova Scotia and educated at the universities of Toronto and Indiana. Associated with the National Museum for many years, honours bestowed since her collecting days, which began in 1928, include Hon. LL.D. (Mount Allison); D.ès L. (Laval); D.C.L. and Fellow of Haliburton (University of King's College). Dr. Creighton is the first woman to receive the latter honour. She has also been named Citizen of the Year by the Kiwanis Club, Dartmouth, been awarded a Centennial Medal and an Honorary Membership to the Nova Scotia Folk Arts Council. In 1942, she attended a Folklore Course at Indiana University courtesy of the Rockefeller Foundation and attended meetings of the International Folk Music Council in Rumania through courtesy of the Canada Council. The author has been awarded several fellowships both from the Rockefeller Foundation and the Canada Council. Her published books include *Songs and Ballads from Nova Scotia, Traditional Songs from Nova Scotia, Twelve Folk Songs from Nova Scotia, Folklore of Lunenburg County, Maritime Folk Songs, Gaelic Songs in Nova Scotia and Bluenose Magic.*